# DEBATING
# RELIGIOUS SPACE & PLACE
## IN THE EARLY MEDIEVAL WORLD
## (C. AD 300-1000)

Sidestone Press

# DEBATING
# RELIGIOUS SPACE & PLACE
## IN THE EARLY MEDIEVAL WORLD
## (C. AD 300-1000)

edited by
Chantal Bielmann
& Brittany Thomas

Published by Sidestone Press, Leiden
   www.sidestone.com

Imprint: Sidestone Press Academics
All articles in this publication have been peer-reviewed. For more information
   see www.sidestone.com

Lay-out & cover design: Sidestone Press
Photograph cover: Jerusalem © Studiodr | Stock.adobe.com
Printed and bound in Great Britain by Marston Book Services Ltd, Oxfordshire

ISBN 978-90-8890-418-9 (softcover)
ISBN 978-90-8890-419-6 (hardcover)
ISBN 978-90-8890-420-2 (PDF e-book)

# Contents

List of Contributors                                                                    7

List of tables and figures                                                              9

Acknowledgements                                                                       11

Introduction: Defining Religious 'Space' and 'Place'                                   13
Brittany Thomas & Chantal Bielmann

The Evolution of Forum Space in Late Antique Hispania: The                            21
Genesis of a New Urbanism?
Pilar Diarte-Blasco

Malta in Late Antiquity: Mortuary Places and Spaces                                   45
Glen Farrugia

A Case for Space: Rereading the Imperial Panels of San Vitale                         61
Brittany Thomas

Early Medieval Places of Worship in the Western Alps: The                             77
District of Verbano Cusio Ossola
Francesca Garanzini

Space and Place: Identifying the Anglo-Saxon Cemeteries                               93
in the Tees Valley, North-East England
Stephen Sherlock

Religious Change vs Cultural Change: The Case of Islamisation                        111
in the Early Medieval Period
Jose Carvajal Lopez

Interactions between the Clerical Enclosure and the                                  127
Extra-Claustral Clergy in Carolingian Francia: A Sacred Space
with Porous Walls
Stephen Ling

**The monastery of Saint Maurice of Agaune (Switzerland) in the first millennium**    143

*Alessandra Antonini*

**Exploring Monastic Space and Place in the Swiss Alps**    159

*Chantal Bielmann*

**Sacred Ground: Community and Separation in a Norse Churchyard, Greenland**    175

*Jess Angus McCullough*

**Light and Life in the Catacombs: Questioning the Early Christian and Early Medieval Pilgrim Experience(s)**    187

*Neil Christie*

**Conclusion: Looking for Beliefs and Visions in Archaeology**    209

*Deirdre O'Sullivan*

# List of Contributors

**Dr Pilar Diarte-Blasco**
*University of Leicester*
pdiarteblasco@gmail.com

**Dr Glen Farrugia**
*University of Leicester*
glen.farrugia@um.edu.mt

**Dr Brittany Thomas**
*University of Leicester*
Bmt0119@gmail.com

**Francesca Garanzini**
*Soprintendenza Archeologia,*
*Belle Arti e Paesaggio per le province di*
*Biella, Novara, Verbano-Cusio-Ossola e*
*Vercelli - Novara/Torino*
francesca.garanzini@beniculturali.it

**Dr Stephen J. Sherlock**
*Professional Archaeologist*
stephen.sherlock@ntlworld.com

**Dr Jose Carvajal Lopez**
*University of Leicester*
jccl2@le.ac.uk

**Dr Stephen Ling**
*University of Loughborough*
s.ling@lboro.ac.uk

**Alessandra Antonini**
*TERA s.à r.l., Travaux, études et re-*
*cherches archéologiques*
a.antonini@terasarl.ch

**Dr Chantal Bielmann**
*University of Leicester*
cb450@le.ac.uk

**Dr Jess McCullough**
*University of Leicester*
doctorjamccullough@gmail.com

**Prof Neil Christie**
*University of Leicester*
njc10@leicester.ac.uk

**Deirdre O'Sullivan**
*University of Leicester*
dmo@leicester.ac.uk

# List of tables and figures

## List of Tables

Table 1.   Radiocarbon dates from Bishopsmill cemetery and Roseberry Road burials, Norton

Table 2.   Dates of conquest of Syrian towns and the date of building of their mosques, according to Guidetti 2014

Table 3.   Swiss monasteries and their noble founders

## List of Figures

Fig 1.     Map of *Hispania* in Late Antiquity

Fig 2.     City Plan: *Caesaraugusta*

Fig 3.     Ercavica. Construction phases and forum activity

Fig 4.     Astigi. Amazona of the sculptural repertoire found in the monumental pool of the forum

Fig 5.     Location of burials in relation to the forum temples of Pollentia, Carteia and Conimbriga

Fig 6.     Map of the Maltese islands

Fig 7.     Example of Maltese late Roman hypogea: Interior of the St. Augustine Catacombs

Fig 8.     The 'imperial panels' of San Vitale – Justinian (top); Theodora (bottom)

Fig 9.     Apse mosaic of San Vitale depicting Bishop Ecclesius (on the right) handing a small model of the church to Christ

Fig 10.    Visual integration map of San Vitale, Ravenna

Fig 11.    The apse of San Vitale, as viewed from the central nave

Fig 12.    Map of Verbano Cusio Ossola, in the Northeastern far end of Piedmont

Fig 13.    San Giovanni Battista al Montorfano. Map of the early Christian period

Fig 14.    San Giovanni Battista al Montorfano. Map of the early Medieval period

Fig 15.    San Giovanni Battista al Montorfano. Frescoes on the apsidal wall of the early Christian Baptistery

Fig 16.    Santi Fabiano and Sebastiano in Verbania Suna. Map of the early medieval phase

Fig 17.    San Pietro in Gravellona Toce. Map of the early medieval phase

Fig 18.    Anglo-Saxon Cemeteries in the Tees Valley and environs

Fig 19.    Map showing the location of the seven sites mentioned at Catterick

Fig 20.    Plan of Hartlepool Headland showing St Hilda's Church and the Saxon sites

Fig 21.    East Mill, Norton: crouched burial in grave 60 with spear beside head

Fig 22.    Reconstruction of the eastern side of the Street House cemetery showing buildings and burial mounds

Fig 23.    Plan of Street House cemetery showing the arrangement of graves and location of objects beside the head

Fig 24.    An example of *muṣallā* found in Qatar

Fig 25.    The Dome of the Rock in the Ḥaram al-Sharīf

Fig 26.    Mosque in abandoned village of al-Jumail, Qatar (19th – 20th centuries)

Fig 27.    Miḥrāb of the Mosque of Cordoba, erected in 961 by order of the Caliph Al-Ḥakam II

Fig 28.    The abbey complex of Saint-Maurice seen to the southwest

Fig 29.    Excavations of Canon Bourban in the courtyard of Martolet (summer 1903)

Fig 30.    Saint-Maurice, layout remains the abbey district in the first millennium (Tera 2014)

Fig 31.    The privileged tomb of ancient necropolis, with the remains of its mark (a)

Fig 32.    The Court of Martolet, looking West (2009). The mausoleum (A) is built on the privileged tomb of ancient necropolis (*)

Fig 33.    The vaulted corridor of the fourth building

Fig 34.    The eastern crypt Martolet (fifth building)

Fig 35.    The court of Martolet looking east

Fig 36.    Schematic section of the pool (north-south, west view)

Fig 37.    The remains of the palace discovered in Agaune

Fig 38.    Map of Switzerland depicting the monasteries building between AD 300 and 800

Fig 39.    Interior of the current abbey of Disentis (image by Peter Berger 2006)

Fig 40.    Abbey of Saint-Maurice viewshed results

Fig 41.    Disentis Abbey viewshed results

Fig 42.    Abbey of St John, Müstair viewshed results

Fig 43.    The Eastern Settlement of Norse Greenland

Fig 44.    Plan of the Churchyard and Burials at Herjolfsnes as seen in Nørlund 1924.

Fig 45.    View of part of the complex interior of the early Christian to Byzantine hypogeum at the Catacombs of St Paul, Malta (Image courtesy of Daniel Cilia, Malta)

Fig 46.    Typical modern photograph of a corridor with loculi and larger tomb recesses in Rome's catacomb of San Callisto

Fig 47.    A sign of the modern pilgrim-cum-tourist experience – a multi-lingual welcome but with lots of 'do not' warnings, from taking photos to littering, using phones or smoking

Fig 48.    A new tour group jostles down the steps into the San Callisto catacombs in Rome, aided by bright lights and new brick steps

Fig 49.    Late Roman ceramic oil lamps behind a grille in the catacombs of San Callisto near the main early papal-saint tombs

Fig 50.    A mid-fourth-century gilded glass bowl base likely once set beside a loculus

Fig 51.    Members of a tour group touching the sides of a gallery and using a pen torch in the catacombs beneath the early medieval church of Sant'Agnese fuori le mura, Rome.

Fig 52.    One sector of the laser-mapped Domitilla catacombs depicting galleries, side chambers, cubicula and intersections (Image courtesy of Prof N. Zimmermann & Vienna University)

# Acknowledgements

This volume has predominantly grown out of discussions generated by a conference held at the University of Leicester from November 22-23, 2014, entitled *Debating Religious Space and Place from Constantine to Cnut*. The two-day conference aimed to reframe the discussion of religious transformations in Late Antiquity and the Early Middle Ages (*c.* AD 300-1000) beyond simple 'Christianisation' or 'Islamisation'. The conference comprised four sessions, arranged roughly by time and region: the Late Antique Mediterranean, Early Medieval Europe, the Byzantine Empire and the Near East, and the North Atlantic World. This encompassed a wide geographic area (from the North Sea to the Holy Land) and a large span of time (six centuries) through which to debate the contentious topic of 'religious space'. Most valuably, this broad framework fostered an environment of interdisciplinarity, bringing Byzantine, Northern European, Mediterranean, and Near Eastern researchers together to discuss themes associated with religious space and place including continuity and change, transformation and transition, experience and memory, visibility and access. While many of the contributors in this volume were presenters at the conference, others have joined our discussion for this publication. Thus this volume is not so much direct 'proceedings' of the conference as it is a continuation of the conference's themes.

The conference was generously funded by the University of Leicester's Graduate Researcher Development scheme, the College of Arts, Humanities and Law, University of Leicester Medieval Research Centre, the School of Archaeology and Ancient History, and by the Society for the Promotion of Byzantine Studies. Travel grants were also provided by the Royal Historical Society (London). Thanks to our session chairs (Dr William Bowden, Prof Joanna Story, Prof Leslie Brubaker, and Deirdre O'Sullivan) for further developing the ideas that eventually became this volume. We also could not have done without our numerous volunteers and the administrative staff support at the School of Archaeology and Ancient History who helped us run a smooth conference. Special thanks are due to Neil Christie for his involvement and advice throughout this long process, and also to Sergio Gonzalez Sanchez for his careful looking over of our manuscript. As editors, we would like to thank all of our contributors for their work on this project and submissions to this volume. We would also like to thank our peer reviewers, and our publishers Sidestone Press for the cover design and typesetting of the book.

*Chantal Bielmann and Brittany Thomas (University of Leicester)*

# Introduction

## Defining Religious 'Space' and 'Place'

*Brittany Thomas & Chantal Bielmann*

*Do walls then make Christians?* (Augustine, *Confessions* 8.2.1)

*Lo! the first Sanctuary (bayt) appointed for mankind was that at Becca* [Mecca]*, a blessed place, a guidance for mankind; wherein are plain memorials (of God's guidance); the place where Abraham stood up to pray; and whosoever enters it is safe. And pilgrimage to the House is a duty unto God for mankind, for him who can find a way there.* (Qur'ran 3:96-97)

*And so holy a place that was, that he would nowise that men should defile the field with blood-shedding, and moreover none should go thither for their needs, but to that end was appointed a skerry called Dirtskerry.* (Icelandic Sagas, Eyrbyggja saga, Chapter 4)

Space and place mattered to the religions of the Early Medieval World; religion automatically forced the issue of whether a space or place had intrinsic sacred value. We can see this in their literature: Augustine asked whether a place of worship was an integral part of what it is to be Christian; Mohammed stated that Mecca was to be a 'blessed place' where people who enter are safe; and a description from the Eyrbyggja saga describes how a built temple made the land around it holy. We can also see the value assigned to holy places in the art, the tradition, and the material culture left behind by medieval people. This observation is not new; books abound on the subject of the meaning of religious space, many of which investigate the connection between space, ritual, and belief (see Hanawalt and Kobialka (eds.) 2000 *Medieval Practices of Space* and Westcoat and Ousterhout (eds.) 2012 *Architecture of the Sacred: Space, Ritual, and Experience from Classical Greece to Byzantium*). Space has been explored in terms of its power (see Rosenwein 1999 *Negotiating Space: Power, Restraint, and Privileges of Immunity in Early Medieval Europe*); its influence on personal experiences such as pilgrimage (see Kristensen and Friese 2017 *Excavation Pilgrimage: Archaeological*

in: Bielmann, C. and Thomas, B. (eds.) 2018: *Debating Religious Space and Place in the Early Medieval World (c. AD 300-1000)*, Sidestone Press (Leiden), pp. 13-20.

*Approaches to Sacred Travel and Movement in the Ancient World)*; and violence (Sauer 2003 *The Archaeology of Religious Hatred in the Roman and Early Medieval World*); and the ever present dichotomy between change and decline (Kaiser and Leone (eds.) 2013 *Cities and Gods. Religious Space in Transition*). Often when we address religion in the fields of Archaeology or Architectural History we understandably focus on the material – the structures for worship and the objects for ritual. However, there is also meaning in the immaterial – the interaction between people and place that creates ritual, sacredness, and significance for the participants. So while it is perhaps surprising to see another volume exploring questions of 'space' and 'place', we argue that it is a good time to return to these ideas as new methodologies and theoretical approaches are producing new answers to old questions.

Before we turn to how this volume answers these questions, we first must outline what is meant by 'space' and 'place'. Tim Cresswell (2004, 1) reminds us that 'place is not a specialized piece of academic terminology', perhaps the reason why these two terms have often been used so interchangeably. Both are used to refer to a variety of relationships that include locations, materials, distances, interactions or communications, and other such qualities that might characterize a 'space' or a 'place'. Place can mean a location like a city or a given area within a city; or something as broadly conceived as a 'landscape' within a place; or a building we use like a church or house; or even an intimate location like a room inside of those buildings. Space is something more abstract. Space can be imagined and remembered, unseen and yet known or understood. It can be a literary space, a mental space, or a place conceived of but not located anywhere. More confusingly still, places can have space between them.

Various frameworks, ranging from the geographical to the metaphysical, the individual to the societal, have sought to define space and place through the ways in which human beings make them meaningful. Of the two words, there seems to be general consensus that 'space' is a more abstract concept than 'place'. A useful overview of these frameworks is that of Leif Jerram (2013, 401). Indeed, Jerram (2013, 401) has argued for a re-examination of the words themselves and how scholars use them:

> *But there is a fundamental problem: very few scholars in any discipline (myself included) have explained precisely what space is, and when they have, it is often treated as a dimension of the human imaginary.*

This confusion, argues Jerram, limits clarity and has the potential to stall discussions about core elements (*e.g.* materiality) in studies that use a 'spatial' theoretical lens to examine a topic within the humanities. Cresswell, for instance, argued that 'space' only becomes a 'place' when human beings attach meaning to it (2004, 10). Tim Ingold (2009), on the other hand, argued against the regular use of the word 'space' at all. Space in Ingold's view reduces life to 'an internal property of things that occupy the world but which do not, strictly speaking, inhabit it' (2009, 29). Place, on the other hand, is defined by movement – knots that only have meaning in the threads with which they are tied. This analogy of place-as-knots results in Ingold's proposal that histories and human experience form a meshwork of sorts (2009, 43), and that any attempt to neatly unravel that meshwork effectively destroys its very meaning. Space, within Ingold's model, has no meaning and signifies nothing. Jerram rejects the claim that humanities have suddenly become interested in space (rather, they have always been interested in it), and proposes a straightforward set of definitions: 'space' is material (proximate physical dispositions of things in relation to other things and to people); 'location' is relational or positional (the location of things on the earth's surface and their scale/density/complexity/distribution); **'place'** is meaningful (values, beliefs, codes, and practices that surround a location). Jerram (2013, 404) believes that if we adopt these three divisions as a means to clearly define these core concepts, it is possible to demonstrate a rich use of 'place' and locational words in historical scholarship, but a confusing and even 'impoverished' use of the word 'space'. In general, Jerram's conflict with the overuse of vague language and the absence of concrete material elements of space and place (*i.e.* things – buildings, locations) is part of the ongoing discussion within this volume.

These examples, albeit brief, demonstrate some of the complexities of approaching space and place in the past. Essentially, we must ask how historians and archaeologists might meaningfully engage with 'space' or 'place', especially, as we shall see throughout this volume, in the absence of direct evidence of how it might have been used. When we ask about 'religious space and place' the complexities arguably increase – even a definition of 'religion' is no simple matter. For example, Insoll's (2004, 6-8) research on archaeology and religion resulted in a (perhaps outrageous) claim that religion is 'undefinable'. However, he follows this up with a broad definition by Meslin (1985, 39): 'a system constructed by a long tradition of thought about fundamental human problems – life, love, good, evil and death'. For this volume, religion is a set of beliefs that are ascribed to the material (the structures, burials, etc.) as well as to the immaterial (*e.g.* the spaces in which the material exist). Ann Marie Yasin (2009, 15) defined the 'place of the sacred' as 'locatable in physical thing or site', while 'sacred space' encompasses 'an area of collective worship defined by the special actions of the community'. Thus, religious (or sacred) space is defined through human activity resulting from belief.

Within this volume, we have not set a standard definition of 'space' or 'place' – each chapter will look at a different aspect of why certain spaces or places were important within their given location. One definition that both Cresswell and Jerram agree upon is that place is meaningful because we make it so through using it. We are now approaching even newer understandings of landscape transformation thanks in part to the employment and interrogation of GIS and isovist technologies, but also the 'opening up' of the topic to interdisciplinary perspectives. Indeed, spaces and places can also be explored beyond the visual – through means such as auditory and olfactory senses, or participatory means such as parades, ceremonies, and burial. And indeed, many of the papers in this volume express these notions. Broadly, the themes that are drawn out throughout the book relate to sacred spaces in three key areas: (1) transformation of spaces and places in which people worship, gather, pray, or perform sacred rites; (2) the phenomenological experience of being in those spaces; and (3) the creation of community around sacred places such as cemeteries and rural churches.

## Transformation of Religious Space and Place

The question of transformation of religious space and place has been examined in considerable detail by both researchers of Late Antiquity and the Early Medieval World.

With respect to the late antique world, the emphasis has been on the transition from 'paganism' to Christianity. A commonly recognised root of the debate for late antique researchers is Peter Brown's seminal work *The World of Late Antiquity* (1971), which challenged the tradition of decline following the collapse of the Roman West and encouraged other historians to pursue similar research (*e.g.* MacMullen 1986, 1997; Lane Fox 1986; Cameron 1993). While these works often examined primary source material to explore how Christianity emerged and became one of the major religions in the West ('Christianisation'), it was soon recognised that the concept of 'Christianisation' and changing sacred landscapes could be examined within an archaeological framework. In other words, what does the material culture tell us about these changes? How did 'Christianisation' as well as 'Islamisation' impact secular and religious space?

There are many different approaches to these questions. The research of Caseau (2001, 2003, 2007), for example, examined changing sacred landscapes by taking case studies across Europe to better categorise the various types of sacred landscapes and describe how they changed over time. Dijkstra (2008) and Goodman (2011), on the other hand, chose to research the reuse of temples as churches within a regional perspective, each revealing patterns within the regions of Egypt and Gaul respectively. Both were able to demonstrate the complexities involved in the transformation of religious spaces, noting how the phenomenon occurred irregularly and slowly. In Italy, Christie (2010; 2006; 2004) approached the question of religious change and its impact on urban and rural spaces within the context of other agencies of change (economies, politics, militaries, *etc.*). We can evaluate these questions from an urban perspective – such as the work of Sami (2010) on Sicily and Bielmann (2014) on Rome. Burial grounds also provide an enormous amount of information about religious change, which is the perspective of **Glen Farrugia**, who uses the burial practices in fourth-century Malta to challenge the idea of blanket Christianisation across the Mediterranean. His paper determines that most communities used a standard style of burial space, whether 'pagan' or Christian, and only the meaning and use of these spaces defined them as belonging to a certain religious group. Further to the impetus of understanding the religious framework of these changes is the examination of religious change within cultural and historical contexts. Here **Jose Carvajal Lopez** explores how 'Islamisation' must be understood within the broader cultural and historical developments, using early Islamic prayer spaces in Syria-Palestine and in the Iberian Peninsula as case studies to demonstrate the broad cultural change happening in medieval Islamic spaces.

However, the study of temple reuse, 'Christianisation', or 'Islamisation' in Late Antiquity and the Early Medieval Period is only one aspect within the wider debate of the transformation of religious space and place. Another key area of research is examining how Christian, Islamic, or other new sacred architecture impacted secular space. The recent work of Osland (2016) on late antique Emerita (Merida, Spain), for example, evaluates how the various religious, social, economic, and political demands of the residents of the centre resulted in a new urban environment with visible roots to its Roman past. The work of **Pilar Diarte-Blasco** contributes to this debate by examining the form and function of buildings in the fora of Roman cities in Spain and concluding that the reuse of classical buildings in early Christian contexts happened only *after* these buildings had long lost their original functions. Another key question is how spaces were continually adapted and changed, resulting in complex archaeological sites. **Alessandra Antonini's** chapter provides an example of this by updating us on the Abbey of Saint Maurice (Switzerland). Recent archaeological excavations here reveal a long history of construction and investment at Saint Maurice from its earliest form as a simple venerated tomb into the grand complex it became after investment by its abbots and bishops, and royal investment by King Sigismund throughout the fifth and sixth centuries. Antonini questions the function of this combined sacred and secular investment and how it affected access to spaces within the monastic complex: which spaces can we read as 'royal' and which were 'episcopal' if their forms borrow from each other? Were some spaces closed to the public? This chapter reveals the complexities of spatial functions and relationships where use was both public and private, monastic and royal.

## Experiencing Sacred Space

The study of space and place often turns to phenomenological discussion of what it means to interact with these spaces and places. Thus, several of the following papers focus on built spaces and how they encoded belief through physical experience. 'Belief' is a set of tenets accepted as true by a group of people, while ritual encodes, enacts, and performs those beliefs (Marinis 2012, 338 after Geertz 1973, 126-131). Most of what can be understood about religious ritual cannot be taken outside of its context. In this sense, ritual is space and place dependent: it must happen within a setting purposefully constructed for its needs, and one that becomes meaningful through the enactment of the ritual itself. Architecturally, religious buildings are sacred spaces with 'platial' functions: they locate the sacred by housing objects and bodies, and they become sacred through the rituals of worship and ceremony. How did built space contextualise interaction with the sacred, or how did it allow people to communicate between and among sacred places?

**Stephen Ling** answers this question by investigating the Carolingian cloister as both place and space – a place where claustral clergy lived and received their education, and a space clergy thought of as the heart of their brotherhood and practice whether or not they lived within the enclosure. His chapter explores the way episcopal writers defined claustral practice to include those brothers who served in the secular world. He concludes that although clergy could be physically and geographically separate, they were bonded through spiritual practices that developed within the sacred space of the cloister.

While phenomenology encompasses all of our senses, the most important in many eras of antiquity and the Early Middle Ages was sight. Seeing was not just a way to understand things, but also a way to *know* things (such as icons, religious art and architecture), or a way to know God or the gods. The articulation of sacred space, then, was not only architectural but also visual (Yasin 2012, 250). Was seeing the sacred or being in proximity to it vital to believing? How did people access and interact with imagery in intimate spaces? **Brittany Thomas** revisits the famous sixth-century imperial portraits inside the church of San Vitale (Ravenna) to question access to and reception of images from a spatial point of view. Her chapter examines the decoration of the church's presbytery as a kind of discourse between the bishop and other powerful individuals in Ravenna, challenging the idea that the worshipping public would have unlimited access to the images in this space. This chapter reveals how the spatial context of these mosaics is key to reading their messages and to mapping the possible liturgies that could have been performed in this building.

Another approach to answering questions of visibility and proximity is through the use of technologies like Geographic Information Systems (GIS). How visible were religious sites? Were monastic sites hidden and isolated as the literature suggests? **Chantal Bielmann** uses spatial archaeology to investigate these questions with respect to monasteries in the Swiss Alps. She argues that the religious centres monasteries in the Swiss Alps were in fact located in places of high visibility, and thus not isolated and hidden islands as the literature suggests.

While sight was a main sense through which people interacted with religious space, other senses (aural, olfactory, *etc.*) were as important to past people's overall experience when interacting with these spaces. This is the central theme of the work of **Neil Christie** who examines the experiences of early Christian pilgrims to Roman catacombs. Combining primary source accounts of late antique pilgrims, archaeological research, and current tourist experiences, he examines how the catacombs were a multi-sensory experience and provides suggestions on future research on the catacombs with respect to the question of pilgrim experiences.

## Interpreting Communities and their Religious Spaces

Religious spaces remain an influential archaeological diagnostic tool – they help us contextualise important places in urban and rural landscapes as centres of activity and ritual. In the Early Middle Ages, religious hubs easily became settlement hubs with faith communities living within large religious structures like monasteries. Equally, religious structures were an expression of community identity and belief. Besides the physical change to a community, what did the construction of a church, a temple, a mosque mean? Who was involved in their construction? What negotiations occurred in the placement of these structures? These questions are explored by **Francesca Garanzini,** who takes us to the Italian side of the Alps to discuss the relationship these churches had with nearby settlements and their placement in the landscape. Her paper demonstrates the Christian nature of the Verbano Cusso Ossola district of Piedmont throughout the Early Middle Ages, but questions any earlier settlement in these high Alpine regions – were the first settlements here built between the sixth and eighth centuries by regional bishops? Why?

The management and use (or reuse) of burial spaces is another aspect of religious space that has influenced our understanding of past communities, as we have already seen in Glen Farrugia's contribution. Changing burial practices have been interpreted as an issue for the living rather than the dead, most prominently by Pearson (1999) in his *Archaeology of Death and Burial.* Collective identity has been an influential model for the interpretation of burials over the early medieval period (such as the contributions offered in Basset (ed.) 1992, and Yasin 2005). Changing practices might reveal changing community attitudes or values, or the presence of transient communities like pilgrims. The work of **Stephen Sherlock** contributes to this perspective by examining the social and cultural significance behind the grouping of burials in the Tees Valley. What do the arrangement of burials mean? What significance (if any) is there in differences in burial tradition within a small region? His research on the Tees Valley in northern England not only explores these questions but also presents us with evidence on how the cemeteries may have been arranged for pilgrimage purposes. The research of **Jess McCullough** similarly explores the significance of burial grounds with respect to community construction and identity in Greenland, using the site of Herjolfsnes as a case study. What did the burials at Herjolfsnes mean to the people who lived nearby? What do the grave goods signify? This chapter demonstrates that these sites acted as 'holy ground' for the community and as a safe space to await salvation in the afterlife.

The book is broadly chronological, ranging from late antique Hispania through to early Medieval Greenland, with **Deirdre O'Sullivan**'s concluding chapter grounding us in the present to question current urban religious experience. Her paper offers an insight into the South Asian communities living in Leicester (U.K.) and the ways in which they have created sacred spaces among reused buildings. She offers this paper not as a direct analogy to medieval space and place, but to showcase the value of ethnographic method for demonstrating that issues of space, place, and sacrality are still extremely relevant among urban groups. O'Sullivan reminds us that 'We cannot experience early medieval sacred places in the same way that the faith communities of the Middle Ages encountered them, but we can strive to understand that experience in intelligent and creative ways'.

Together, we, as editors, feel that the rich and varied papers presented in this volume demonstrate the many complexities within studies of late antique and early medieval religious spaces across Europe and the Near East; overall, they provide a valuable contribution to the fields of Archaeology, Art and Architectural History, Medieval History, Visual Studies, and Culture and Memory Studies. Each of the authors challenges or revisions traditional models of 'religious change' within their respective areas of expertise. They show the possibilities for new approaches and ways of thinking about the meaning of space and place in history, and how religious spaces in particular have developed across cultures. As a whole, this volume offers us a current discussion for furthering the work in these fields.

# The Evolution of Forum Space in Late Antique Hispania

## The Genesis of a New Urbanism?

*Pilar Diarte-Blasco*

## Introduction

The progressive loss of the use of Roman urban public buildings and spaces and their later reuse with new functions is one of the essential characteristics of the transformations that cities underwent in Late Antiquity. In Hispania, as in the rest of the Empire, these transformations were fundamental to the genesis of the new urban reality of Late Antiquity (Gurt 2000-2001, 443-444; Kulikowski 2004, 85-129; Diarte-Blasco and Gurt 2015). The changes bestowed a diverse appearance to these ancient spaces which had long been symbols of *Romanitas*. Reuse is, as will be seen, fairly common; a contrast lies with circuses, which, often detached from the main city nucleus, generally saw no structural adaptation and were quarried (Diarte-Blasco 2009, 71-84; 2012, 287-290).

Roman public buildings are architectural units that are difficult to ignore inside the urban core because of their design and bulk, the large space they occupied and the scale of material used in their construction. These facts alone made them hard to discard, even as their primary roles were lost. However, some buildings were not reoccupied and others witnessed a reduced later occupation, leading to an image of virtual abandonment. This situation occurred mainly in the cities that failed to survive into Late Antiquity, but was present also in some that did. In the latter, however, such buildings lay away from the main late antique focus of the urban layout – a space that usually coincides with the Classic urban centre.

Location was therefore significant to the fate and evolution of classical public structures. 'Non-core' units like circuses might be lost, but 'core' or more centrally-sited units generally endured, if modified. This process can be observed in different types of Roman public spaces. Thus, theatres located near the urban heart, such as those of Corduba or Caesaraugusta, appear to always have seen activity in their immediate vicinity; whereas in cities such as Singilia Barba, Acinipo, Regina, Pollentia and Carteia,

in: Bielmann, C. and Thomas, B. (eds.) 2018: *Debating Religious Space and Place in the Early Medieval World (c. AD 300-1000)*, Sidestone Press (Leiden), pp. 21-44.

theatres lay in more peripheral spaces (both in the High Empire and in Late Antiquity), and their 'fringe' location was, arguably, a central factor in the lack of redevelopment in the area after the building lost its original function.

This question of location and frequentation and later fortunes is critical for many Roman public structures such as entertainment buildings, baths, temples, or any other public space, but not for the city fora. Indeed, the forum is the only Roman public building complex which can be definitely excluded from this maxim, since its central location meant that it surely largely remained a frequented space, a focus of roads and planning alike – set in the geometric centre where the Kardo Maximus intersected the Decumanus Maximus. In cases where its position was somewhat removed from the topographic heart of the city – something that is in contravention of Vitruvius' (*De Arch.*1,7,1) advice about its central position in the urban fabric – this space was the fulcrum of Roman city-life, with a major role in political, social, religious and economic life. In Hispania, as in other provinces of the Empire, fora were the most characteristic and centralizing element of Roman urban planning and were designed to be a multifunctional public space. Without this focal element, Roman cities would have probably dissolved into scattered poles of attraction.

Despite this indisputable pre-eminent position, there are issues such as topography, accessibility, appropriate communications or other significant buildings of local interest that might cause a variation in the forum location (Etxebarria 2008, 41-97). Nevertheless, the importance of the forum derives from the function it fulfilled – perhaps varied but in all cases complementary (De Ruggiero 1922, 198-215; Walde and Hoffman 1965, 537ff; Coarelli 1985, 126ff; Etxebarria 2008, 26-30) – which conformed precisely to the *dignitas forensis* so characteristic of this space.

In Roman Hispania, most fora occupy a central position. This shows a fixed, parallel architectural development established once the model had been practically consolidated, comprising the temple, built on a high *podium*, aligned on the principal axis of the arcaded square. This model began to be consolidated from the second century BC, as evident in the forum of Pompeii or in the Forum of Caesar (Domínguez 2009, 29-30). The temple, set on a high podium, is defined, for example, as the centre piece of a large arcaded square or piazza whose space is delimited on one side by a basilica. This building is also the one that broadly defines the two main groups that are seen among Hispanic fora (Jiménez 1987, 115-116; Jiménez 2009): (i) fora with a basilica located on the side opposite to that which housed the focal religious building, leaving its longest side perpendicular to the longitudinal axis of the forum, as is the case of Caesaraugusta, Clunia, Baelo Claudia or Segobriga; (ii) fora featuring the basilica on the long side of the square, set parallel to the longitudinal axis, such as at Conimbriga and Turobriga, and perhaps also Tiermes. The main change after their initial planning normally related to insertions of imperial cult space, the real vehicle of the new political ideology, which found a privileged setting in the fora. In Hispania, the phenomenon of the cult of the emperor and the imperial family was finally settled in the time of Tiberius, when it became a 'matter of state' and was expressed strongly through the images.

Beyond these relatively minimal differences in form, these spaces had in common the importance they held within their respective cities. A majority of Hispanic fora in fact remained virtually intact until the third century when the first changes took place and when, most importantly, the forum structure, buildings and spaces began to undergo a slow but progressive transformation, which would, in fairly rapid time, lead to a new, late antique reality.

## Late Antique Evolutions: A Timeline of Change

The loss of the original functionality of fora in cities across the Mediterranean is recognised as an event which extended over the broad chronological period from the fourth century to the seventh century, but with special emphasis of change during the fifth and sixth centuries. This transition was one that was greatly affected by the evolving appearance of the towns. The old functional and power structures suffered adversely in many cases due to this new development: state civic laws emphasized the need to maintain the decor of the public areas, whether fora and entertainment buildings, and also, in the earlier phase, pagan temples and altars, but above all the need to prevent public areas falling into private hands (Ellis 1998). However, the interpretation of such legislation is extremely complicated because, while the frequent repetition of such laws could indicate that the illegal occupation of public land was a widespread problem, we cannot determine if that repetition in fact demonstrates the ineffectiveness of the legislation itself; furthermore, we cannot be certain whether the laws were only properly implemented in the wealthier, larger towns, where civic controls were presumably stronger.

Beyond Hispania, in Arles (France), for example, from the fifth century, archaeology has shown the occupation of the forum by houses and also how materials from the complex come to be reused for the construction of housing. This situation must have involved a major change of mindset in the citizen body, one which had long been maturing, since already a century earlier the high imperial mausolea and the circus were being transformed into areas of habitation (Sintes 1994; Loseby 1996, 45-70). Similarly, at Luna (modern Luni, Italy), although neglect and decay of the monumental centre began in the late third century, it was not until the sixth century when the first houses occupied parts of the forum zone (Ward-Perkins 1978, 313-321). In Antioch (Turkey), however, such occupation of the forum space takes place in the fourth century, and is characterized by having a stronger commercial and craft character (Liebeschuetz 1972). The chronology, as we will see, can vary from place to place, although the process of occupation of this public space, so fundamental a component of the classical city, occurs in all urban centres of all the Empire. Certainly, some of the original functions of these monumental civic squares continued during these centuries, remaining an important part of Mediterranean urbanism and not disappearing in the fourth and fifth century, but rather suffering a definitive eclipse between the sixth and seventh centuries. Indeed, before the complete neglect of theses spaces, diverse commercial and social activities persisted in them and, in addition, some fora witnessed restorations, such as repairs to paving and porticoes. Nevertheless, many of these works of maintenance – which by themselves denote the ongoing value of these squares – are attested in fora / agorai in the Eastern Empire (Lavan 2006), yet appear almost completely absent in the Western Empire from the fifth century.

In Hispania (Fig. 1), the third century ushered in, in most of the known city fora, a series of transformations took place which allows us to foresee the process that lead

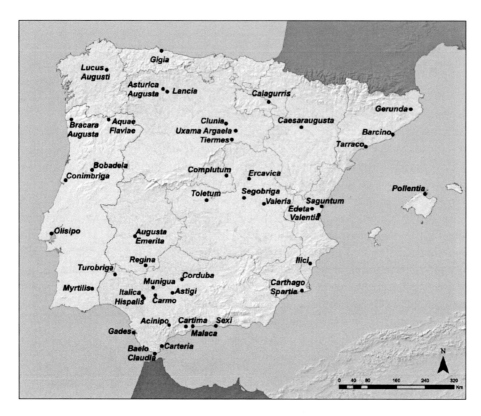

*Figure 1: Map of Hispania where we find the cities analysed in this article.*

to the end of the public spaces that typified the classical city of the High Empire. This fact, confirmed in most archaeological records, for too long was attributed to the impact of the widespread third-century crisis, which, in addition to the extensive economic and social hardships across the Empire, included incursions – mentioned by historical sources – by groups of both Franks and Alemanni extending into the Iberian Peninsula (Arce 1978, 264-265; Arce 1982). Excavations in recent years, however, have shown that if these major raids really took place, they have (as yet) no direct translation in the archaeological record.

From the mid-third century, without indications of any kind of violence or destruction, in cities like Caesaraugusta, Segobriga, Valentia and Complutum,[1] the perception of public urban spaces began to be altered with the walling up of some porches / porticoes, the burgeoning abandonment of spaces and even some areas of landfill – and yet the forum continued to function with apparent normality. In fact, honorary statues

---

1   Very few cities feature clear levels of destruction that may be associated with invasions. Efforts have been made to link them, for example, to those found in Pompaelo and Turiaso, although the only clear case seems to be Tarraco, as the historian Victor Aurelius recalled (*Liber de Caesaribus*, XXXIII, 3): 'After looting Gaul, Frank tribes took over Hispania, devastating and almost sacking the city of Tarraco, and occasionally having managed to obtain boats, some of them arrived as far as Africa'. However, the destruction has been observed only in the archaeological record of the harbour area and other areas outside the walls, and never inside the city (see Macías 2000, 260-261).

*Figure 2: Caesaraugusta. Plan of the city in which the new features that the forum acquires between the third and fourth century are represented: domestic, productive, trade and as a space for landfills. Below, the late antique structures located in the portico of the temple (Photo: Hernández and Bienes 1998 / Plan: P. Diarte-Blasco).*

and their pedestals continued to be dedicated, which shows that the *monumentum* and symbolic value of the forum remained active.

But it is important to recognize that the sequence is not uniform. Thus, in the case of Caesaraugusta (Fig. 2), its forum – built under Emperor Tiberius – kept its ground plan largely intact throughout the fourth century, although the sewer that ran under the forum and extended towards the river Ebro was blocked up at the end of the previous century (Mostalac and Perez 1989, 106-111). However, despite recognized improvements to the ornamentation of the forum between the end of the third century and the earlier fourth century, it seems that from the second half of the third century changes had commenced in this public space, including some blocking walls and repairs to the pavement (Aguarod and Mostalac 1998, 22-23). In contrast, in Valentia a fire in the forum-basilica left the building in ruins and it then seems to have become a quarry for building materials, a new honorary inscription dedicated to the emperor Probus was set up in the forum square (CIL, II, 14, 20; Ribera 2000, 19-20).

In both cases, it is clear that these early processes of change did not lead to a rupture. Instead we can interpret these as simply the result of the adaptation of the space to changes brought by the passage of time. We should not dismiss changes prior to this time, but it is noticeable that archaeologists have too frequently seen changes to be emblematic of wider changes in the Empire, namely the 'Third Century Crisis'.

Yet, as noted, the actual functionality of these spaces endured. Obviously, the picture is not uniform and there are some other examples in the Iberian Peninsula where the start of the transformations in fact brought about the end of the original use of this public space. This is particularly true of those towns that suffered calamitous events, such as Munigua and Baelo Claudia, which were affected by the earthquake that shook Baetica in the second half of the third century leading to premature urban loss/decay. A few other urban centres faltered even without natural disasters, such as those that did not survive into Late Antiquity, such as Clunia, or those whose survival underwent moments of great difficulty, such as Cartima and Saguntum (where forum activity fell away across the second century). Management and control activities were very likely moved from the upper part of the city to the lower part, to the area of porta Ferrissa (Aranegui 2004, 127). In these cities the more typical urban forum transformations, which began elsewhere in the third century and intensified in the fourth and fifth century, would show a remarkable acceleration.

Although in principle we may think that in these cases the factors that influenced the evolution of the fora of these cities – generally secondary towns in the network of Hispanic cities – are similar, the fact remains that they did not develop in exactly the same way. While in Cartima the forum was ruined as a result of violent destruction at the end of the second century (Melero 2007, 344-345; Berlanga and Melero 2009, 178-179) and apparently saw no effort at reconstruction, we can observe in Clunia that not all areas of the city were treated in the same way: thus although the forum features the first stages of transformation – for example the boarding-up of the spaces between columns – and a loss of its original function (Palol and Guitart 2000, 63-85; De la Iglesia and Tuset 2008, 83-84), Clunia's theatre complex underwent intense remodelling during this same period, showing the population's enduring engagement with leisure facilities (Gutierrez *et al.* 2006, 303; Tuset *et al.* 2009, 18-25).

Apart from these cases, characterized by the start of their transformation in the High Empire, or the examples of towns affected by natural disasters, it seems that in Hispania most forum spaces entered the third century still performing the functions for which they were conceived, even if their architectural structures were already undergoing their first evident or marked changes. Although there is no doubt that the third century was pivotal, the process did not affect all fora with the same intensity. We have noted that the majority of towns that began and fully completed their redevelopments in the third century, that is to say, those whose architectural and structural evolution was so intense that it completely prevented usual activity in the forum, were precisely those cities whose continuity of life was interrupted between Late Antiquity and the early Middle Ages. Or, put another way, the precocious demise of those urban centres had been heralded by an early and complete transformation of their fora.

This was, for instance, the case at Carteia (Bernal 2006, 448ff), Uxama (García Merino 2007, 204), Turobriga (Campos and Bermejo 2007, 257-258), Regina (Álvarez and Mosquera 1991, 364) and Pollentia (Orfila *et al.* 1999, 111-112), where it seems clear that the evolution of cities influenced the development of their fora and not the other way around. The maximum development of these towns gave way to an intense process of losing the characteristic features of the Classical city, which mainly affected public spaces and especially their fora, preventing them from keeping the functionality for which they were created.

In these urban centres which survived into Late Antiquity, the third century only led to some modifications that changed the appearance of some areas of the forum space, but not the elimination of its functionality. This is the case of the aforementioned Valentia or Caesaraugusta but also and above all, the provincial capitals of Augusta Emerita, Tarraco and Corduba. These three cities underwent specific changes and were affected by different situations, such as the earthquake that occurred in third century in Corduba. However, all three maintained their structural and functional forum spaces into the fourth century and even into the fifth.

In Tarraco, the Provincial Forum-Circus complex maintained its original and official function until at least the mid-fifth century, as signified by epigraphic evidence: the last inscription documented is dedicated to the emperors Leo and Anthemius (468-472). The epigraphic record alone, obviously, cannot demonstrate that the forum maintained all the original functions, but it seems clear that its representative character endured and that there was a civic administration which still wanted to decorate the space. Before that time, however, the first modifications had appeared in this space, with robbing of the Flavian era structures evident from the second quarter of the fifth century. This plundering caused the formation of large landfills (TED'A 1989, 447-448; Macías 1999, 182-192), which in some areas were placed directly in the square, after the robbing of the stone slabs of the pavement. The presence of two open rubbish dumps within the *temenos*, however, does not necessarily mean that the entire provincial forum had lost its official capacity (Bosch *et al.* 2005, 169). In fact, the appearance of these landfills in the square did not prevent the continued display of epigraphic (and no doubt sculptural) materials in the forum.

The Provincial Imperial Cult complex at Emerita Augusta maintained its role until the mid-fifth century, after which the temple and the porches were abandoned (Mateos and Palma 2004, 45-47; Mateos 2006, 353-354). However, it seems likely that in the fourth century the forum had already lost some of the representative quality of its past, since the robbing of materials apparently began in that period, when civic control of this space became weaker, as manifested in the abundant graffiti, mainly consisting of drawings and personal names, which were carved or applied on the marble trim at the base of the temple. Some of those base-pieces were later reused in the walls of houses during the Visigothic settlement in the area. One block of stone features graffiti representing a Chrismon, which could be viewed as an attempt to Christianise or purify the temple – unless, of course, simply a carving by a bored Christian (Alba and Mateos 2006, 356-360).

The active endurance of the Colonial Forum of Corduba does not match that of the Tarraco and Emerita Augusta fora. During the fourth century, honorary epigraphs were still being dedicated to the emperors by senior officials of the diocese (Garriguet 1997, 73-80; Marquez 2009, 105-121), indicating the ongoing functionality of the space (Hidalgo 2005, 403). However, from the second half of that century, silt was being deposited over the pavement of the piazza, and we can also trace the insertion of domestic facilities that reused architectural materials from buildings in the forum area (Carrasco 2002, 207).

High administrative status for such towns, therefore, seems to have had significance in terms of the longevity of classical public spaces, whether fora, entertainment structures or market structures. The survival of these spaces is surely symptomatic of the reality of cities whose central role in the management and control of their provinces prevented, before the fourth century and in some cases well into the fifth century, the cessation of the established function of their fora. Augusta Emerita, Tarraco and Corduba are cities that had a close and formal relationship with the Empire and, above all, managed to maintain their role as hubs and control centres. Consequently, we might assume that old political, judicial and social functions also endured longest in these elevated Hispanic centres.

But there are anomalies: the two cities of Hispalis and Barcino, neither of which were provincial capitals or had a priori little in common, both show good survival of their fora. This survival seems extraordinary when we compare the towns with others of comparable, secondary size and role. However, what can be highlighted is that, from the fourth century, both cities were made Episcopal Sees. Moreover, later, first Barcino and then Hispalis, acquired, albeit only for a short while, the seat or centre of the Visigothic monarchy, while Hispalis also became the metropolitan see of Baetica at some point in the second half of the fifth century (Ordoñez Agulla, 2005). Their selection for such roles must relate to these towns having gained much in importance in the late Roman period. Noticeably, archaeological evidence from their fora suggests that municipal power remained active at least until the fourth century. Hispalis new forum, following the most favoured scholarly hypothesis (Beltrán *et al.* 2005, 70-73), would have been built *c.* AD 300; unlike the earlier Republican forum, this was not located where the Kardo and Decumanus Maximus crossed. Its plan seems to have placed the basilica on the minor side of the square, now under the church of San Salvador (Campos and González 1987, 123-158; Campos 1993, 198-201). Excavations in the area have uncovered various inscriptions, with the latest one dedicated to the emperor Constantius, between the years 293 and 305. No subsequent inscriptions are yet documented but intensive changes did take place in that space.

In Barcino, the last epigraph comes much later than at Hispalis and was dedicated to Numio Emiliano Dextro, former proconsul of Asia, between AD 379 and 385. In fact, according to recent investigations it could be Dexter, the son of Bishop Paciano (Rodà 2001, 30-31). The fourth century sees the first notable transformations in the forum which included the building of a domestic space, known as the *domus* of Sant Honorat, which occupied part of the forum, specifically, the opposite area of the temple (Florensa and Gamarra 2006, 189-209).

Despite these data of indicators of forum survival in some centres, we can state that in Hispania, around the mid-fifth century, there were no longer any fora which retained their original functionality and none that had not changed their original form. In most forum spaces, however, we can recognize that this process of structural change, redesign and even dispersal began in the third or fourth century and, although it might be seen as a gradual phenomenon – and not a uniform one -, it was taking place at a time when new urban references began to appear in what can begin to be defined as the late antique city form.

## A New Functionality

The loss of the basic layout and architectural features of the forum spaces in the Hispanic cities thus began long before the primary roles had disappeared. In fact, in many cases, we see that the disappearance of this original functionality was a gradual process that was usually only a result of the consolidation of the private use of space. Although, in principle, this did not directly interfere with the use of the forum, it eventually caused the demise of the ancient public space. The process, however, was not uniform throughout the Iberian Peninsula and, as noted, there were cities where the interruption of forum use was caused by natural catastrophes or violent destruction such as fire or earthquakes, as occurred in Baelo Claudia and Munigua. It also seems evident in the Pollentia forum, where, between AD 270 and 280, a major fire devastated the entire area, and destroyed the insula of taverns and various other residential zones close to the forum (Arribas and Tarradell 1987, 133; Equip d'excavations de *Pollentia* 1994, 142; Orfila *et al.* 1999, 111-112). Although in this and other cases the process is sudden, this brought about the initial phase of privatization of the space. Elsewhere this new private function did not always terminate the public use of the zone, since the process was progressive and permitted the co-existence of the original functions of the forum and the emergent new ones.

The combination of various uses in these spaces was more common than might be expected. It was not unusual, for instance, to find compact domestic spaces built between the portico and between the columns of the forum or even occupying part of the square, even while some, if not all, forum activities continued (Diarte-Blasco 2015). This variety of activity seems evident in both Segobriga (Abascal *et al.* 2002; Abascal *et al.* 2004) and Caesaraugusta (Hernandez and Núñez 2000, 185), to name just two of the outstanding examples.

These houses are remarkable in many cases for their modest form and also for being directly associated with small workshops; however, among them can be seen some larger and important households, as for example in Uxama Argaela. In this case, it seems that the called Tiberian forum was active only until the Flavian period

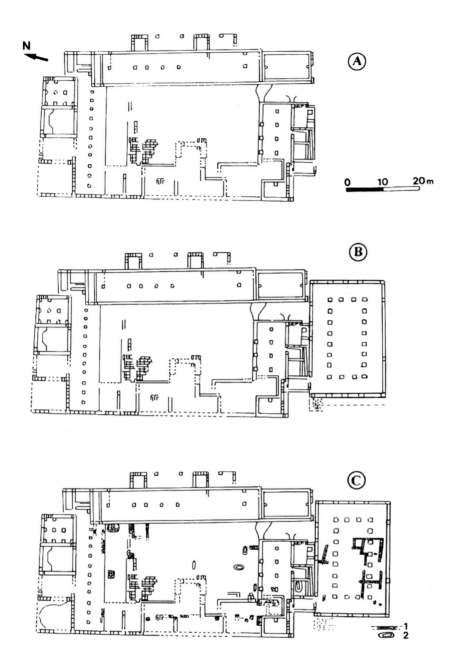

*Figure 3: Ercavica. Construction phases and forum activity: A) Augustan era; B) construction of the basilica; C) Reoccupation of the forum in Late Antiquity, where #1 represents the establishment of structures with masonry walls and #2 represents graves (Lorrio 2001).*

(García Merino 1987, 87-88; Núñez and Curchin 2007, 604). However, the cessation did not transform the forum into private use, and certainly until the late third century or early fourth century, the building maintained its public use. From this period, and although we must emphasize that it has not been excavated in its entirety, it appears that the forum structures were abandoned and the *temenos* portico was reused for the construction of a large *domus*, which seems to belong to a person of some importance – perhaps a public official (García Merino 1991, 253; 2000, 181). This domestic complex in fact exploited the layout of the pre-existing structures, with the old square adapted as a large peristyle which was paved with mosaics (Morenas de Tejada 1914, 339-349; García Merino 1987, 86-87; 2007, 208).

Gradually, the original function of this forum diminished in the face of the new private uses. It is difficult to determine whether the process was spontaneous or not, although it has been suggested – a hypothesis mainly supported by the limited number of domestic units – that it was a disorganized process, a consequence of a distinct lack of control of the municipal administration. But it is difficult to determine whether there was some kind of 'program' in this process or not. However, taking into account that the encroachment of these public spaces began in many cases before the fora's full public roles had faltered, it is likely that the process had followed some sort of pre-set plan or, at least, had had the approval of municipal powers.

The establishment of houses and small workshops around the forum was, nonetheless, a major transformation of the original features of these complexes, even if many components of the old complex were retained – such as the perimeter walls serving as the load-bearing walls of new buildings. In Carteia, for example, there was an intense late occupation, centred on the third, fourth and fifth centuries, which seemingly relates to such 'domestic intrusions' (Bernal 2006, 423) in the forum. Or we can look to Ercavica (Fig. 3), where the basilica fell out of use and came to be occupied by domestic units, marked by simple partitioning using masonry walls, which were, in some cases attached directly to the original foundations (Osuna 1976, fig. VD; Lorrio 2001, 1 0).

Besides this domestic use, rubbish dumps were created in some fora, sometimes inside buildings, but sometimes directly in the square itself, as in the colonial forum of Augusta Emerita and at Corduba. In many cases, this characteristic became the final attack on the *dignitas* of what had been the most significant urban focal point of *Romanitas*. There is no doubt that these dumps relate closely to the new housing that had been set up, and to the waste generated by the occupants; at the same time, they represent one of the first stages of plundering that affected these spaces (Gurt and Diarte-Blasco 2011, 7-22). They also signify a breakdown in civic control of intramural waste disposal. The quarry works and the subsequent reshaping of ashlar stone or other architectural elements were crucial to the new look of the old forum spaces in Regina (Álvarez and Mosquera 1991, 364-370), Tarraco, Carthago Nova[2] and Valentia (Ribera and Rossello 1999, 14-15).

These were cities with very different administrative classes, size and importance in the Hispanic urban landscape, but on whose fora workshops for milling, stone work and even quarries to obtain lime were installed. In any case, apart from the exceptions of Gerunda and Myrtilis, two towns where the fora were reconverted into spaces whose political-administrative function was paramount – in the first case, marked by the cre-

2    The *Carthago Nova* Forum is a rather unique case, since although significant degradation starts in the second century with the abandonment of some of its most emblematic spaces, in the fourth century some areas were revived as forum space. In the second century, for example, a redevelopment of the northern pavement of the square was carried out taking advantage of reused materials from other structures (De Miguel and Roland 2000, 32-37). The looting continued during the third century, and even in the fourth century, when the forum area saw some recovery, while some of the pedestals of the forum were used to refurbish the Honda Street Baths (see Noguera *et al.* 2009, 279-281).

ation of the residence of the *comes ciuitatis* (Nolla *et al.* 2009, 128), and in the second, of a palace complex (Macías 2005, 318-319) – in other cities we see a trend towards the privatization of forum spaces which certainly can be viewed as the first signs of the formation of the late antique city.

## Christianisation: The Definitive Transformation of Forum Spaces

Following this first phase privatisation of the former public area, in many cities the ancient forum spaces underwent a process of Christianisation. Although not forming a majority, the examples are sufficient and important enough in the Iberian Peninsula to consider this transition as part of the process of adapting the old fora to a new, late antique reality. Except for Astigi (Fig. 4), where an iconoclastic process may have put an end to the forum,[3] in other Hispanic cities, a direct relationship between the termination – both structural and functional – of the forum space and the establishment of Christianity is practically non-existent. After all, as seen, changes had been underway long before the full acceptance of Christianity. Christianisation, therefore, did not affect intact and active forum structures, but developed, certainly not before the fifth century, in spaces that had long lost their original role.

When talking about a Christianisation of space we are referring primarily to the establishment of burial sites, but also to the construction of churches. Regarding burials, these were not always articulated as full necropoleis, as do occur in the fora of Pollentia, Ercavica, Carteia and Astigi, but often the buried were dispersed in ones or twos or in small groups only in the former public spaces, such as in the forum of Tarraco – in both Colonial and Provincial fora, some burials appeared (Mar and Salom 1999, 79-81; Gurt and Macías 2002, 96) – or the example of Carthago Nova (Noguera *et al.* 2009, 284-285). These latter examples would signify only a partial phenomenon of intra-mural burial of the dead, without substantially affecting urbanism. But in other cities, burial activity was intense, with fora covered by necropoleis extending of much of the square, making it impracticable for any other function here besides burial, funerary rites and, conceivably, worship too, with an expectation of a church being built in the proximity to the necropolis.

In Pollentia, for example, while burials took over the piazza and some other structures from the old forum, it seems that the Capitol area was specifically or deliberately excluded from burial activity (Arribas and Tarradell 1987, 135). Although it is difficult to determine to what period we may ascribe this necropolis – identified as late Roman, early Christian and even medieval – the latest research indicates that it most likely began in the sixth century (Riera 2009, 102). This building, therefore, would have remained visible when the necropolis was established, thus raising the possibility that it might have been converted into a church.

---

3    The existence of a possible iconoclastic episode in the city is a hypothesis that arises from the discovery of a number of pieces of sculpture in the forum's large monumental pool. These high quality pieces were deposited together at the beginning of the fourth century when the pool became clogged. This date was determined through the African ceramics – Hayes 45, 46, 50 and B, and imitations of Hayes 23 B, 181 and 182 (see Romo 2002, 168).

*Figure 4: Astigi. Amazona of the sculptural repertoire found in the monumental pool of the forum.*

This situation can be extended to Conimbriga and Carteia, where the hypothesis of the reused temple for Christian worship can be made, since the burials were located at the foot of the podium of those buildings (Fig. 5) (Roldán 1992, 38; De Man 2005; Bernal 2006, 454; Roldán *et al.* 2006). Moreover, in the case of Carteia, the hypothesis becomes stronger as the temple perimeter walls were reconstructed, perhaps for this new use.

The relationship between necropolis and reuse of ancient Pagan temples as churches is a hypothesis yet to find secure archaeological confirmation; we rely on spatial connections and on stray, presumed Christian sculptural evidence such as latticework and screens. When a necropolis is lacking, the assumed transformation of the temple into a church is even harder to prove. However, in the capital of the Diocese, at Emerita Augusta, despite the absence of a necropolis, it is possible that the so-called Temple of Diana of the colonial forum, which was converted into a mansion in the medieval and modern periods, was used as a place of Christian worship (Mateos and Sastre 2004, 397-415). The building's pagan religious use failed between the fourth and fifth century, but it maintained its main architectural features. This fact, coupled with the installation of a sizeable Visigothic structure on the adjacent pool and, above all, an abundance of sculptural material of late Roman tradition – with some pieces displaying clear religious symbolism – discovered in the vicinity, suggest that perhaps one of the motivations that facilitated

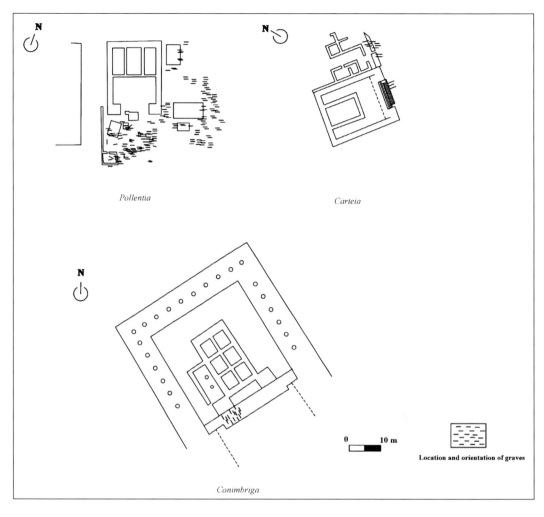

Figure 5: Location of burials in relation to the forum temples of Pollentia, Carteia and Conimbriga. The plan draws from the following sources: Orfila et al. 1999; Roldán et al. 2006; Correia and Alarcão 2008 (plan: P. Diarte-Blasco).

the survival of the temple structure was, in fact, its revised use as a church in Late Antiquity.[4]

A crucial element to take into account when looking at the permanence of sacredness (from pagan to Christian) is the continuity in religious use of a former forum unit and, specifically, its temple. However, the available data are by no means certain and there are many scholars who ignore these examples (Arce 2006, 115-124). In fact, there are only two fora in which we can affirm archaeologically that a church was imposed: Tarraco, where the area of the provincial cult temple was replaced by a church (TED'A

---

4  The Christian use of the Temple of Diana is still difficult to prove. However, we believe that the fact that a Chrismon, the mystic lamb and a cross appear in the sculptural materials, as well as the discovery of Christian tombstones in the area, make it likely, as indicated by P. Mateos and I. Sastre, that a Visigoth church could have existed either within the temple or adjacent to it.

DEBATING RELIGIOUS SPACE AND PLACE IN THE EARLY MEDIEVAL WORLD (C. AD 300-1000)

1989, 447; Mar and Salom 1999, 79-81; Bosch *et al.* 2005, 170) and Valentia, where the new religious area, in no strict relation to the pagan temple, was located in a peripheral position with respect to the principal axis of the forum.

There are also some potential examples, most often associated with the continuity between the forum space and the subsequent mosques and medieval churches – as at Caesaraugusta[5], Aquae Flaviae (Rodríguez 1999, 36-40; Rodriguez and Alcorta 1999, 782), Hispalis (Tarradellas 2000, 281; Beltrán *et al.* 2005, 73) and perhaps Toletum. The best case is that of Toletum, although the actual space occupied by the forum is unconfirmed. It has been observed that the upper zone of the city, occupying a large levelled area where the late medieval Cathedral and main square are located, appears the ideal place for the forum (Palol 1991, 788; Rubio 2005, 139-140). Indeed, P. De Palol has argued that the Catholic cathedral dedicated to St. Maria and the Episcopal see must have existed since the fifth century AD on the former area of the forum. It has been further highlighted that the site of the church of Santa Maria was later replaced by a mosque in the Muslim period, and eventually by the present Gothic cathedral, could also have been the location of the temple dedicated to the imperial cult (Palol 1991, 788-789; Barroso and Morín 2007, 104).

The Christianisation of the forum space was crucial to establish the importance that the old forum space still held within the urban fabric – and above all we should not forget its usual position in the centre of the classical town. There are many cases, however, where such Christianisation of forum space never occurred. Yet, in contrast, the first phase transformations of Late Antiquity were common for all Hispanic fora. Although there are some sites which, having gone through both phases, such as Pollentia or Conimbriga, did not survive into the Middle Ages, it seems that the majority of those cities that only experienced the privatisation of the old forum (first phase), without then featuring a subsequent Christianisation, were precisely those that disappeared in this period, as is the case for Regina, Uxama or Turobriga. In this sense, a lower rate of Christianisation of the urban topography would signal reduced or little interest towards that town on the part of the Church, and consequently a lesser architectural development was followed by a lower urban development. The reasons for such choices need further study – for example, did the Church, *i.e.* the bishops, have a say in possible urban relocation or a merging of communities in more secure seats?

However, such generalizations are dangerous, because we have cases of cities – such as Barcino – that underwent the first phase of the process of change, but did not go through the Christianisation process, and yet still endured through Late Antiquity into the Middle Ages. In this particular case, it seems that the old forum was kept as a geographical landmark within the city, although some of its building elements were

---

5    On the basis of an inscription found in the area of the curia and dated to the fourth century, plus the review of the stratigraphic and architectural contexts of the area, A. Mostalac recently postulated that some areas of this forum may have played a different role, perhaps related to Christianity, after AD 350. This hypothesis is based on the epigraph where the word 'aula' can be read, referring perhaps to a church and, above all, the fact that the curia underwent a variety of architectural remodelling during this period (Mostalac 2009, 96). However, as recently pointed out by V. Escribano, as well as the lack of clear archaeological traces to confirm this hypothesis, its possible location in the forum space would lead to the assumption that there was an Episcopal Church on the forum in the years 378/379, as deduced from the First Council of Zaragoza. In principle, this date seems too early (Escribano 2009, 156).

dismantled and dispersed, as evident for a number of honorary pedestals employed in the construction of the Episcopal palace in the early fifth century AD (Bonnet and Beltran De Heredia 2001, 74-97; Beltran De Heredia 2009, 142-169).

Therefore, we do find exceptions, but in general terms, we can trace two successive and converging phenomena which resulted in the formal dissolution of fora. The two phases of this evolution – privatization and Christianisation – were part of the complex processes – social, economic, political, religious and mental – which resulted in the emergence of a new space, one which could be said to be in part the inheritor of the forum of the High Empire, becoming a focus of diverse social attraction for the new, late antique city in Hispania.

## Conclusion

The loss of their original public use is the most significant factor in the evolution of the forum in Hispania in Late Antiquity. With only a few exceptions, from the third century AD – but sometimes even from the second century – we can trace what can be termed an unstoppable transformation of the forum, whereby structures (first) and functions (later) were gradually discarded as the townscapes overall evolved into a new, late antique form. The appearance and establishment of domestic units over the forum space became a clear urban and social trend in which – though it seems rather excessive to talk about 'planning' – permission from the ongoing civic authorities was at least surely necessary. In fact, in many cities, when the first such invasive domestic structures appear, and when walls or their materials come to be reused for the first time, we can observe that the fora had not totally lost their original functionality. Thus, it is incautious to speak of a watertight process in which the forum spaces first ceased to be fora and only then were re-occupied by houses and/or workshops. Indeed, in many cases, their use as civic squares and commercial spaces endured even as domestic structures were becoming established in these sectors and so it is possible to claim a co-existence of public and private functions and activities during the fourth and fifth centuries. In reality, the processes overlapped and most of the public spaces investigated had already started their transformation before Late Antiquity. That is why it is most likely that the dissolution process of the socio-political and religious activity that took place in fora happened when the modifications in the architectural structures and spatial ornamentation occurred.

The privatisation phase was certainly one of the first peculiarities of late antique urbanism. It took place in a gradual and progressive way, except in those cities where violent actions or natural catastrophes accelerated the evolution, provoking abrupt changes. However, we must not consider the transformation process in the fora as unique or isolated, because other public spaces, including their communicating streets and porticos, were in many instances also taken over for private use. In this widely changing context, it is possible to detect a change in mentality: public spaces were ceasing to be interpreted in a Classical way, and losing their reason to exist, as new necessities emerged.

As a consequence, the Christianisation of some fora did not directly affect the overall old Roman structure, but always took place as a secondary reoccupation of the space formerly used by the forum, which then, in many cases, become an area for habitation.

Though it would often keep part of the original distribution of the space, when the necropolis and churches began to be built, the fora had already lost their functionality and, in most instances, also their physiognomy. Occupied by houses, small workshops and sometimes even rubbish dumps, they started a Christianising process which did not take full shape until the fifth or sixth century. For this reason, Christianisation cannot be considered decisive in the cessation of forum function.

Nor did such Christianisation occur in all Hispanic fora. This fact is significant in showing that Christianisation of the space did not assure its survival as an essential space in the late antique urban organization; however, its absence tended to occur in cities which had a weaker urbanization in Late Antiquity and, therefore, a lower chance of survival.

The appearance of a new form of power was fundamental in the organization of a new urbanism. However, it was not until the *curiae* had been weakened, or had vanished, that the Church could start to take hold of the spaces where the *curiae* had previously exerted their power. This fact, even if likely, does not yet have clear confirmation in the archaeological record and thus it is preferable to simply point out that many fora have spaces that continued to be used, first by the city curiae and later by the Church. It is highly significant that, in cities as different as Tarraco, Pollentia or Valentia, the new powers took over a space which, despite it having lost the representativeness it had possessed in the classical past, must have maintained some type of *memoria*, since the inclusion of the old forum within the new topography of power seems neither casual nor brought about by chance. This topography, on the other hand, dictated that the old public space continued to have a pre-eminent position in the urban fabric, and above all – by means of the old fora – directly linked the Classical city with the new urban forms of Late Antiquity.

As we have seen, therefore, the transition of the Hispanic cities into the late antique period - both the urban 'project' that was fading and the new type of city that was forming – can be identified in clear fashion with changes to and in their fora. But, while the archaeology shows change, we need still to speculate on the agents of change in the first phase – are changes due to a debilitated *curia*? Or is this reflective of towns lacking sponsors? Or perhaps space was even being sold to help fund empty urban coffers? These questions are difficult to answer from the archaeology, although it seems that the weakened *curia* may well have allowed certain intrusions, with specific zones the first given over to private activity: perhaps the market square remained open for market stalls, but porticos were sold off first. In this sense: Was stone robbing actually legal? Or should we see the sale of specific old and unmaintained structures first and then a progressive robbing elsewhere? In Hispania, it seems evident that especially in the first moment, the robbed materials drawn from public buildings were reused in the construction of other public structures, which leads us to conclude that between the third and the fifth century, the phenomenon might have been controlled by the urban authorities. We cannot rule out sales to private citizens and, perhaps, after the fifth century, certain processes of looting became widespread. The initial control of the process, in any case, does not prevent us from wondering if the townscape came to look 'shabby' and untidy as a result. On the other hand, this might be nothing more than a modern perception of the researchers that does not correspond with the reality of those inhabitants of Late Antiquity. It is difficult to establish whether those were the declining standards, but what is clear is that beyond the concept of decline, in the late antique cities of Hispania the fora changed and would never be the same again. In sum, the archaeological data are growing but so are the questions about the lives and fates of the fora.

## Acknowledgements

This paper was written as part of the MED-FARWEST project based at the University of Leicester and funded by the European Union's Horizon 2020 research and innovation programme under the Marie Sklodowska-Curie grant agreement No 658045. My thanks go to Professor Neil Christie of the University of Leicester; his expertise and understanding substantially improved the latest version of this paper.

Furthermore, I am hugely grateful to J. M. Gurt, Professor of the University of Barcelona, for his invaluable support in the guidance of my first years of pre-doctoral research and for much advice since.

## Bibliography

### Primary Sources

CIL= *Corpus Inscriptionum Latinarum.* Berlin, 1863-.

Vitruvius, M.L. *De Architectura libri decem.* Translated from Latin by F. Granger (ed.). Cambridge. Harvard University Press, 1934.

Victor, S.A. *Liber de Caesaribus.* Translation from Latin by P. Dufraigne (ed.). Paris: Les Belles Lettres, 1975.

### Secondary Sources

Abascal, J.M., Almagro, M., and Cebrián, R. 2002. Segobriga 1989-2000. Topografía de la ciudad y trabajos en el foro. *Madrider Mitteilungen* 43, 123-161.

Abascal, J.M., Cebrián, R., and Trunk, M. 2004. Epigrafía, arquitectura y decoración arquitectónica del Foro de Segóbriga, in: Ramallo S.F. (ed.), *La decoración arquitectónica en las ciudades romanas de Occidente.* Murcia: Universidad de Murcia, 219-256.

Alba, M. and Mateos, P. 2006. Epílogo: transformación y ocupación tardoantigua y altomedieval del llamado foro provincial, in: Mateos, P. (ed.), *El "Foro Provincial" de Augusta Emerita: un conjunto monumental de culto imperial.* Madrid: Anejos de Archivo Español de Arqueología, 355-380.

Álvarez, J.M. and Mosquera, J.L. 1991. Excavaciones en Regina (1986-1990), in: *I Jornadas de Prehistoria y Arqueología en Extremadura (1986-1990).* Mérida: *Extremadura Arqueológica II*, 361-371.

Aguarod, C. and Mostalac, A. 1998. *Historia de Zaragoza, Vol.4: La Arqueología de Zaragoza en la Antigüedad Tardía.* Zaragoza: Ayuntamiento de Zaragoza, Servicio de Cultura: Caja de Ahorros de la Inmaculada.

Aranegui C. 2004. *Sagunto: "oppidum", emporio y municipio romano.* Barcelona: Bellatera.

Arce J. 1978. La crisis del siglo III d.C. en Hispania y las invasiones bárbaras. *Hispania Antiqua* VIII, 257-269.

Arce, J. 1982. *El último siglo de la España romana: 284-409.* Madrid: Alianza Editorial.

Arce, J. 2006. *Fana, templa, delubra destrui praecipimus*: el final de los templo de la Hispania romana. *Archivo Español de Arqueología* 79, 115-124.

Arribas, A. and Tarradell, M. 1987. El Foro de Pollentia. Noticia de las primeras investigaciones, in: *Los foros romanos de las Provincias Occidentales.* Madrid: Ministerio de Cultura, 121-136.

Barroso, R. and Morín, J. 2007. La *Civitas Regia* Toletana en el contexto de la Hispania de la séptima centuria, in: Carrobles, J. Barroso, R. Morin J. and Valdes F. (eds), *Regia Sedes Toletana. La topografía de la ciudad de Toledo en la Antigüedad Tardía y Alta Edad Media.* Toledo: Real Fundación de Toledo, 95-161.

Beltrán, J., González, D. and Ordóñez, S. 2005. Acerca del Urbanismo de *Hispalis.* Estado de la cuestión y perspectivas. *Mainake* XXVII, 61-88.

Beltrán de Heredia, J. 2009. Arquitectura y sistemas de construcción en Barcino durante la antiguedad tardía. Materiales, técnicas y morteros: un fósil dierctor en el yacimiento de la Plaza del Rey. *Quaderns d'Arqueologia i Història de laCiutat de Barcelona* 5,142-169.

Berlanga, M.J. and Melero, F. 2009. Cartima a través de las fuentes arqueológicas y epigráficas, in: González, J. and Pavón, P. (eds), *Andalucía romana y visigoda. Ordenación y vertebración del territorio.* Roma: L'Erma di Bretschneider, 167-190.

Bernal, D. 2006. *Carteia* en la Antigüedad Tardía, in: Roldán, L. Bendala, M. Blánquez J. and Martínez S. (eds), *Estudio histórico-arqueológico de la ciudad de Carteia (San Roque, Cádiz), 1994-1999, I.* Sevilla: Andalucía, Consejería de Cultura, 417-464.

Bonnet, C. and Beltrán de Heredia, J. 2001. Origen y evolución del conjunto episcopal de Barcino: de los primeros tiempos cristianos a la época visigótica, in: Beltrán de Heredia, J. (ed.), *De Barcino a Barcinona (siglos I-VIII). Los restos arqueológico de la plaza del Rey de Barcelona.* Barcelona: MHCB, Ajuntament de Barcelona, Institut de Cultura Barcelona,74-93.

Bosch, F., Macías, J.M., Menchon, J.J., Muñoz, A. and Teixell, I. 2005. La transformació urbanística de l'acròpolis de Tarragona: avanç de les excavacions del Pla Director de la Catedral de Tarrgona (2000-2002), in: Gurt, J.M. and Ribera, A. (eds), *VI Reunió d'Arqueologia Cristiana Hispànica. Les ciutats tardoantigues d'Hispania: cristianizació i topografia.* Barcelona: Monografies de la Secció Històrico-Arqueològica, 167-174.

Campos, J.M. 1993. La estructura urbana de la *Colonia Iulia Romula Hispalis* en época imperial. *Anales de Arqueología Cordobesa* 4, 181-219.

Campos, J.M. and Bermejo, J. 2007. Manifestaciones de culto imperial en el foro de la ciudad hispanorromana de *Turobriga*, in: Nogales, T. and González, J. (eds), *CultoImperial: política y poder.* Roma: L'Erma di Bretschneider, 253-273.

Campos, J. and González, J. 1987. Los foros de *Hispalis. Colonia Romula. Archivo Español de Arqueología,* vol. 155-156, 123-158.

Carrasco, I. 2002. Intervención arqueológica de urgencia en un solar sito en calle Góngora número 13 esquina a calle Teniente Braulio Laportilla (Córdoba). *AnuarioArqueológico de Andalucía 1997* (III), 199-208.

Coarelli, F. 1985. *Il Foro Romano II. Periodo repubblicano e augusteo*. Roma: Edizioni Quasar.

Correia, V.H. and Alarcão J. 2008. *Conimbriga:* um ensaio de topografia histórica. *Conimbriga* 47, 31-46.

De Man, A. 2005. Sobre a Cristianizaçãode um *Forum. Al-madan* 13, electronic adendum.

De Miquel, L. and Roldán, B. 2000. Actuaciones arqueológicas en el área meridional del Molinete en 1999, in: *XI Jornadas de Patrimonio Histórico y Arqueología Regional, Murcia, del 2-5 de Mayo de 2000*. Murcia: Dirección General de Cultura, 32-37.

De Ruggiero, E. 1922. *Forum*, in: De Ruggiero, E. (ed.), *Dizionario epigrafico di antichità romane*. Roma: Pascualucci, 198-215.

Diarte-Blasco, P. 2009. La evolución de las ciudades romanas en Hispania entre los siglos IV y VI d. C.: los espacios públicos como factor de transformación. *Mainake* XXXI, 71-84.

Diarte-Blasco, P. 2012. *La configuración urbana de la Hispania tardoantigua: transformaciones y pervivencias de los espacios públicos romanos (s. III-VI d. C.)*. Oxford: BAR International Series (2429).

Diarte-Blasco, P. 2015. La convivencia de lo público y lo privado: el establecimiento de unidades domésticas y artesanales en los espacios cívicos hispanos, in: Brassous, L. and Quevedo, A. (eds), *Urbanisme civique en temps de crise. Les espaces publics d'Hispanie et de l'Occident romain entre le IIe et le IVe siècle*. Madrid: Casa de Velázquez, 289-307.

Diarte-Blasco, P. and Gurt, J.M. 2015. La percepción del espacio en el urbanismo tardoantiguo: características evolutivas en el ejemplo hispano. *Isidore de Séville et son temps. Antiquité Tardive* 23, 307-328.

Domínguez, A. 2009. Espacios públicos en transición: del ágora griega al foro romano, in: Noguera, J.M. (ed.), *Fora Hispaniae. Paisaje urbano, arquitectura, programas decorativos y culto imperial en los foros de las ciudades hispanorromanas*. Murcia: Editum, 24-35.

Ellis, S. 1998. Power-broking and the refuse of public buildings in Late Antiquity, in: Cambi, N. and Marin, E. (eds), *Acta XIII Congressus Internationalis Archaeologiae Christianae. Split-Porec (25.9-1.10.1994)*. Vatican City-Split: Pontificio Istituto di Archeologia Cristiana,233-239.

Escribano, V. 2009. La sacralización cristiana de los espacios. El caso de Zaragoza, in: Mostalac, A. and Escribano, V. (eds), *El cristianismo primitivo en Aragón*. Zaragoza: caja de Ahorros de la Inmaculada, 145-159.

Etxebarría, A. 2008. *Los foros romanos republicanos en Italia centro-meridional tirrena. Origen y evolución formal*. Madrid: Consejo Superior de Investigaciones Científicas.

Florensa, F. and Gamarra, A. 2006. L'excavació del jaciment arqueològic del carrer Sant Honorat 3, de Barcelona. *Tribunal 'Arqueologia* 2003-2004,189-209.

García Merino, C. 1987. Desarrollo urbano y programación política de *Uxama Argaela. Boletín del Seminario de Estudio de Arte y Arqueología* LIII, 73-107.

García Merino, C. 1991. La casa urbana en *Uxama Argaela*, in: *La casa urbana hispanorromana. Ponencia y comunicaciones*. Zaragoza: Institución Fernando el Católico, 233-259.

García Merino, C. 2007. Crecimiento urbano, abastecimiento de agua y territorio en *Uxama Argaela*, in: Navarro, M. and Palao, J.J. (eds), *Villes et territoires dans le bassin du Douro à l'époque romaine*. Bordeaux: Diffusion de Boccard, 202-235.

Garriguet, J.A. 1997. Un posible edificio de culto imperial en la esquina SE del foro colonial de Córdoba. *Antiquitas* 8, 73-80.

Gurt, J.M. 2000-2001. Transformaciones en el tejido de las ciudades hispanas durante la Antigüedad Tardía: dinámicas urbanas. *Zephyrus* LIII-LIV, 433-442.

Gurt, J.M. and Diarte-Blasco, P. 2011. Spolia et Hispania: alcuni esempi peninsulari. *Hortus Artium Medievalia* 17, 7-22.

Gurt, J.M. and Macías, J.M. 2002. La ciudad y el *territorium* de *Tarraco*: el mundo funerario, in: Vaquerizo, D. (ed.), *Espacios y usos funerarios en el Occidente romano*. Córdoba: Universidad de Córdoba, Seminario de Arqueología, 87-112.

Hernández, J.A. and Núñez, J. 2000. La ordenación del espacio de la Zaragoza prerromana y romana. *Salduie* I, 181-202.

Hidalgo, R. 2005. Algunas cuestiones sobre la *Corduba* de la Antigüedad Tardía, in: Gurt, J.M. and Ribera, A. (eds), *VI Reunión de Arqueología Cristiana Hispánica (Cartagena, 2003).* Barcelona: Monografies de la Secció Històrico-Arqueològica, 401-414.

Iglesia, M.A. de la and Tuset, F. 2008. Clunia centro de poder territorial, in Burón, M. (ed.), *Patrimonio cultural y territorio en el Valle de Duero. Actas Coloquio Internacional*. Valladolid: Junta de Castilla y León, 75-85.

Jiménez, J.L. 1987. *Arquitectura forense en la Hispania romana*. Zaragoza: Universidad de Zaragoza.

Jiménez, J.L. 2009. Los foros en las provincias de Hispania: estado de la cuestión, in: Noguera, J.M. (ed.), *Fora Hispaniae. Paisaje urbano, arquitectura, programas decorativos y culto imperial en los foros de las ciudades hispanorromanas*. Murcia: Editum, 35-64.

Kulikowski, M. 2004. *Late Roman Spain and its Cities*. Baltimore: The Johns Hopkins University Press.

Lavan, L. 2006. Fora and Agorai in Mediterranean cities during the 4th and 5th c. A.D., in: Bowden, W., Gutteridge, A. and Machado, C. (eds.), *Social and Political life in Late Antiquity*. Leiden and Boston: Brill, 195-249.

Liebeschuetz, J.H.W.G. 1972. *Antioch: City and imperial administration in the later Roman Empire*. Oxford: Oxford University Press.

Lorrio, A. 2001: *Ercavica. La muralla y la topografía de la ciudad*. Madrid: Publicaciones Universidad de Alicante.

Loseby, S.T. 1996. Arles in Late Antiquity: *Gallula Roma Arelas and Urbs* Genesii, in: Christie, N. and Loseby, S.T. (eds), *Towns in Transition. Urban Evolution in Late Antiquity and the Early Middle Ages*. Aldershot: Scolar Press, 45-70.

Macías, J.M. 1999. *La ceràmica comuna tardoantiga a Tàrraco. Anàlisis tipològica i històrica (segles V-VII)*. Tarragona: Tulcis. Monografies Tarraconenses.

Macías, J.M. 2000. *Tarraco* en la Antigüedad Tardía: un proceso simultáneo de transformación urbana e ideológica, in: Ribera, A. (ed.), *Los orígenes del cristianismo en Valencia y su entorno*. Valencia: Ajuntament de València, 260-261.

Macías, S. 2005: *Mértola, O último porto do Mediterrâneo*. Mértola: Campo Arqueológico de Mértola.

Mar, R. and Salom, C. 1999. La transformació de l'acròpoli de Tàrraco, in: de Palol P. (ed.), *Del Romà al romanic. Història, art i cultura de la Tarraconense Mediterrània entre els segles IV i X.* Barcelona: Enciclopèdia Catalana, 79-81.

Márquez, C. 2009. Transformaciones en los Foros de *Colonia Patricia*, in: Noguera, J.M. (ed.), *Fora Hispaniae. Paisaje urbano, arquitectura, programas decorativos y culto imperial en los foros de las ciudades hispanorromanas.* Murcia: Editum, 105-121.

Mateos, P. (ed.) 2006. *El "Foro Provincial" de Augusta Emerita: un conjunto monumental de culto imperial.* Madrid: Anejos de Archivo Español de Arqueología.

Mateos, P. and Sastre, I. 2004. Mobiliario arquitectónico de época tardoantigua en el entorno del templo de Diana de Mérida. Una propuesta sobre su ocupación entre los siglos VI-IX. *Mérida. Excavaciones arqueológicas* 2001, 397-415.

Mateos, P. and Palma, F. 2004. Arquitectura oficial, in: Dupré, X. (ed.), *Mérida, Colonia Augusta Emerita.* Roma: L'Erma Di Bretschneider, 44-45.

Melero, F. 2007. El estudio de la *Cartima* romana (Cártama, Málaga) a través de los nuevos hallazgos. *Mainake* XXIX, 339-355.

Morenas de Tejada, G. 1914. Divulgaciones arqueológicas. Las ruinas de Uxama. *Por esos mundos*, 338-344.

Mostalac, A. and Pérez, J.A. 1989. La excavación del Foro de Caesaraugusta, in: *La Plaza de La Seo.Zaragoza. Investigaciones Histórico-Arqueológicas.* Zaragoza: Estudios de Arqueología urbana, 81-155.

Noguera, J.M., Soler, B., Madrid, M.J. and Vizcaíno, J.2009. El foro de Carthago Nova. Estado de la cuestión, in: Noguera, J.M. (ed.), *Fora Hispaniae. Paisaje urbano, arquitectura, programas decorativos y culto imperial en los foros de las ciudades hispanorromanas.* Murcia: Editum, 217-302.

Nolla, J.M., Palia, L., Sagrera, J., Sureda, M., Canal, E., García, G., Lloveras, M.J. and Canal, J.2009. *Del fòrum a la plaça de la Catedral. Evolució històrico urbanística del sector septentrional de la ciutat de Girona.* Gerona: Història Urbana de Girona.

Núñez, S.I. and Curchin, L.A. 2007. *Uxama Argaela*, in: Navarro M. and Palao, J.J. (eds), *Villes et territoires dans le bassin du Douro à l'époque romaine.* Bordeaux: Diffusion de Boccard, 600-609.

Ordóñez Agulla, S. 2005. Hispalis. Perfil histórico, in: *La catedral en la Ciudad (I). De Astarté a San Isidoro.* Sevilla: Catedral de Sevilla. Aula Hernán Ruiz

Orfila, M., Arribas, A. and Cau, M.A. 1999. La ciudad romana de *Pollentia*: el foro. *Archivo Español de Arqueología* 72, 99-118.

Osuna, M. 1976. *Ercávica I. Aportación al estudio de la Romanización de la Meseta.* Cuenca: Patronato Arqueológico Provincial.

Palol, P. 1991. Resultados de las excavaciones junto al Cristo de la Vega, basílica conciliar de Santa Leocadia de Toledo. Algunas notas de topografía religiosa de la ciudad, in: *Actas del Congreso Internacional del XIV Centenario del Concilio III de Toledo (589-1989).* Toledo: Arzobispado de Toledo, 787-813.

Palol, P. and Guitart, J. 2000. *Los grandes conjuntos públicos. El foro colonial de Clunia.* Burgos: Diputación Provincial de Burgos.

Ribera, A. 2000. *Valentia* del paganismo al cristianismo: siglos IV y V, in: Ribera, A. (ed.), *Los orígenes del cristianismo en Valencia y su entorno.* Valencia: Ajuntament de València, 19-32.

Ribera, A. and Roselló, M. 1999. *L'Almoina: el nacimiento de la Valentia cristiana*. Quaderns de Difusió Arqueològica 5. Valencia.

Riera, M. 2009. Enterramientos de la Antigüedad Tardía en las islas de Cabrera y Mallorca, in: López, J., Martínez, A. and Morín, J. (eds), *Morir en el mediterráneo Medieval*. Oxford: British Archaeological Report, 99-151.

Rodà, I. 2001. Barcelona desde su fundación hasta el siglo IV d. C, in: Beltrán de Heredia, J. (ed.), *De Barcino a Barcinona (siglos I-VIII). Los restos arqueológico de la plaza del Rey de Barcelona*. Barcelona: MHCB, Ajuntament de Barcelona, Institut de Cultura Barcelona, 22-31.

Rodríguez, A. 1999. *Aquae Flaviae* II. Chaves.

Rodríguez, A. and Alcorta, E. 1999. Aquae Flaviae (Chaves), ciudad romana: balance y posibilidades, in: Rodríguez, A. (ed.), *Los orígenes de la ciudad en el noroeste hispánico: actas del Congreso Internacional, Lugo 15-18 de mayo de 1996, Vol. 2*. Lugo: Diputación Provincial de Lugo, 779-806.

Roldán, L. 1992. *Técnicas constructivas romanas en Carteia (San Roque, Cadiz)*. Madrid: Monografías de Arquitectura Romana.

Roldán, L., Bendala, M., Blánquez J. and Martínez S. 2006. *Estudio Histórico-arqueológico de la ciudad de Carteia (San Roque, Cádiz) 1994-1999*. Sevilla: Andalucía, Consejería de Cultura.

Romo, A.S. 2002. Las termas del foro de *Colonia Firma Astigi*, Écija (Sevilla). *Romula* 1, 151-174.

Rubio R. 2005. Toledo Romano: balance y nuevas perspectivas en la investigación, in: Romero, A. (ed.), *Arqueología romana en Toletum: 1985-2004*. Toledo: Consorcio de la Ciudad de Toledo, 137-139.

Sintés, C. 1994. La réutilisation des espaces publics à Arles: un temoignage de la fin de l'Antiquité. *Antiquité Tardive* 2, 181-192.

Tarradellas, M.C. 2000. Topografía urbana de Sevilla durante la Antigüedad Tardía, in: Gurt, J.M. and Tena, N. (eds), *V Reunió d'Arqueologia Paleocristiana Hispánica, Cartagena 1998*. Barcelona: Monografies de la Secció Històrico-Arqueològica, 279-290.

TED'A 1989. El Foro Provincial de *Tarraco*. Un complejo arquitectónico de época Flavia. *Archivo Español de Arqueología* 62, 141-191.

Tuset, F., Iglesia, M.A. de la and Elkin, M. 2009. Clunia: Roman failure, archaeological marvel. *Current World Archaeology* 32, 18-25.

Walde, A. and Hoffman, J.B. 1965. *Lateinisches Etymologisches Wörterbuch*, I, 4. Heidelberg: Indogermanische Bibliothek.

Ward Perkins, B. 1978. Luni. The decline and abandonment of a Roman town, in: Blake, H.McK., Potter, T.W. and Whitehouse, D.B. (eds), *Papers in Italian Archaeology I*. Oxford: British Archaeological Reports, 313-321.

# Malta in Late Antiquity

## Mortuary Places and Spaces

*Glen Farrugia*

### Introduction: Confrontation or Transition?

Plenty of ink has arguably been spilt over the subject of Christianisation. Gibbon's (1782) ageless *The History of the Decline and Fall of the Roman Empire* and Brown's (2012) recent *Through the Eye of a Needle: Wealth, the Fall of Rome, and the Making of Christianity in the* West are just two examples of published works on the subject of early Christianity, albeit linked to the fall of Rome. Indeed, while these were written centuries apart, they demonstrate the continuing fascination scholars have with the topic of early Christianity and its seemingly rapid rise from a persecuted religion to the sole faith of the empire and the various kingdoms of Western Europe. Once only explored within a historical framework, research has exploded within archaeological (*e.g.* Ferrua 1953 Rutgers 2000), anthropological (*e.g.* Fletcher 1999), and even psychological and political (*e.g.* de Ste. Crois 1963; Theide 1992) disciplines, all of which have impacted our understanding of 'Christianisation'. This topic has also attracted the attention of scriptwriters seeking to romanticise the events. We can recall the 1951 Hollywood film directed by Mervyn LeRoy *Quo Vadis* which shows lions in the Roman amphitheatre tearing apart the limbs of early Christians condemned for their faith, while the pagan spectators cheered and enjoyed themselves. In 2009, the film 'Agora' depicted Rachel Weisz as Hypatia during the turmoil and social unrest of fourth-century Alexandria. While these dramatisations are of course exaggerations of the time period, researchers also argue that the historical accounts were embellished. Candida Moss (2013), for example, argues that some of the story of Christian persecution is fictitious, although we know that public executions of early Christian communities happened during the time of the Julio-Claudian dynasty until the Constantine. This was due to a fear that the new, fast emerging, religion and community could put the Roman Empire, its beliefs and its politics in jeopardy. To this end, a political campaign in the first century AD took its toll on the Christians and those who acknowledged such faith (Chohick 2010, 82).

in: Bielmann, C. and Thomas, B. (eds.) 2018: *Debating Religious Space and Place in the Early Medieval World (c. AD 300-1000)*, Sidestone Press (Leiden), pp. 45-60.

The oppression on those embracing Christian faith lasted until AD 313 when Constantine the Great declared the Christian faith as legitimate in the edict of Milan. However, conflicts surely did not stop there, especially since the majority of the Roman citizens living in the Empire till the end of the fourth century AD still embraced a polytheistic religion. Indeed, the destruction of the Serapeum in Alexandria in AD 391 is often seen as a classic example of continued hostilities between Christians and pagans during the late Roman period.

This chapter thus sets out to first review the available source material which deals with evidence of tolerance of the new Christian community towards other religions and ideologies across the fourth century AD. Here I consider how early Christian texts are read and whether we can evaluate these texts as historical documents relating them to historical circumstances in which they were generated. I then consider the results of this review in relation to the Maltese islands and the archaeological data derived from past and recent excavations – do we see any evidence of competition for space, or, as a result, religious conflict between various communities living in Malta in the fourth century AD? Two case studies will be discussed which highlight the religious origins of inscriptions and symbolism found in Maltese mortuary spaces: the first concerns inscriptions and frescoes found at hypogeum number two in the St. Agatha catacombs, and the second example constitutes two inscriptions located on the walls of the South-East hypogeum at Tac-Caghki secondary school. In addition, this chapter analyses the archaeological and epigraphic record for any new evidence which can shed light on the religious transition. The inclusion of data from the archaeological record is not aimed at critiquing volumes, such as Young's (2014) *The Cambridge History of early Christian History*, but rather to set objectives to complement, or perhaps, fill in any gaps in this subject. What additional information can the archaeological record reveal about early Christianity and its inception as an official religion? Excavations in one of these catacombs during the mid-1950s revealed fourth-century frescoes and epitaphs: these are of high archaeological importance as their content reveals important information about religious beliefs of the time. Furthermore, the positioning of these frescoes potentially shed light on the relationship between pagan, Jewish and Christian communities living on fourth-century Malta and how they chose to use (or reuse) and share mortuary spaces.

## The Maltese Islands: Historical Context

With a total area of 316 square kilometres, the Maltese archipelago consists of three islands – Malta, Gozo and Comino. Malta is largest of the three and covers an area of almost 243 square kilometres. Here human activity can be detected as early as the fifth millennium BC. The second island of the trio is Gozo. This is relatively small; however, evidence shows a flourishing community living here as early as the fourth millennium BC. Lastly, Comino is the smallest of the three. No archaeological evidence of early settlements is noticed here expect for one single tomb which dated back to the Phoenician period, that is, the seventh – eighth century BC (Buhagiar 1986; Said-Zammit 1993; Trump 2005). Malta's geographical position in the centre of the Mediterranean attracted ancient civilisations that ended up colonising the islands recurrently. Following the prehistoric community, the Phoenicians and Punic communi-

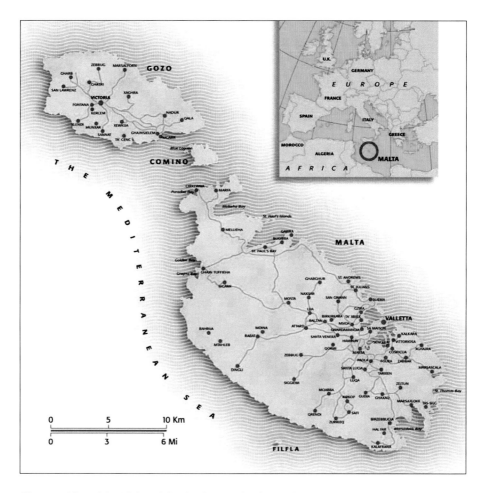

*Figure 6: Map of the Maltese islands (Orange Smile travels).*

ties occupied the islands for around six centuries (eighth – third century BC) and then the Roman when took over the archipelago in the 218 BC (Bonanno 2005) (Fig. 6).

According to the ancient Roman historian Titus Livius, the Maltese islands fell under Roman rule in 218 BC. Although the literary sources of the first two centuries of Roman rule are quite numerous (Bonanno 2003, 142), the political situation of the late Empire is somewhat blurred by lack of documentary data (Bonanno, 2003). Were the Maltese islands considered by Romans as part of the western or the eastern Empire? This gap makes it difficult to understand the social setting of Malta during this period as well as the political and religious ideologies of the local people. One inscription provides some context to the status of one of the islands in early fourth century. The inscription was erected by the city of Gozo (*Gaulus Isula*) to Constantius Chlorus (AD 293-306), Augustus of the western empire and Galerius (AD 305-311), August of the eastern empire (*CIL* X.7504; *cf.* Rizzo 1976-77, 201*)*:

> *D(OMINO)N(OSTRO) C(AIO) AUR(ELIO) VALERIO / CONSTANTIO AUG(USTO), / R(ES) P(UBLICA) GAUL(ITANORUM), CUR(ANTE) / F(?) POLLIONE* [ET] *RUFO / M(?) F[---] IIIVIRR(IS) / [---].*

*'To our lord Caius Valerius Aurelius Constantius Augustus; the city ( res publica )*
*of Gaulus [set this up], under the supervision of F(?) Pollio and Rufo M(?) F(...),*
*members of the board of three men...'*

While the inscription provides indication of Gozo's political status and administration, that is, the status of the city as a *'res publica'* not a *municipium,* it however does not provide any clues on which jurisdiction the island fell (Bonanno 2003, 260).

Perhaps, more revealing is the discovery of a hoard of bronze coins dating to *c.* AD 275. The hoard was discovered in 1937 in Rabat, Gozo, by workers who were constructing parts of St. George's basilica (Bonanno 2005, 227). Although the coins are not in a good state of conservation, the low relief on one of the sides seem to depict the prominent head of Claudius II, who was Roman Emperor between the AD 268 and AD 270, while on the other side of the coin, the depiction is almost unrecognisable; however, one can notice what seems to be a bearded man dressed as a soldier holding military equipment in hand. This may indicate the goddess *Fides* which was commonly depicted on the *Antoninianus* – the currency of that time. Maltese researchers, such as Bonanno (2005) attributed these coins to an eastern-province mint and suggested that this might be indicative that the Maltese Islands were part of the Eastern Roman empire in the late third/early fourth century. Although this evidence should not be ignored, it would certainly be incorrect to draw firm conclusions on the jurisdictional placement of Maltese islands based on this discovery, especially since the type of coins discovered were mostly minted in Rome and Mediolanum (modern Milan). Later mints were also stuck in *Siscia* and Antioch (Sellars 2013, 349-350). However, the parallels that can be drawn with the Maltese types, at least those referred to and illustrated by Bonanno, seem to be of western provenance.

## Religious Context: Pagan, Jewish, and Christian Communities

When it comes to the religious status of the islands, the information here is more revealing. Epigraphic evidence shows that up to the second century AD a strong pagan belief was prominent on Malta: inscriptions in Mtarfa and Mdina (North-West of Malta) refer to a temple of Prosperina and its restoration in the first century AD and the construction of a temple dedicated to Apollo in the second century AD respectively:

> *(CHRE)STION AVG B P(ROC)/ (INSU)LARUM MELIT ET (GWL)/*
> *(COLUMNA)S CUM F(ASTI)DIIS/ ET PA(RIETI)BVS/ TEM(PLI) DEAE/*
> *PROSPERINAE VETVSTATE/ RVINAM INMINEN(TI)BVS/ RESI (TITUI)*
> *T (RI)MVI ET PILA(M)/ INAVRAVIT (CIL X.7494; cf.* Bonanno 2005,203).

> *'Chrestion, procurator of the islands of Melite and Gaulus, damaged columns and*
> *walls at the old temple of Prosperina risking to collapse. Things included small*
> *cracks in the golden ball.'*

Ancient literary sources of the second century AD refer to other pagan temples, notably, the ones dedicated to *Herakles* and *Hera.* This information is written in Ptolemy's *Geography* where he refers to the Maltese Islands and their respective cities, that is, Melite and Gaulos (Bonanno 2005, 197). Ptolemy used his system of coordinates to locate these places, and when modern geographers translated these into the modern longitude and latitude system they found this to be slightly off location but not considerably out of the way to indicate that Ptolemy was referring to another place (Bonanno 2005, 200). Unfortunately, no specifics are given about the temples or the communities using them. This ancient catalogue of places was probably compiled around the mid-second century AD and published centuries later (Bagrow 1945, 329). Archaeological evidence from another prominent site known as Tas-Silg, suggest that the Pagan 'temple-culture' was still strong during the fourth-fifth century AD. The stratigraphy suggests that this site, which is mainly composed of religious spaces, was used and re-used by different communities in different eras – starting from the prehistoric period (3000-2500 BC) and ending with the early Christian phase whose plan hints at an early basilica dating to the fifth century AD (Bonanno *et al.* (eds) 2000, 69-71). The latter is perhaps the only early Christian establishment found on the Maltese islands which indicates worship activities taking place above grounds.

The 'cultural profile' of the Maltese community from the fourth to the sixth century AD is not known. Maltese archaeologist describe this period as 'one of the darkest of Maltese history' (Bonanno 2003, 259; *cf.* Dalli 2006, 38). Here the term 'cultural profile' mainly refers to the religion, language and type of administration adopted by the Maltese communities during late antiquity. Such profile could provide important information on the peoples' interaction with religious architecture and the overall feeling of a religious transition which, according to the archaeological context, interrupted a millennium-old polytheistic tradition and led to the conversion of a prominent pagan temple, notably the one dedicated to goddess Astarte into a Christian establishment (Buhagiar 1996, 6). Similar conversions, although not very common, took place in the Roman world during the fifth and sixth century AD as part of the Christian campaign started by Constantine the Great in the fourth-century AD, particularly at the Temple of Athena in Syracuse and the church of *San Lorenzo Vecchio* in Pachino Southern-most part of Sicily and approximately 110 kilometers North-East of the Maltese islands (Bayliss 2005, 17). It is important to point out, however, that there is little evidence indicating the implementation of drastic measures towards the conversion of Pagan temples into Christian establishments. In fact, archaeological evidence shows that in certain cases (*e.g.* the Temple of Khnum in Elephantine, Egypt and the sanctuary of Pan in Caesarea Philippi) non-Christian establishments where neglected and left in a desperate state to the extent that these were never reused (Lavan 2011, xix).

Interestingly, the subterranean architecture of Late Antiquity did not suffer the same faith of some of the pagan temples, and architectural conversion or neglect here is somewhat undetected. The archaeological record in Malta and elsewhere in the Mediterranean reveals that catacombs were the most common way of burying the death among (different) religious communities. With the exception of the Jewish catacombs, the distribution and setting of Pagan and Christian tombs presents a challenge to archaeologists in identifying possible relationships between religion and funerary space since there seems to be an intermingling of tombs, sometimes within the same chambers (Fig. 7).

Past scholars (Vassallo 1876; Bellanti 1924; Ferrua 1949) have paid too much attention to dating the Maltese catacombs and given little importance to the material

*Figure 7: Example of Maltese late Roman hypogea: Interior of the St. Augustine Catacombs (Photo by Daniel Cilia).*

culture and other archaeological features which could have possibly provided further evidence on the socio-religious environment of the time. Their interest in dating the catacombs ties to the culture-history theoretical framework – namely the matching of the archaeological record with historical documents – which the Maltese archaeologists were sure working under. In particular, the Maltese and foreign archaeologists were attempting to align the dates of the first or second century AD. If accurate, it would confirm the religious influence St. Paul had on the community during his three-month stay in Malta. This narration is found in chapter 28 of the Acts of the Apostles dated to around AD 62:

> *'Once we had come safely through, we discovered that the island was called Malta. The inhabitants treated us with unusual kindness. They made us all welcome by lighting a huge fire because it had started to rain and the weather was cold. Paul had collected a bundle of sticks and was putting them on the fire when a viper brought out by the heat attached itself to his hand. When the inhabitants saw the creature hanging from his hand they said to one another, "That man must be a murderer; he may have escaped the sea, but divine justice would not let him live". However, he shook the creature off into the fire and came to no harm, although they were expecting him at any moment to swell up or drop dead on the spot. After they had waited a long time without seeing anything out of the ordinary happen to him, they changed their minds and began to say he was a god. In that neighbourhood there were estates belonging to the chief man of the island, whose name was Publius. He received us and entertained us hospitably for three days. It happened that Publius' father was in bed, suffering from fever and dysentery. Paul*

*went in to see him, and after a prayer he laid his hands on the man and healed*
*him. When this happened, the other sick people on the island also came and were*
*cured; they honoured us with many marks of respect, and when we sailed they put*
*on board the provisions we needed. At the end of three months we set sail in a ship*
*that had wintered in the island; she came from Alexandria and her figurehead was*
*the Twins.'* (Catholic Online translation, Acts of the Apostles 28.1-11).

Despite this event being documented in the Bible, no archaeological evidence to date has shown that Malta's early Christian catacombs were a direct consequence of this considering the later dating of these sites, that is, the fourth century AD (Buhagiar 1986, 38-41). Therefore, the Christianisation of Malta might have occurred gradually from indirect influence of nearby communities such as the ones living in Sicily or North Africa. The topic of Christianisation has been briefly discussed in the first part of this chapter and was based on literary evidence; however, when speaking of religious transition, ancient documents often contain bias and political agendas which may distort the interpretation of archaeological evidence if not handled with utmost objectivity.

Before discussing the archaeological evidence for the different religious communities present in fourth-century Malta, it is crucial to identify these religions, their derivation and chronological context. First, I consider the broad range of belief we label as 'pagan'. Although the term *paganus* is related to the classical period, a similar polytheistic religion has been present on the Maltese islands since the early Phoenician period, that is, seventh century BC, when communities' *colonists* from the Near Eastern shores ventured to the western Mediterranean in research of mineral resources (Aubet 2001, 2). Unlike the previous traditions, which seemed to be inclined towards a monotheistic god of fertility, the Phoenicians brought with them a different faith which is evident in the archaeological record. Inscriptions, amulets, pottery and burial practice illustrate a quasi-Egyptian religious belief with some of the same gods, such as Horus and Anubis, being venerated (Bonanno 2005, 63). This polytheistic religion survived all the way through the Punic period (500-218 BC) as well as during Roman rule. No doubt, with the Roman annexation, more gods, such as Apollo, were introduced to the islands. However, excavations at the multi-period site of Tas-Silg in the South East of Malta reveal, as Bonanno states 'an uninterrupted continuity of function of the place as the most important sacred shrine on the islands, as suggested by Cicero, as well as the survival of the Punic language way into the Roman period' (Bonanno 2005, 155). Archaeological evidence highlights the importance of the pagan temples to the Maltese communities and their administrators. Information comes mostly in the form of inscriptions on slabs commemorating restorations of temples such as that of goddess *Prosperina*, and another inscription dedicated to Julia Augusta, wife of Augustus. This inscription reveals the divine connotation which Roman rulers and their wives were given. Another important inscription found in Rabat Malta, commemorates the construction of a temple dedicated to Apollo and refers to the considerable sum of money which the benefactor paid for its completion. The name of the benefactor went missing but the inscription refers to him as the chief of the island (*CIL.* X8313; *cf.* Bonanno 2005, 232).

The Maltese catacombs reveal another religion certainly present during the fourth century AD, namely, the Jewish faith. In *The Jews of Malta*, Cecil Roth (1928) argued that way before the introduction of Christianity 'some adventurous Hebrew' made his way to the Islands during the Phoenician commercial activities and that is how the Jewish faith rooted itself and survived up to and beyond the fourth-century AD (Roth 1928, 188). Roth suggested that the latter event could perhaps be the reason for the 'Semitic imprint which was never subsequently lost, in spite of repeated conquests and changes in the rule' (1928, 188). An interesting observation by Roth (1928, 189), but one which discredits her own 'theory' that a Jewish community was established on the Islands sometime between 700 and 218 BC, is the landing of St. Paul in Malta around AD 62. Chapter 28 of the Acts of the Apostles, written by St. Luke, describes the Maltese community then as 'βάρβαροι' (Acts of the Apostles, 28, 2) or barbarians, which in a Judeo-centric context refers to a community with a pagan culture without knowledge of either Greek or Latin language. So, if this chapter in the Acts of the Apostles really refers to Malta, a Jewish Community was not established one of the islands prior to the mid-first century AD.

The last religion that can be identified archaeologically in the fourth century is Christianity. While scholars have tried to date its establishment to the first century AD, the archaeological evidence of the early Christian does not match this date (Buhagiar 1986, 38-41; Bonanno 2005, 262). In fact, early Christian material culture ranging from pottery to burial places as well as the limited epigraphic evidence was relatively small compared with that of nearby Sicily and North Africa. Furthermore, the majority of these finds date to the fourth century or early fifth century AD, with the earliest being the 'standard North-African red-ware lamp' (Buhagiar 2007, 46) excavated from the early Christian establishment of Tas-Silg dating to AD 400 or even later. Without debating the validity of the narrative documented in Chapter 28 of the Acts of the Apostles, it is unlikely that a single event like this left an instant cultural blueprint which is reflected in the archaeological record.

### Sharing Mortuary Spaces

Thus, based on this brief review of the archaeological evidence alongside previous perceptions for the inception of these religions, we can argue that these three religious communities were contemporaneously present on the Maltese Islands during the fourth century. With pagan, Jewish and Christian ideologies, communities, and people all found on islands, one would suppose that these communities were bound by specific socio-religious obligations stipulated by the Roman law. Therefore, in order to evaluate the legal obligations of the different communities towards each other, it is useful to note two important works: Salzman's (2010) *Ambrose and Usurpation of Arbogastes and Eugenius: Reflections on Pagan-Christian Conflict Narratives* and Johnson's (1997) *Pagan-Christian Burial Practices of the Fourth Century: Shared Tombs?* I start with the latter which reviews Roman law and church decrees in light of the problems of fourth century burial customs and funerary practices between different religious communities. These two particular works have been chosen as they strike an important balance between the literary sources available about the Pagan-Christian relationship during the religious transition period and the actual archaeological evidence. This allows the reader to corroborate literary sources with more tangible evidence especially in view of the shared or contested spaces during religious and political turbulence.

Johnson (1997) emphasises that over the twentieth century scholars have dedicated much time writing about fourth-century 'Christian-Pagan' hostilities (*e.g.* Symmachus' and Ambrose's dispute over the removal of the Altar of Victory from the Senate House) and the Christianisation of the pagan communities (1997, 39). However, Johnson rightly laments that the literature has failed to explore and expand in detail the study of the many burial sites, including necropolis, catacombs, churchyard burials, and more. It is in this vein that Johnson explores whether the 'Christian-Pagan' conflict, which he assumed as obvious, continued also after the death of the individuals of different faiths. He accomplishes this by reviewing the synodical canons and Roman law. However, a preliminary review of the latter revealed that such rules and regulations were not standard between the fourth and sixth centuries but rather in a 'state of evolution' (Johnson 1997, 49). Furthermore, Johnson believes that the evidence of 'reserved' burial spaces and areas for specific religious communities is not completely evident before the sixth century (1997, 49). The use of shared spaces and reutilisation of the same tombs may be corroborated by Gregory of Tours' reference to ritual proceedings such as the blessing or consecration of the place of burial before the body is laid to eternal rest.

Johnson's analysis outlined that there is absence of evidence to suggest that Christians and pagans were not buried together. In fact, he uses the *Via Latina* catacombs of Rome as a perfect example of how tombs of both religious communities can be found in the same space. But he stresses that the sources 'are limited in number and do not permit a complete view of early Christian attitudes towards death and burial. For this reason, an examination of the archaeological evidence is required to complete the picture' (Johnson 1997, 49).

Johnson notes that the Christian cemeteries developed from previous pagan burial grounds (1997, 50). An example of this common development can be detected from the catacomb of Sant'Agnese on the Via Nomentana where galleries underneath pagan *mausolea* were converted into Christian catacombs (Johnson 1997, 51). In most cases, it can be observed that Christian burial structures reused or adapted older remains to fit the needs of the new religious communities. Whether in North Africa, the Northern or Western Mediterranean, archaeological evidence shows a continuity of religious space. This is especially true for burial spaces during Late Antiquity. This fact importantly shows that families and communities living in urban and rural areas likely had different religions but this did not initially compromise their relationships nor their attitudes towards space.

Salzman's 2010 work challenges the notion that the conflicts of the fourth century, especially between the Western and Eastern Roman administration was purely because of different religious beliefs. The author reviews theories put forward by previous scholars (McLynn 1994 and Cameron 2010) about the causes that led to the Battle of Frigidus in view of the socio-political situation of the fourth-century AD (Salzman 2010, 223). Her study aims at explaining that beneath this conflict laid another important reason which went beyond religion, that is, pure political ambition and the conquest of land and space. Theodosius, who won the Battle of Frigidus, officially restored Christianity across the Empire. Even though this event clearly shows that the Christian-Pagan conflict was used as prerogative for the extension of power and rule, it finally had serious repercussions on the relationship between the different religious communities living under Roman rule.

Although Salzman's work does not delve directly into the issue of contested and shared spaces between the different religious communities of the time, evidence indicates that one of the main causes which triggered the uprising was related to the pagan religious spaces, notably, the temples. In fact, in *c.* AD 422, Eugenius started funding the restoration of these temples. These religious establishments suffered considerable neglect due to the lack of funding following the legalisation of Christianity and the administration's endeavour to construct new Christian establishments (Salzman 1997, 197). This 'funding-scheme' was considered as a sort of bribe by Eugenius to the pagan community and powerful elites in return to their political support. However, this was seen as unethical and unacceptable move by the Christian community – mostly by Ambrose, the bishop of Milan who asked for the intervention of Arbogastes to cease such practice.

Some sort of conflict surely occurred between different religious communities in other provinces located in prominent areas ruled by the Romans during the fourth century. This was not purely driven by the different religious dogmas but rather by the instability produced by the high ranking Roman administrators who continuously sought to acquire power through the support of different religious communities within their empire. Sometimes this political support came at the stake of transforming prominent religious spaces to satisfy the spiritual needs of the community. The establishments that experienced transformation include: the Temple of Aphrodite in Turkey which was converted into the church of St. Michael; the temple of Zeus in Cilicia, Turkey, transformed into a Christian church of Syrian architectural influence (Bayliss 2005, 17); and the conversion of the temple of Juno(?) at Tas-Silg, Malta (Buhagiar 2007, 43).

## The Late Antique Hypogea of the Maltese Islands

The term 'hypogeum' refers to an underground chamber used for burial purposes. Temi Zammit, who was appointed curator of the museum archaeology in 1903, has initially used this term in his first Museum Annual Report of 1904 to refer to the prehistoric temple found in Paola, South-East of Malta. In similar reports (such as those published in 1917 and 1922) Zammit speaks about late Roman funerary complexes as catacombs or tombs but not as hypogea. It was not until the 1949 when Antonio Ferrua, an authority in the field of Palaeochristian archaeology, wrote about the small size and highly-elaborate early Christian tomb complexes:

*'Chi visita la prima volta e catacomb di Malta deve aspettarsi qualche cosa di nuovo e d'insolito, anche s'egli e' un commune turista; meglio ancora se non e' digiuno di archiologia Cristiana o se di questa disciplina ha fatto, come si dice, la sua specialita. / Chi ode dire catacomb corre subito con il pensiero a vasti labirinti sotteranei, fatti di gallerie interminabili che s' incrociano fra di loro in modo inestrivabil. Cosi' infatti sono per esempio molto di quelle di Roma. / In realta' le piu grandi di essi ['catacombe' Maltesi], quelli detti di S. Paola e quelle che si svolgono sotto la Chiesa di S. Agatha – non s'estendono al di la' di cinquanta metri*

*in ampiezza. Ancora quest'ultime, xhe ora appaiano come un unico complesso catacobale, sono in effetto diversi ipogei, anticamente distinti fra loro e solo di recente artificialmente collegati insieme'* (Ferrua 1949, 505-506).

*'Those visiting the Maltese catacombs for the first time will see something unusual – it is even better if the visitor has no knowledge of Christian archaeology. When one speaks about catacombs, the first thing that comes to mind is a system of labyrinths crossing each other. This is the case with most of the Roman catacombs; however those found in Malta such as the one of Saint Paul and the underground tombs found underneath Saint Agatha church do not extend more than fifty meters in length. Furthermore, those of Saint Agatha are in fact a number of individual hypogea which were only recently and 'artificially' connected to each other.'*

Following Ferrua's article, the term *hypogeum was* introduced as a 'standard' terminology when referring to late Roman and Byzantine tomb complexes. In 1976, Vincent Borg preferred using the term 'miniature catacombs' to avoid confusion with the prehistoric hypogeum in Paola.

Late Roman and Byzantine hypogea, or catacombs, are fairly numerous in the Maltese islands, especially in the western part of Malta where 92 hypogea have been documented by Buhagiar (1986). The first known documentation on Maltese catacombs is to be found in Marc Antonio Axiaq's accounts of the Maltese Islands date back to AD 1610. Similar to Jean Quintin, who wrote the first detailed description of the Islands including its ancient heritage in 1536, Axiaq was a high ranking official serving as surgeon on the galleys of Order of St. John in the beginning of the 16th century (as cited in Buhagiar 1983, 291). He was taken to what he describes as 'grottos' where he could notice human bones in rock-cut spaces. From this period onwards, scholars kept visiting such sites, writing accounts, uncovering tombs and collecting artefacts from the burial places. Unfortunately, as a result of these visits occurring before the time of rigorous archaeological recording, the provenience for many of the artefacts collected from these sites has been lost.

With the setting up of Malta's Museum of Archaeology, its committee of management and the obligatory submission of the Museum Annual Reports to the Governor as from 1904, the artefacts retrieved from the catacombs, such as oil lamp, started being documented and made available to local and foreign scholars for further study and dating. The study carried on the material culture relied heavily on relative dating and comparative analysis. Although this methodology provided a good indication on the chronological context, commercial ties and foreign influences, the dating of these artefacts remained at large un-calibrated and sometimes questionable. As a consequence of this, most of the scholarly effort focused on the cataloguing, dating, surveying and illustrating of the funerary spaces and material culture in an effort to take stock of the amount of evidence available for the fourth century AD for comparative purposes. This has, in return, left a gap in the analysis of other aspects which has been discussed in the first part of this chapter such as the relation between different religious communities and the funerary space. Despite the limited evidence available, it is felt that the epigraphic and visual resources found inside Malta's late Roman hypogea can help in this regard, and if the hypothesis which is being presented here – that the proximity of tombs owned by different religious families is indicative of the social behaviour (conflict or peaceful coexistence) between the deferent religious communities – is considered to be naïve, it will, at least, serve as a basis for other researcher to explore other methodologies, such as that of 'mapping' late Roman and Byzantine inscriptions and art in relation to their spatial context. Therefore, I shall use this methodology and discuss two examples from two catacombs: that of St. Agatha and the other from Tac-Caghki catacombs, both located in Rabat. This, of course, shall be discussed in view of the preliminary review which has been presented in the first part of this chapter and which discussed the socio-political situation and tensions in late Roman period.

In1956 proper archaeological documentation was conducted at Saint Agatha catacombs. This was not originally envisaged by the Museums Department but has been carried out as part of a post-WWII survey commissioned by the British Empire to evaluate the damage suffered by various cultural heritage sites (Sagona 2015, 14). These catacombs span over 4100 square meters and contain over 500 tombs. Archaeological excavation here revealed interesting frescoes and inscriptions which date back to circa AD 300 (Camilleri 2001, 40). Among the most important are the frescoes uncovered in 1958 by Antonio Ferrua on the walls of tomb number 10 and which included the depiction of pelicans and floral wreaths. When it comes to the inscriptions, in some cases the content reveals the nature of the religious ideologies of those writing them, however most of them do not provide any information except for names such as the one knows as the inscription of *Leoniae* and which according to Ferrua reads: '*..ante.. calendas septembres deposition Leoniae*' or 'Before the Calends of September, Leonias was buried' (Camilleri 2001, 39).

This inscription located in the tomb identified as number three in Buhagiar's catalogue is decorated in late Hellenic art. Surely, the inscription alone does not provide the information on the religion of the person buried, however, there is another important symbol painted on the lower part of the side wall. This can be identified as the symbol of the pagan goddess Tanit or Juno. Unlike the common shared symbolism between Christians and Pagans, such as the Good Shepherd, the olive branches, the doves and others, the symbol of Tanit was exclusively used by pagan communities. Tomb number four, which is located in the same catacomb and abutting with tomb number three, contains 'the best preserved painted decorations in the Maltese Hypogea' (Buhagiar 1986, 74), namely, a simple line drawing of two pelicans and two garlands on the internal walls of this tomb. The interpretation that has been given by Ferrua (1949, 510) was that both frescoes depicted Christian symbolisms. These frescoes and the inscription of Leoniae date to around AD 400 (Camillerri 2001, 39-41). If Ferrua is correct in his interpretation, then a pagan tomb and a Christian tomb were deliberately placed near each other with the families of the dead buried in these particular tombs caring less for each other's religion and belief in the afterlife.

Approximately 200 meters away from St. Agatha catacombs one finds the site known as tac-Caghqi Secondary School Hypogea. This small complex of tombs, which was discovered by architect Harold Borg during the laying of foundations for the school in 1952 and later cleaned and documented by the Charles G. Zammit, who acted as curator of the Arcaheology in the mid-1960s, is no less susceptible for generating similar characteristics than the one found in tombs number four and ten at St. Agatha catacombs (Buhagiar 1986, 185). In fact, the South-East hypogeum at Tac-Caghki is characterised by six small chambers accessible through their own independent entrance from a central hall. Each chamber contains three *arcosolia* (an arch cut into the walls with its base serving for placing two or more bodies) excavated in its walls. This hypogeum contains two different inscriptions. The first has been written in Neo-Punic style and was painted above the window door of a cubicle and when translated reads: 'by virtue of the gift [grave goods] offered to you, oh spirit, you that are strong, do not worry and let go'. The emphasis on the spirit, the surrounding tone, and the objects placed within the burial imply a pagan eschatology. The second inscription is located in the same catacomb and has been inscribed in the same style of writing; however, this time the tone and meaning are completely different. According to Borg and Rocco this inscription reads 'Qum' which means rise or 'Wake Up' (1972, 65). While the first inscription is written in a tone of consolation from someone who acknowledges that the tomb is the eternal resting place, the second inscription is more assertive and it is written in the imperative, as if someone is commanding the soul of the deceased to rise and continue its journey to the afterlife. The latter has connotations with the Christian belief of resurrection. Buhagiar (1986, 183) argues that it is uncertain if such inscription can be linked to Christian belief despite the presence of the symbol of the palm tree, which accompanies these two letters. Perhaps Buhagiar is too cautious in his interpretation; however, the absence of direct symbolism, such as the cross, might reflect the earliest phase of Christianity in the Maltese islands where the community still embraced a Punic culture. Despite this preference, it is unlikely that a Christian tomb (even if reutilised from a previous pagan burial) featured an inscription referring to a pagan eschatology. Therefore, a possible reinterpretation of this could be that these two tombs were either used contemporaneously by a pagan and a Christian family in around AD 300, or the pagan tombs were abandoned and not re-utilised by the Christian families. In any of the case, this indicates that if the interpretations provided by Borg and Rocco (1972) are correct, the individuals buried here and their families did not have reservation on the funerary space to be used by different religious communities.

Unlike Christians and Pagans, the Jewish communities in Malta seemed to have their own hypogea with private entrances. This is evident from the inscribed symbol of the menorah which indicates Jewish burial at each entrance of the catacombs such as hypogeum 17 at St. Agatha catacombs. This hypogeum was discovered during the construction of the Missionary Society of Saint Paul Mother House (Buhagiar 1986, 91). Archaeological excavation has also revealed that Jewish Hypogea rarely interconnected with other hypogea unless the one adjacent was owned by another Jewish family. No archaeological evidence has been found so far which show the reutilisation of tombs, especially in light of the unfinished tombs which could be noticed near tomb nine of the same chamber. In view of such evidence no assumptions can be made on the relationship between the Jewish community and the rest of the community except that religious conflict in general was unlikely considering the very close proximity of the Jewish catacomb with the rest of the hypogea.

## Conclusion

The evidence presented above, although limited, is fore-grounded by the concept of 'the territorial modalities of the communalisation of religion' discussed by Hervieu-Leger in his 'Space and Religion: New approaches to Religious Spatiality in Modernity' (2002) where he explores how different religious communities behave in establishing their spaces (2002, 99). Although the context of this study focuses on an early modern period, the same concept might apply to earlier periods. Hervieu-Leger argues that tension created for contested spaces existed since the development of early Christian communities. In most Roman colonies conflict was the order of the day even after the legalisation of Christianity in AD 313, where some Christians 'remained comfortably within the ambit of the synagogue…', 'others became virulently anti-Jewish', and a segment of the Christian community perceived their religious role as one to resist Roman power (Fredrisken 2006, 605). All this led to political and social instability until the fourth-fifth century AD.

The same cannot be said for the Maltese Islands. The 'model' I have proposed here sheds light on the argument that there was no conflict in Malta between different religions – particularly between pagans and Christians – by conceptualising spatial distribution and the setting of tombs within the same hypogea. How likely would it have been for two religious communities who were in conflict to accept burial in such close proximity? The evidence here points to the conclusion that this would have been very unlikely. The first part of this chapter discussed ancient literary sources showing that although Malta was under Roman rule, it did not hold political importance. This probably led to high religious tolerance and a flexible administration. This may have affected the way the Maltese communities, embracing different ideologies and religions for centuries, coexisted in peace while adapting to new currents that slowly arrived from overseas such as Christianity. And this is surely reflected in the second part of this chapter, where we see in the archaeological record that there seems to be no evident spatial limitations determined by religious conflict between the religious communities present on the Maltese islands in Late Antiquity.

## Bibliography

*Primary Sources*

CIL= Mommsen, T. and der Wissenschaften, P.A. (eds), 1883. *Corpus inscriptionum latinarum* (Vol. 10, No. 1). Berlin: Gregorium Reimerum.

Catholic Online translation. n.d. *Acts of the Apostles 28.1-11. http://www.catholic.org/ bible/book.php?id=51&bible_chapter=28* (Accessed: 10 April 2016).

*Secondary Sources*

Aubet, M.E. 2001. *The Phoenicians and the West: politics, colonies and trade*. Cambridge: Cambridge University Press.

Bagrow, L. 1945. The origin of Ptolemy's Geographia. *Geografiska Annaler* 27, 318-387.

Bayliss, R. 2005. From Temple to Church: Converting Paganism to Christianity in Late Antiquity. *Minerva* September/October, 16-18.

Bellanti, P.F. 1924. *Studies in Maltese History*. Malta: Empire Press.

Bonanno, A., Frendo, A.J. and Vella, N.C. 2000 (eds). *Excavations at Tas-Silg, Malta: a preliminary report on the 1996-1998 campaigns conducted by the Department of Classics and Archaeology of the University of Malta.* Msida: Malta University Press.

Bonanno, A. 2005. *Malta: Phoenician, Punic, and Roman.* Malta: Midsea books.

Borg, V. 1976. Une île et ses hypogées de l'ère des premiers chrétiens: Malte. *Les Dossiers de l'Archéologie* 19, 52-67.

Borg, V. and Rocco, B. 1972. L'Ipogeo di Tac-Caghqi a Malta. *Sicilia Archeologica Rassegna periodica di studio notizie e documentazioni a cum dell' E.P.T. di Trapani,* June, 64-74.

Brown, P. 2012. *Through the Eye of a Needle: Wealth, the Fall of Rome, and the Making of Christianity in the West, 350-550 AD.* New Jersey: Princeton University Press.

Buhagiar, M. 1983. The study of the Maltese paleochristian catacombs. *Melita Historica* 8/4, 291-298.

Buhagiar, M. 1986. *Late Roman and Byzantine catacombs and related burial places in the Maltese Islands.* British Archaeological Reports 302. Oxford: British Archaeological Reports Ltd.

Buhagiar, M. 1996. The Early Christian Remains at Tas-Silg and San Pawl Milqi, Malta. A Reconsideration of the Archaeological Evidence. *Melta Historica* 12, 15.

Buhagiar, M. 2007. *The Christianisation of Malta: catacombs, cult centres and churches in Malta to 1530.* British Archaeological Reports 1674. Oxford: British Archaeological Reports Ltd.

Cameron, A. 2010. *The last pagans of Rome.* Oxford: Oxford University Press.

Camilleri, V.J. 2001. *Saint Agatha: An Archaeological Study of the Ancient Monuments at St Agatha's Building Complex, Crypt, Catacombs, Church, and Museum.* Malta: Missionary Society of St. Paul.

Chohick, L.H. 2010. Jews and Christians, in: Bingham, D.J. (ed.), *The Routledge Companion to Early Christian Thought.* London: Routledge, 68-86.

Dalli, C. and Cillia, D. 2006. *Malta: The Medieval Millennium.* Malta: Midsea books.

De Ste. Croix, G.E.M. 1963. Why were the early Christians persecuted? *Past and Present* 36, 6-38.

Ferrua, A. 1949. Antichità cristiane. *Le catacombe di Malta.La Civilta'Cattolica 1949a* 3, 505-515.

Fletcher, R.A. 1999. *The barbarian conversion: from paganism to Christianity.* California: University of California Press.

Fredrisken, P. 2006. Christians in the Roman Empire in the first three centuries CE, in: Fredrisken, P (ed.). *A Companion to the Roman Empire.* Oxford: Blackwell Publishing, 587-606.

Gibbon, E. 1782. *The History of the Decline and Fall of the Roman Empire, Volume I.* A. Strahan & T. Cadell: London.

Hervieu-Léger, D. 2002. Space and religion: new approaches to religious spatiality in modernity. *International Journal of Urban and Regional Research* 26/1, 99-105.

Johnson, M.J. 1997. Pagan-Christian burial practices of the fourth century: shared tombs? *Journal of Early Christian Studies* 5/1, 37-59.

McLynn, N.B. 1994. *Ambrose of Milan: church and court in a Christian capital.* Oakland: University of California Press.

Lavan, L. 2011. Introduction, in: Lavan, L. and Mulryan, M. 2011 (eds), *The archae-ology of late antique 'paganism'*. Leiden: Brill.

Moss, C. 2013. *The Myth of Persecution: How Early Christians Invented a Story of Martyrdom*. Broadway: Harper Collins.

Rizzo, F. 1976. Malta e la Sicilia in età romana. Aspetti di storia politica e costituzionale, in: *Attidel IV Congresso Internazionaledi Studi Sulla Sicilia Antica*. Kakalos 22-23, 173-214.

Roth, C. 1928. The Jews of Malta. *Transactions (Jewish Historical Society of England)* 12, 187-251.

Rutgers, L.V. 2000. *Subterranean Rome: in search of the roots of Christianity in the cata-combs of the Eternal City*. Leuven: Peeters Pub & Booksellers.

Sagona, C. 2015. *The Archaeology of Malta: From the Neolithic Through the Roman Period*. Cambridge: Cambridge University Press.

Salzman, M.R. 2010. Ambrose and the usurpation of Arbogastes and Eugenius: reflections on pagan-Christian conflict narratives. *Journal of Early Christian Studies* 18/2, 191-223.

Said-Zammit, G.A. 1997. *Population, land use and settlement on Punic Malta: a con-textual analysis of the burial evidence*. British Archaeological Reports 680. Oxford: Archaeopress.

Sellars, I. 2013. *The monetary system of the Romans*. eBook: distributed by Lulu.

Thiede, C.P. 1992. *Heritage of the first Christians: Tracing early Christianity in Europe*. Oxford: Lion Books.

Trump, H.D. 2005. *Malta: Prehistory and Temples*. Malta: Midsea Publishers.

Vassallo, C. 1876. *Dei monumenti antichi nel gruppo di Malta, cenni storici. Periodo fenicio ed egizio*. Malta: Malta Government Press.

Young, F., Ayres, L. and Louth, A. 2004 (eds). *The Cambridge history of early Christian literature*. Cambridge: Cambridge University Press.

# A Case for Space

## Rereading the Imperial Panels of San Vitale

*Brittany Thomas*

### Introduction

The imperial panels in the church of San Vitale in Ravenna – dual portraits of the Byzantine Emperor Justinian and his wife, Empress Theodora (Fig. 8) – are perhaps the most famous depiction of the Byzantine court in the early medieval world. These two panels have been scrutinized a number of times with an almost equal number of possible interpretations (Von Simson 1948; Grabar 1960; Deichmann 1969 and 1976; Kitzinger 1977; MacCormack 1981; Maguire 1987; Barber 1990; Andreescu-Treadgold 1994; Andreescu-Treadgold and Treadgold 1997; Bassett 2008). While almost all the previously cited literature has confronted the interpretation of these panels through formal analysis and some even through post-structuralist deconstruction, they have all also assumed that the panels were in plain view and broadly available to a large audience. In this chapter I would like to unpack considerations of access to and control of what is a contentious space within the church itself: could all citizens enter, view, and marvel at the artwork of San Vitale's inner sanctuary? While it seems obvious that these mosaics were meant for the glorification of the emperor we must also be aware that access to and interpretation of these mosaics varied greatly throughout the multi-period use of this building. Rank and participation in liturgical rituals, gender, and social status dictated who was allowed into certain church spaces and therefore who was allowed to view these decorative programmes from close up. What we can access today as tourists does not necessarily reflect the internal arrangement or viewing access of this church in the sixth century. The mosaics in San Vitale may have functioned primarily as power discourse for the local archbishop Maximian (AD 546-557), rather than for the imperial family. This chapter therefore questions the church of San Vitale as an arena of power discourse between the Byzantine imperial family, Bishop Maximian, and the people of Ravenna in the mid-sixth century by exploring current approaches to ancient viewership and access to ecclesiastical spaces.

in: Bielmann, C. and Thomas, B. (eds.) 2018: *Debating Religious Space and Place in the Early Medieval World (c. AD 300-1000)*, Sidestone Press (Leiden), pp. 61-76.

*Figure 8: The 'imperial panels' featuring Emperor Justinian (top) and Empress Theodora (bottom) (Photos by Robert Culos, distributed through Wikimedia Commons).*

The city of Ravenna and its artwork have become almost iconic of Late Antiquity itself. The Justinian mosaic in particular is ubiquitous in modern scholarship as the cover art for books centring on the 'Later Roman', 'Early Byzantine', and/or 'Byzantine' Empires (and even, rather erroneously, the Roman Empire) – thus, an image which seems to represent the history of nearly nine centuries (for example: Elsner 1995; Bowersock *et al.* (eds) 1999; Moorhead 2001; Rautman 2006; Luttwak 2009; Heather 2013).

Was this portrait originally meant to be so famous and so representative of the imperial image during the early Byzantine period in the West? This question is revisionist in nature, it asks us to rethink our construction of ancient viewership and the idea of constructed tourism. It is essential to remember that these images could not have been disseminated widely in antiquity in the absence of printing or film. Images of the Emperor may have been circulated from the imperial capital (at the time of San Vitale's construction this would have been Constantinople) in antiquity to local gov-

|

ernors for the commissioning of imperial portraits which were based on this 'official' type (Højte 2005, 86); however, we have no evidence concerning the way in which the commissioning process of these particular mosaics worked nor do we know exactly the type of reproductions that could have been circulated (Fejfer 2009, 408-410). We may speculate about whether or not painted copies of these mosaic portraits could have been available to the public, but largely in order to see them one would have to have travelled to Ravenna in person – a luxury generally available to elites, clergy, and po-tentially to pilgrims. While later texts do suggest these mosaics were well known at least within Italy, we have few indications that San Vitale was somehow an ancient 'tourist' location or that people were widely aware that the imperial panels existed in the same way that we know ancient people admired public monuments in Rome.

I argue in this chapter that rather than the Emperor Justinian – who never lived in the Western Empire, did not commission these mosaics, and never set foot in Ravenna at all – it was the Bishop Maximian who had greater reason to stamp his name on the decorations of San Vitale. This is not necessarily a new argument; it was an observation first made by Otto Von Simson in his early assessment of the Byzantine art of Ravenna in 1948, although his major interpretations of the San Vitale mosaics have been re-ex-amined by later scholars. Two of the more often cited interpretations of the panels con-cern the presence of 'imperial power': first that they were completed in a post-Gothic Ravenna and thus represent a re-conquest of space and proclaim the returned glory of the 'Roman' Empire (McCormick 1986, 120; Elsner 1995, 177; Reece 1999, 66); and second that the portraits in the sanctuary are meant to be seen as exact representations of the Emperor and Empress participating in the Little Entrance at the start of the liturgy (Mathews 1971, 146-147; Barber 1990; cf. Elsner 1995, 179).

In response to the first argument, I would take into consideration the fact that the building was most likely begun during Ostrogothic rule, and the general time-line for completion and decoration is, as we shall see, debatable. San Vitale was a newly built church, on a bishop's private property, in the north-western quadrant of the city – nowhere near any of the Ostrogothic buildings – all things considered this was a very inoffensive location to build a church. As far as the second interpretation goes, Von Simson (1948, 30) argued that perhaps these mosaics were meant to depict what Byzantine Emperors do, as he interpreted the whole of San Vitale as definitely 'Byzantine' in its artwork. However, Von Simson (1948, 30, 37) also notes that the participation of the Emperor in offertory rites was common practice in the East, but at least since the time of Bishop Ambrose and Theodosius I in the late fourth century this was not common in the West. This might suggest that San Vitale was one of the churches in which a completely Byzantine liturgy was practiced. If not, it would have been odd for Ravennate locals to interpret the panels based on a Byzantine motif that takes literal the presence of the Emperor. However, the introduction of eastern devo-tional practices by eastern migrants is one measurement by which historians often class Ravenna as being a wholly Byzantine city. Barber (1990) perhaps most thoroughly explored this interpretation through analysing the panels as two separate and distinct representations of not just what Emperors do, but what imperial men and women do: he concluded that each panel fulfils the social and gender norms within which the Byzantine Emperor and Empress were received.

A third, sometimes casually offered, argument for the panels is that they are a general representation of imperial rule (Barber 1990, 34), unspecific to Justinian and Theodora, but specific to the role imperial power needed to play in relation to the rest of the decorative scheme (indeed – this is perhaps a more enduring interpretation). In his discussion of the transformation of imperial images Elsner (1995) argued that the imperial panels represent the 'end' version of imperial imagery, the transcendent representation of the Emperor: abstract, scriptural, and hierarchically inferior to the image of Christ enthroned depicted in the vault of the apse. However, I suggest a more complete approach to viewership inside specific spaces that questions modes of commission, production, and placement in addition to Elsner's model of 'mystic viewing'. I would like to turn to more spatially (and 'platially') oriented discussion; most pressingly, all of these interpretations beg the question of how visible these portraits actually were to the worshipping public, and who was allowed to view them up close. Further, how has the dissemination of these images in the nineteenth and twentieth centuries shaped our understanding of their 'power'?

## Constructing an Imperial and Episcopal Capital

To better understand the historical context in which the imperial panels were created, we must briefly consider Ravenna's role as the Late Roman capital and, further, the role of the Ostrogothic king Theoderic the Great in the creation of the city's structure and power centres prior to the Byzantine re-conquest. Ravenna's life as the Western capital began when Emperor Honorius moved the imperial seat from Milan to Ravenna around the year 402. Ravenna remained more or less the imperial residence under Honorius' nephew, Valentinian III, until his move back to Rome *c.* 445. There is considerable debate over how much time Late Roman Emperors actually spent in Ravenna, as Rome remained the cultural heart of the Empire and seat of the Senate throughout the fourth and fifth centuries (see Gillet 2001 for catalogue of imperial itineraries from Honorius up to Romulus Augustulus). We have evidence that laws were issued from Ravenna not long after the Visigothic sack of Rome in 410 (*Cod. Th.* 14.1.6; 15.1.48). However, after the death of Valentinian III in 455 at Rome, a twenty-year gap exists in the residency of any authority other than the reigning bishop up until the usurpation of the Western throne by the Romano-Germanic military commander Odoacer in 476.

It was only after Odoacer's dethronement by Theoderic the Amal (later, the Great) in 493 that Ravenna became a thriving capital city as the seat of the (briefly) united Ostrogothic and Visigothic Kingdoms. By 511 Theoderic controlled two Gothic seats, the Western Roman capital, and held hegemony over the Burgundian and Vandal kingdoms on his borders. In this year, he sent an embassy to Constantinople asking for the imperial vestments which Odoacer had earlier sent East to be returned to him in Italy (Heather 2013, 78-79). Theoderic's building programme was easily the most substantial and enduring phase of Ravenna's growth. It included construction of various buildings in a palace and church complex, support for an Arian cathedral and baptistery, repair of the city's Roman aqueduct, erection of the only honorific statue in the city, and of the only free-standing 'imperial' mausoleum. These structures would have made a lasting impression of Ravenna as a Gothic capital, and Ravenna remained Theoderic's city in the eyes of the Eastern court. This preoccupation with the idea of

Italy ('Rome') as a Gothic kingdom eventually spurred the Gothic War that resulted in the re-conquest of Ravenna by the Byzantine Empire.

Following Theodoric's death in 526 the Amali rule Italy lasted little more than a decade. Justinian took the throne in the East in 527, and from the 530s onward campaigned in the heart of the old Roman West (Moorhead 2001, 133). By 536 his general Belisarius had captured Sicily and turned his army north. Ultimately Italy succumbed to the Byzantine forces, with Ravenna officially surrendering in 540 (Procopius, *Wars* 6.23-30). No new Emperor was ever elevated in the West again. Rather, Ravenna became the seat of the Byzantine exarchate of Italy, an administrative city situated between the Western cultural centre of Rome and the Eastern power centre in Constantinople.

Re-conquest also saw the bishopric of Ravenna (previously a metropolitan) upgraded to an Archbishopric, signalling the growth of power and wealth granted to the Church. Maximian was the first Bishop of Ravenna to receive the title 'Archbishop' after his nomination by Emperor Justinian. When the city's Bishop Victor died in 545, the citizens of Ravenna petitioned Justinian to replace him with a local Ravennate candidate of their choosing. Instead of respecting this petition, Justinian (after nearly a year of deliberation) rewarded Maximiam, a native of Pula (modern Croatia), with the episcopal chair (*LPR* 70). Although Maximian eventually made peace with the people of Ravenna and became one of their city's greatest patrons, he drew his legitimacy predominantly from the Eastern Court and the Byzantine Emperor. The rapidly changing political climate in the West had recently polarized the elite community in Ravenna between those favouring the previous Gothic regime and those sympathetic to the Eastern Emperor. This also shed light on institutional and regional loyalties such as the professional army, mostly made up of ethnic 'Goths', and the increasingly blurry lines between the communities of 'Arian' Goths and Catholic 'Romans' (Amory 1997, 168, 258-259). In the latter half of the sixth century, the Byzantine Emperor increasingly supported Ravenna's autonomy over Rome, a tradition more prominent throughout the seventh century (Cosetino 2015, 58). To this end, it was important to Maximian to tie himself to the legitimate 'Roman' Emperor, though it is unclear how much immediate influence Byzantine rule had on the local population culturally or demographically as early Byzantine administration largely followed late Roman settlement and urban patterns (Brown 1984; Brown and Christie 1989, 386). In the atmosphere of the year 540, the religious monuments and artwork may have provided a reasonable arena for Maximian to showcase the rise of episcopal power and rank in Ravenna coupled with a message of legitimacy.

## San Vitale as a Bishop's Church

Ravenna's Byzantine period is often regarded as the high point of Byzantine imperial artwork in the West, Christian imperial iconography, and a return to 'Roman' imperial power in the Mediterranean (most prominently by Von Simson 1948[1987 revised]; McCormick 1986; Elsner 1995). It was during this transition from the Gothic period into the Byzantine period in the mid-sixth century that the decoration and consecration of the church of San Vitale took place. Thus, the panels depicting the Emperor Justinian and his wife Theodora are thought to broadly represent the blatant and visible re-conquest of space (Elsner 1995, 177; Reece 1999, 66). As discussed above, this interpretation is not wholly incorrect, but we must also consider the circumstances of the building's construction and the major players involved both before and after the city's administrative turnover in order to gain a clearer view of who Maximian's audience was.

The local ninth century chronicler Agnellus tells us in his *Liber Pontificalis ecclesiae Ravennatis* (*LPR*) that the church was founded under the Bishop Ecclesius (522-532), and 'by Julian the banker together with this bishop' (*LPR* 52), thus during the Gothic period. Our understanding of the construction of San Vitale is hindered by how little we actually know about it, despite its survival. If Ecclessius' role was simply to give permission to build on his land, it is possible that proper construction began under his successors Ursicinus (533-536) or more likely under Victor (538-545), whose monogram appears on several carved column capitals on the lower storey. If so, the whole project may have been delayed or interrupted by the outbreak of the Gothic War from 535-540. Fredreich Deichmann, the German scholar who conducted the first thorough study of Ravenna's early Christian architecture and mosaics, argued that construction actually only began after 540, with the coming of the Byzantine re-conquest and the Byzantine Archbishop (Deichmann II, 1976; cited by Verhoeven 2011, 47). Deichmann's assessment came largely from his argument that Ravenna was a Byzantine city and so San Vitale must have only been constructed by the Byzantine bishop. However, it does seem rather clear that Ecclesius was viewed as the church donor because his portrait appears in the apse handing a small model of the church to Christ (Deliyannis 2010, 225). Andreescu-Treadgold and Treadgold's (1997, 716) detailed study of the mosaic programme in the sanctuary from scaffolds revealed that work on all of the mosaics was indeed interrupted at some point, and the workload of all of the mosaics was divided as a result of the distribution of labour by the mosaic workshop.

What we do know for certain is that Archbishop Maximian consecrated the church in 547:

> 'Julian the banker built the basilica of the blessed martyr Vitalis from the foundations, authorized by the vir beatissimus Bishop Ecclesius, and decorated and dedicated it, with the vir reverendissimus Bishop Maximian consecrated it April 19, in the tenth indiction, in the sixth year after the consulship of Basilius [AD 547]'
> (LPR 77)

The wording of the full inscription has been much debated: it is unclear whether this means that construction of the building itself began under Ecclessius, or simply that Bishop Ecclesius gave permission or land to Julian to begin work on the church because it was built near or upon his legal property as mentioned in *LPR* 57 (Deichmann 1976, 7-33 proposed that the words for 'authorized', 'built' and 'dedicated' in the inscription are actual legal terms to describe the procedure for commissioning a church in the sixth century, see Deliyannis 2010, 225 for discussion). This means at most the whole building took twenty-five years (if begun at the start of Ecclesius' reign), and at least it took seven (if begun the year of the Byzantine conquest). Only Ecceslius and Maximian are named in the inscription, and are also the only two bishops featured in the decoration of the apse (Fig. 9), leaving out Ursicinus and Victor (and Julian,

*Figure 9: The apse mosaic depicting Bishop Ecclesius (on the right) handing a small model of the church to Christ, perhaps the first decorative motif of this type (Photo by author).*

the mythical financier). However, within two years of the consecration of San Vitale Maximian would also dedicate Sant'Apollinare in the port city of Classe, which would depict his predecessors Severus, Ursus, Ursicinus, and Ecclesius in the apse. The tradition of depicting bishops in their own churches was common in Ravenna, and arguably began there in the sixth century (Deliyannis 2014, 52-53). As the Church grew wealthy its bishops were increasingly prone to embarking on elaborate building and decorative campaigns (Janes 1998, 60). While seemingly at odds with the Christian ideal 'blessed are the poor' (Matthew 5:2), these prestige buildings were somehow expected of a culture that was the direct descendant of Roman splendour. The rich decoration of San Vitale and Sant'Apollinare also acted as showpieces for the new Archbishopric as a whole, and it cannot be forgotten that as a place of worship they were also a testament to the splendour of God.

From Agnellus' account, we gain a clear picture of Maximian as a patron of the city, and Byzantine Ravenna as a place busy with construction (*LPR* 70, 72-77, 79, 80, 82-83). Maximian is named as the builder, decorator, or consecrator of five different churches, and it appears that a church was finished (or at least consecrated) every two years in the early part of his episcopacy. Maximian brought the splendour of the Byzantine court with him; he had access to good building and decorative material from the East, and sent for expert craftsmen from Constantinople when the builders in Ravenna were unable to complete their projects due to lack of materials. Agnellus in fact says that Maximian brought in so much material overnight that 'they would hardly be able to fashion in eleven months' the amount of good stone and brick delivered to the city (*LPR* 73). Maximian also gave his personal wealth to the city, a wealth which Agnellus says 'we possess up to today' (*LPR* 76). This suggests that Ravenna was not greatly damaged by the Gothic War, and that it recovered within the decade largely due to the presence of the new bishop and that this recovery and prominence of the church survived locally well into the ninth century. It is also important to mention here that San Vitale itself was not financed by the Church or State, but by a private banker – Julian 'Argentarius' (*LPR* 52). Banking was a particularly thriving business in sixth century Ravenna, with nearly three times as many active *argentarii* here as in Rome (Cosentino 2014, 248, 250). We know almost nothing about Julian, save that he was called 'the banker' and financed three churches: San Vitale, Saint Apollinare in Classe, and a church devoted to San Michele that is no longer extant (see Cosentino 2006 for a discussion of how he amassed his wealth). This suggests a great deal of cooperation between Julian and Maximian, and that church financing in this period is both a private and public affair.

Maximian was a highly visible patron in Ravenna's cityscape. The *LPR* records that he built the church of St. Stephen where 'in the vaults of the apse his image is fixed in multicolored mosaic, and is surrounded by wonderful glasswork' (*LPR* 72) and that he put his name on two dedications inside the church, and constructed a small *monasteria* nearby where 'above the capitals of all the columns the name of this Maximian is carved' (*LPR* 72). He decorated St. Andrew and gifted it with martyr relics, consecrated both San Michelis and San Vitale, and consecrated Sant'Apollinare in Classe. Agnellus gives much attention to the inscriptions and dedications in the churches, but most especially to the long list of saint and martyr relics Maximian personally brought to the city. In contrast, he offers only this one short sentence about the decoration of San Vitale: 'And in the apse of San Vitale the image of this same Maximian and of the emperor and empress are beautifully created in mosaic' (*LPR* 77). It appears that at least at the time of Agnellus in the ninth century the panels were noteworthy, but the decoration of San Vitale was neither more nor less special than any of the other churches in which Maximian was depicted or named.

Of the design of San Vitale itself Agnellus notes that 'No church in Italy is similar in structures and in mechanical works' (*LPR* 59). Whether this is a construction of rhetoric or in fact a comment on the uniqueness of the building as a whole is a matter of debate. In her edition of the *LPR*, Deliyannis (2004, 329) notes that the phrase '*mechanicis operibus*' indicates a work that was complicated or of high quality, which could be a reference to the interior decoration rather than the building as a whole. Unfortunately, the only parts of the interior decoration belonging to the sixth century are those mosaics in the main sanctuary. Most of the church's interior was redecorated in the Baroque period, and the original decoration of the other vaults, including the central dome, is completely unknown (Verhoeven 2011, 46, 195). Agnellus was correct in his assertion in that the octagonal structure for a church was unique to the West, although this design was in fashion in the East during the later Roman period (Karutherimer 1986, Antioch: 76; Syria, general: 138; Palestine and Jordan: 157; Ravenna as a rarity: 232). However, the octagonal design had been use in Ravenna at least since the late fifth century not for churches, but for the shape of both the Neonian and Arian baptisteries (Krautheimer 1986, 176). Whether San Vitale's design came directly from local inspiration or was an Eastern import cannot be known for certain. Richard Krautheimer (1986, 236) believed the architect was a Westerner, who, in his view, 'designed the one truly great building of the West in the sixth century'.

## Considering Space: San Vitale as the Viewer

We can recognize, therefore, San Vitale as a richly decorated and endowed construction that surely drew many visitors. But here we can turn back to the question of access – how was the decoration viewed or even seen? One approach to understanding how people understood this building and its iconography is to turn to the primary sources, a method applied by Jaś Elsner in several of his studies of the Roman world (1995, 1998, 2007b). This method takes the abstraction of what is in the mind of the viewer and draws it directly out of a source that wrote about certain works of art, buildings, or monuments. As this chapter has demonstrated thus far, the dominating historical text for sixth century Ravenna is actually Agnellus' ninth century series of the lives of Ravenna's bishops. Agnellus, however, represents just one particular view: he is an elite and well-educated clergyman who saw these mosaics with the aid of historic consciousness, and may have had access to places an ordinary person would not. It is harder to accept that every person had easy viewing access to the panels at all: the portraits flank the side of the high altar such that someone sitting or standing in the church's central space would have a hard time getting a clear view. It is entirely possible these panels were made more specifically for viewing from within the sanctuary, or from the Bishop's chair in particular. This demonstrates the impact of the individual agency of figures like Maximian on the power discourse within San Vitale and Ravenna more widely. Although we think of them as 'imperial' panels, they are better thought of in their ecclesiastical setting.

This is certainly not to say that ordinary people did not understand the monumentality or overall general message of imperial power in this church. And certainly they knew their Emperor – he was depicted on common coinage all over the empire. Rather, I argue that we take into account the immediate spatial context of such a famous portrait and frame it within the building itself and the building's history. If we take into account the changes to the cityscape that happened in the three hundred years that passed between Maximian's reign as bishop and Agnellus' penning of his *LPR* then it is appropriate to note that Agnellus can only tell his readers what he sees with his own eyes, or what he has read and heard about structures or decorations that no longer exist. So he, like the modern tourist, experiences the city through immediate context. For Agnellus these mosaics were also inevitably bound up in ninth-century politics: particularly Ravenna's rivalry with Rome and the Papacy, an issue that was just barely recognisable in the sixth century and only came to fuller fruition between the mid-seventh and eighth centuries (see Ortenberg West-Harling 2016 for discussion).

The available text sources for early Byzantine Ravenna are very few. Procopius' *The Buildings*, a hybrid *ekphrasis* and traditional panegyric, would have been a rather obvious choice for physical descriptions of Ravenna's churches, as Jas Elsner (2007a, 38) pointed out: 'the great advantage of buildings as a choice of subject was the geographical scope by which the emperor's works could be used to represent the extent of his empire'. Unfortunately Procopius' account stops short of Italy, as he worked eastward from Constantinople. But perhaps a selection from a Byzantine author would not lead us to any clearer a picture of the impact of the Ravenna programmes due to the problem of rhetorical language used in Byzantine writing. As Liz James (2007, 4) argued, these descriptions often express attitudes and reception rather than reality – meaning they do not describe what they physically see. The same problem holds true for other historical sources – travel writers, medieval bishops, and Grand Tour era travellers who give us some insight into access to images inside of churches – while these are expressions of various modes of viewing (and are valuable for those reasons), they rarely comment on things like location or placement, visibility, or whether or not the elements in the programme were complete or in the process of being finished or restored. These small details are often lost to the archaeological and historical records.

However, there is room to explore some alternative solutions to the problem of the lack of sources by turning to recent approaches to viewing with 'space syntax' or 'isovist analysis' methods. 'Space syntax' simply means the field of view directly visible from a given location, or can be used to talk about the horizontal 2D plane of site at the eye level of the viewer (Turner *et al.* 2001, 103; Palious and Knight 2013, 230). These methods can be used to generate visual integration or visibility graphs that are intended to show us how much everyday people might see in the church. In pursing this, we first have to take into account that San Vitale is an unusual church. As already mentioned, the floor plan of this basilica is octagonal and so does not have a central hall or nave the way other Roman-style basilicas do. There is no central aisle that draws the viewer's attention toward one part of the church in particular, unless a performance or mass was happening in the sanctuary space. Paliou and Knight's mapping (2013) of San Vitale for visual integration (Fig. 10) showed red values are 'high integration' blue values are 'low'. Their graph shows us what we might expect: namely that the very centre of the room, under the central dome, is the most 'visually integrated' space in the building – in other words, it can be seen from relatively numerous viewpoints. Paliou and Knight used this method to discuss viewer access from the gallery (second storey) to the ground floor, and to ask questions about what kind of sensory experience people (mostly women, who were often made to stand in the gallery) on this level might have. Paliou and Knight were asking not specifically about the decoration, but the entire performance of a mass or ceremony within the church including auditory and olfactory senses.

While this method presents some interesting results and possibilities for investigating sensory perception, a graph of this type cannot show us precisely how things looked on the ground or how much of the decoration one could actually see (and, as they note in their paper, this graph in particular is only useful in 2D analysis). For the case of the imperial panels in particular this graph reveals two problems: first, the panels flank the inside of the high altar, meaning that they are in one of the areas of relatively low 'integration' (with a pale green colour). If a member of the congregation were to look directly at the sanctuary from the central dome area, they would not be able to see the panels except at a severe angle (Fig. 11). Second, standing under the central dome in the main nave seems an unlikely place for the congregation to stand at all given that this space is the most 'visually integrated' on the ground floor, although this space is the one from which most tourists would view the sanctuary.

It is useful to consider this insight in light of the performance that could have taken place in San Vitale. Marinis (2012, 348) noted that the floor plan of some of the tenth to thirteenth-century ambulatory-style churches in Constantinople posed a problem for Byzantine liturgy: it involved a series of circular processions through the nave during which the clergy brought the Gospel books from the altar into the nave and back to the altar again in a 'U' path. Thus, a church with a floor plan which inhibits these proces-

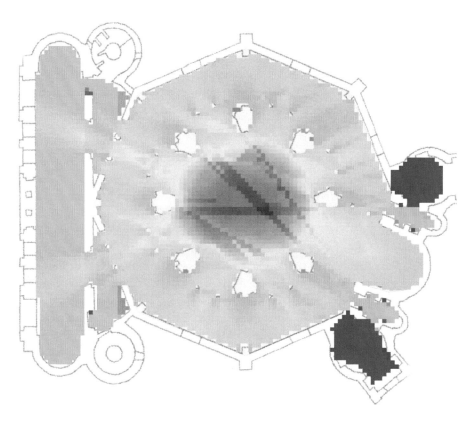

*Figure 10: Visual integration map of the ground floor of San Vitale. Red values = high integration, blue values = low integration. From Paliou and Knight (2013), reproduced with permission.*

*Figure 11: The apse, as viewed from the central nave (Photo by author).*

sions or blocks the view of the congregation would not have been the location of such a ceremony. San Vitale, however, seems perfectly adapted to such a performance, if we assume that most people congregated in the ambulatory and faced inward *toward* the space under the central dome in order to watch the processions (the space that is, after all, most visible), rather than standing in the centre of the church and facing the apse. This indicates that viewers could have possibly seen one or the other panels from the ambulatory if they were close enough to the sanctuary and if no choir, chancel, or rood screens inhibited their view. As previously discussed, women were usually 'regulated' to the second storey gallery, where their viewing experience would be very different to those on the ground floor. The best place for an audience to view the panels would be to the left or right of the sanctuary, very close to the mass, and even then, only one of the two panels would be completely visible. If we take into account the many people attending services and consider the performance of the liturgy in the sanctuary then we can get an idea of how busy the inside of the church was during regular worship. People in attendance of the mass would not have been there to contemplate the decoration, but rather to participate in the performance. We do not know how much or how often an ordinary spectator would have been contemplating the decoration or its meaning as opposed to paying attention to the mass. The decreased visibility of these decorations from the point of view of the audience leads back to the original point: these panels are seen most perfectly from directly inside of the sanctuary, precisely where the Bishop himself and presumably other important members of the elite ecclesiastical ranks and administration would be sitting.

Otto Von Simson summarised his analysis of Ravenna's mosaics by arguing that churchgoers experienced the decoration as part of the setting for a liturgical performance (1948, 98). A decade later, Paul Zanker (1997, 183) echoed this argument more broadly by stating that Roman people only ever experienced art or architecture as it was part of a performance or parade or any other ceremony, whether secular or sacred. These two arguments suggest that the way people interact with public art is through cognitive experience and performance rather than simple appreciation and reception. While images held one meaning for their patrons and benefactors (namely to legitimize, commemorate, or praise), they could hold entirely different meanings for viewers once they became part of a certain kind of performance.

## Conclusion

Arguably those closest to the performance of the mass were Maximian in his bishop's throne and others allowed in the sanctuary during ceremonies, and it does have to be considered that the purpose of any church was not predominantly for public discourse, but for worship. To return to San Vitale's historical context, it is worth noting this church was not built in isolation. The early Byzantine period in Ravenna was exceedingly busy with building, much of it done just in the single decade of Maximian's reign. Sant'Apollinare in Classe and San Vitale in Ravenna are the largest and arguably most beautifully decorated churches in the region. Individual agency impacted upon space as much as ritual, belief, and socio-cultural structures (Marinis 2012, 339). Maximian may have chosen to only speak to those Ravennate elites who might have had a hard time accepting his appointment as their new Bishop. San Vitale is very much a Bishop's church, if we take its full dating; it was constructed under two, but possibly up to four, of its sixth-century bishops and decorated with over-life-size portraits of two of these bishops. The individual agents of Ravenna in the sixth century were most prominently its Bishops rather than the imperial family.

As this chapter has shown, it is important to consider and view these mosaics not through the eyes of a modern tourist (or indeed to a modern academic), but to try to comprehend their contemporary setting. It means considering the performance of the liturgy, the social status of the participants, and the general makeup of Ravenna's congregation. After all, we do not really know how 'public' churches in Late Antiquity were, and we do not know who was allowed into these spaces beyond the most important members of the ceremony – the 'ordinary' person may well have been excluded except during certain occasions. We also do not know what the internal arrangement of the sanctuary was, whether there were chancel screens or rood curtains, how big the ambo or altar pieces were, or if these things moved frequently or obstructed the view. If so, then perhaps it is fair to suggest the ordinary person who did not usually see these works of art was greatly impressed and their awe was heightened by the rarity of seeing it, much as we are today. By contrast, regular attendance to this church for weekly mass could lead to over-familiarity and loss of a concrete message. A study done by Chadford Clark (2007) and his team offers one possible method for analysis visibility from the congregation to certain liturgical focuses (the altar, the ambo, the Bishop's chair). In what he called a 'modest visual experiment', using the ruins of Byzantine churches in Jordan he had participants stand at measured distances from the altar and then created a scale of visibility for how clearly participants could distinctly make out fine details (hand gestures, facial features, *etc.*) (Chadford Clark 2007, 87-88). His paper effectively showed that certain points within the church are more distinctly visible than others depending on the size of the hall and location of the focuses, and he concluded that churches were built to maximise the visibility of the liturgies (Chadford Clark 2007, 98). The performative nature of church services was the focus of the mass, and whether or not the public were allowed into the church outside of the mass is unknown.

Together these considerations lead us to a rereading of San Vitale's decorative programmes as a sort of private message between the Bishop and his elite constituents as a kind of permanent claim to legitimacy and power through image, and all future bishops seated in that chair would see his portrait stamped with his name (*cf.* Andreescu-Treadgold and Treadgold 1997, 722 who feel he might have only cared about impressing his contemporaries). It also speaks to the integral cooperation of a private citizen like Julian with local ecclesiastical powers like Maximian: the way this message translated to the public in antiquity is a matter of debate, though the overall monumental impression of such a richly decorated church surely impacted its viewers. They are also affected by Ravenna's relationship with both of the other Sees, Rome and Constantinople. Modern scholarship and the modern public have largely been impacted by the dissemination of photographs of the panels which put you at eye-level with Justinian or Theodora, as though they are paintings in a gallery rather than inscribed artwork in a building. Another consideration I would like to put forward is that we often use these panels as a diagnostic feature of early Byzantine power relations: representations of the Byzantine court are, as far as I know, very rare, even from Constantinople. We go back to these images so often because they are almost the only ones available, certainly the only ones of their particular medium. This is a rather deceiving view of a complex setting: imperial images are always negotiated through local means, and the presence of 'imperial power' within these images is almost taken for granted. Imperial portraits in an otherwise episcopal city do seem particularly significant, but framing them within episcopal space reveals that the 'imperial panels' are an ecclesiastical message which make use of the symbols of imperial power, and not necessarily an imperial message which makes use of the symbols of ecclesiastical power. Context and space are paramount to our understanding of these mosaics and deserve further consideration in the re-'reading' of late antique decorative programmes.

## Bibliography

### Primary Sources

Agnellus of Ravenna. *The Book of Pontiffs of the Church of Ravenna*. Translated by D. Mauskopf Deliyannis. Washington: The Catholic University of American Press, 2004.

*Theodosian Code*. Translated by C. Pharr. Princeton, NJ: Princeton University Press, 1952.

Prokopius. *The Wars of Justinian*. Translated by H.B. Dewing, Revised by A. Kaldellis. Indianapolis/Cambridge: Hackett Publishing, 2014.

### Secondary Sources

Amory, P. 1997. People and Identity in Ostrogothic Italy, 489-554. Cambridge: Cambridge University Press.

Andreescu-Treadgold, I. 1994. The Emperor's New Crown and St. Vitalis' New Clothes. *Corsi di cultura sull'arte ravennate e bizantina* 41, 149-186.

Andreescu-Treadgold, I. and Treadgold, W. 1997. Procopius and the Imperial Panels of S. Vitale. *The Art Bulletin* 79, 708-723.

Bassett, S. 2008. Style and Meaning in the Imperial Panels at San Vitale. *Artibus et Historiae* 29, 49-57.

Bowersock, G.W., Brown, P. and Grabar, O. (eds) 1999. *Late Antiquity: A Guide to the Postclassical World*. Harvard: Harvard University Press.

Brown, T.S. 1984. *Gentleman and Officers: Imperial Administration and Aristocratic Power in Byzantine Italy AD 554-800*. British School at Rome. Hertford: Stephen Austin and Sons.

Brown, T.S. and Christie, N. 1989. Was there a Byzantine Model of Settlement in Italy? *Melanges de l'Ecole Francaise de Rome. Moyen Age* 101/2, 377-399.

Chatford Clark, D.L. 2007. Viewing the Liturgy: A Space Syntax Study of Changing Visibility and Accessibility in the Development of the Byzantine Church in Jordan. *World Archaeology* 39, 84-104.

Cosetino, S. 2006. Le fortune di un banchiere tardoantico. Giuliano argentario e l'economia di Ravenna nel VI secolo, in: Augenti, A. and Bertelli, C. (eds), *Santi Banchieri Re: Ravenna e Classe nel VI secolo San Sever oil tempio ritrovato*. Milan: Skira, 43-48.

Cosentino, S. 2014. Banking in Early Byzantine Ravenna. *Journal of Medieval and Humanistic Studies* 28, 243-254.

Cosentino, S. 2015. Ravenna from imperial residence to episcopal city: processes of centrality across empires. *Rechtsgeschichte Legal History* 23, 54-67.

Deichmann, F.W. 1969. *Ravenna, Haupstadt des Spätantinken Abendlandes. Band I: Geschitche und Monumente*. Wiesbaden: Franz Steiner.

Deichmann, F.W. 1976. *Ravenna, Haupstadt des Spätantinken Abendlandes.Band II, 2: Kommentar 2: Die Bauten desJulianus Argentarius: Ubrige Kirchen*. Wiesbaden: Franz Steiner.

Deliyannis, D.M. 2010. *Ravenna in Late Antiquity*. Cambridge: Cambridge University Press.

Deliyannis, D.M. 2014. Ecclesius of Ravenna as Donor in Text and Image, in: Danielson, S. and Gatti, E.A. (eds), *Envisioning the Bishop: Images of the Episcopacy in the Middle Ages*. Turnhout: Brepols.

Elsner, J. 1995. *Art and the Roman Viewer: The Transformation of Art from the Pagan World to Christianity*. Cambridge: Cambridge University Press.

Elsner, J. 1998. *Imperial Rome and Christian Triumph: The Art of the Roman Empire AD 100-450*. Oxford: Oxford University Press.

Elsner, J. 2007a. The Rhetoric of Buildings in the *De Aedificiis* of Procopius, in: James, L. (ed.), *Art and Text in Byzantine Culture*. Cambridge: Cambridge University Press, 33-57.

Elsner, J. 2007b. *Roman Eyes: Visuality and Subjectivity in Art and Text*. Princeton: Princeton University Press.

Fejfer, J. 2009. *Roman Portraits in Context*. Berlin: Walter de Gruyter.

Gillet, A. 2001. Rome, Ravenna and the Last Western Emperors. *Papers of the British School at Rome* 69, 131-167.

Grabar, A. 1960. Que lest le sens de l'offrande de Justinien et de Theodora sur les mosaiques de Saint-Vital? *Felix Ravenna* 81, 63-77

Heather, P. 2013. *The Restoration of Rome: Barbarian Popes and Imperial Pretenders*. Oxford: Oxford University Press.

Højte, J. 2005. *Roman Imperial Statue Bases: From Augustus to Commodus*. Aarhus: Aarhus University Press.

James, L. 2007. Introduction: Art and Text in Byzantium, in: James, L (ed.), *Art and Text in Byzantine Culture*. Cambridge: Cambridge University Press, 1-9.

Janes, D. 1998. *God and Gold in Late Antiquity*. Cambridge: University of Cambridge Press.

Kitzinger, E. 1977. *Byzantine Art in the Making: Main Lines of Stylistic Development in Mediterranean Art, 3rd-7th Century*. Cambridge, MA: Harvard University Press.

Krautheimer, R. 1986. *Early Christian and Byzantine Architecture*. London: Yale University Press.

Luttwak, E. 2009. *The Grand Strategy of the Byzantine Empire*. Harvard: Harvard University Press.

MacCormack, S. 1981. *Art and Ceremony in Late Antiquity*. London/Berkeley: University of California Press.

Maguire, H. 1987. *Earth and Ocean: The Terrestrial World in Early Byzantine Art*. University Park: Pennsylvania State University Press.

Mathews, T. 1971. *The Early Churches of Constantinople: Architecture and Liturgy*. University Park: Pennsylvania State University Press.

McCormick, M. 1986. *Eternal Victory: Triumphal Rulership in Late Antiquity, Byzantium, and the Early Medieval West*. Cambridge: Cambridge University Press.

Marinis, V. 2012. Structure, Agency, Ritual, and the Byzantine Church, in: Wescoat, B. and Ousterhout, R. (eds), *Architecture of the Sacred: Space, Ritual and Experience from Classical Greece to Byzantium*. Cambridge: University of Cambridge Press, 338-364.

Moorhead, J. 2001. *The Roman Empire Divided: 400-700*. Harlow: Longman.

Ortenberg West-Harding, V. 2016. The Church of Ravenna, Constantinople and Rome in the Seventh Century, in: Herrin, J. and Nelson, J. (eds), *Ravenna: its role in medieval change and exchange*. London: Institute of Historical Research, 199-210.

Paliou, E. and Knight, D.J. 2013. Mapping the Senses: Perceptual and Social Aspects of Late Antique Liturgy in San Vitale, Ravenna, in: Contreras, F., Farjas, M. and Melero, F.J. (eds), *Proceedings of the 38th Annual Conference on Computer Applications and Quantitative Methods in Archaeology*. British Archaeological Reports Series 2494. Oxford: Archaeopress, 229-236.

Rautman, M. 2006. *Daily Life in the Byzantine Empire*. London: Greenwood Press.

Reece, R. 1999. *The Later Roman Empire: An Archaeology AD 150-600*. Stroud: Tempus Publishing.

Turner, A., Doxa, M., O'Sullivan, D. and Penn, A. 2001. From isovists to visibility graphs: a methodology for the analysis of architectural space. *Environment and Planning B: Planning and Design* 28, 103-121.

Verhoeven, M. 2011. *The Early Christian Monuments of Ravenna: Transformation and Memory*. Turnhout: Brepols.

Von Simson, O. 1948/1987. *Sacred Fortress: Byzantine Art and Statecraft in Ravenna*. Princeton: Princeton University Press.

Zanker, P. 1997. In Search of the Roman Viewer, in: Buitron-Oliver, D. (ed.), *The Interpretation of Architectural Sculpture in Greece and Rome*. Washington: The National Gallery of Art, 179-191.

# Early Medieval Places of Worship in the Western Alps

## The District of Verbano Cusio Ossola

*Francesca Garanzini*

### Introduction: The Verbano Cusio Ossola District of northwestern Italy

Over the last three decades, the former Soprintendenza Archeologica del Piemonte (renamed 'Soprintendenza Archeologia, Belle Arti e Paesaggio') has been supervising excavations inside churches across the entire northwestern part of Italy and, frequently, also supervising the archaeological investigations of the outcomes from these excavations. This rescue archaeology, although at times unplanned, has provided new information about early Christian churches, notably those uncovered in the district of Verbano Cusio Ossola. These new datasets, including details on architectural plans, construction material, and artistic elements, contribute to a wider understanding of church typologies of Northern Italy as well as a richer understanding of the links between architecture and liturgy. It also raises various questions. How are these sites placed within the landscape? What can their locations tell us about the settlement history and their function? Do the plans of the churches reveal any regional similarities or local distinctiveness?

The Verbano Cusio Ossola is an Alpine district within the Piedmont region that shares international borders the Swiss cantons of Ticino and Valais. While the region lacks primary source data on villages dating back to the Roman period, the Anonymous Geographer of Ravenna (*c.* AD 700) does report the existence of a *civitas* within the region: *Oxilia*, now known as Domodossola (Lieb and Wüthrich 1967, 105-107). While assumptions about the real meaning of the word *civitas* in the Geographer's statement and the corresponding site location are still to be clarified (especially as settlements known as *civitas* are often linked to bishoprics), such a reference may produce further evidence of a local community around Domodossola, so far unsupported by archaeological evidence (Caramella and De Giuli 1993, 46-51).

The Geographer lists other settlement types in the region of Piedmont (in which the Verbano Cusio Ossola District sits). These include forts (*castra*) and towns (*civ-*

in: Bielmann, C. and Thomas, B. (eds.) 2018: *Debating Religious Space and Place in the Early Medieval World (c. AD 300-1000)*, Sidestone Press (Leiden), pp. 77-92.

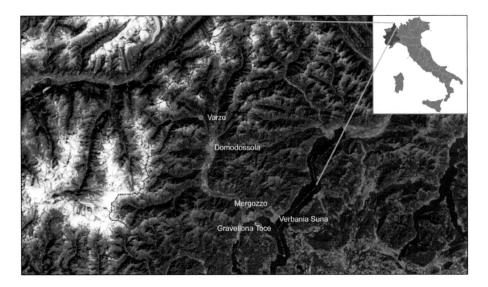

*Figure 12: Location of the main sites reported in this paper. In the box, the district of Verbano Cusio Ossola, in the Northeastern far end of Piedmont.*

*itates*), apparently built along a back line of defence of the Alps as to safeguard the strategic routes. According to Settia (1993, 105-112), these settlements may date to the period Theodoric (493-526) was in control of Northern Italy. This theory, however, is contradicted by Micheletto (1998, 65) who suspects the settlements listed by the Geographer date to the Lombard period (568-774). The lack of primary source material on the region's settlement history results in a need to rely on secondary source material including archaeological investigations. However, these databases are likewise lacking: most of the available information derives from 19th and 20th centuries discoveries and are often unproven. No significant evidence of early medieval settlements has been revealed by excavations but just secondary findings like small groups of graves, rare artefacts (pottery, soapstone, *etc.*) and, twice, coins and jewellery. One common feature of the local early medieval settlements is that they are placed in the valley floor, below 800 meters. Therefore, the available archaeological database tends to confirm the ongoing life of these settlements in the same place from the Roman period to the early Middle Ages up to date (for a comprehensive database review: Garanzini, *in press*).

Thus, our understanding of the Verbano Cusio Ossola district remains unclear. As far as we know, the district has always been part of the Diocese of Novara, whose first bishop Gaudenzio is mentioned from the late fourth century (Cantino Wataghin 1999; Perotti 2007); the oldest material evidence related to the local diocese – in particular related to the Episcopal group – is dated to the middle of the fifth century (Pejrani Baricco 1999; Brant 2012, 398-440). So far, a clear proof of the events that led to the current conformation of the diocese, among the largest in Northern Italy, is not available (Andenna 2007; Perotti 2007). This chapter is thus focused on furthering our understanding of the district's settlement history by evaluating a number of early medieval rural churches: San Giovanni Battista in Montorfano, near Mergozzo, SS. Fabiano e Sebastiano in Verbania Suna, San Pietro in Gravellona Toce and San Giorgio in Varzo (Fig. 12). The former church of Santa Maria – no longer preserved – in the

DEBATING RELIGIOUS SPACE AND PLACE IN THE EARLY MEDIEVAL WORLD (C. AD 300-1000)

*castrum* of Mattarella, near Domodossola, is also briefly mentioned among the sites. For each church, the chapter provides general data and information together with the reference literature for a comprehensive overview of the archaeological contexts. Based on this review, this chapter argues that the churches and sixth-century Christian funerary inscriptions are evidence of an increasing penetration of Christianity in the district.

## Archaeological Data

### San Giovanni Battista in Montorfano

The early Christian baptismal complex of San Giovanni Battista, excavated between 1980 and 1982 (Pejrani Baricco 1999; 2001), is placed at the foot of Montorfano, on a south-facing plateau. The church features a single-nave with an apse, oriented from the east to the west, interestingly joined to a baptistery (across Northern Italy baptisteries are quite common in independent buildings) with a similar plan and size (around 6.5 × 5.5 m), with an annex on the northern side (Fig. 13A). Construction material consists of rough-cut local stone, like in the other cases described in this chapter. The baptismal font, embedded in the floor, is placed almost in the centre of the nave: its octagonal exterior encompasses an interior circular shape. The deep apse was separated from the nave by a barrier and held a recess under the altar for relics. The foundation of the baptismal complex of San Giovanni is dated between the late fifth and early sixth century; this timeline has been recently confirmed by the study of the artefacts discovered during the archaeological excavation (Garanzini and Proverbio 2016). Later (date unknown), the font was replaced with a smaller one and slightly rotated (Fig. 13B): a new floor *in cocciopesto* (lime mortar with crushed bricks) was built up, in relation to reconstruction of the barriers, now supported by a masonry base and four small pillars.

Therefore, the south church underwent radical reconstruction, clearly visible in the presbyterial area divided into three apses with a horseshoe-shaped internal profile (Fig. 14). The existence of residential buildings has hindered the completion of the archaeological investigations on the western side of the church intended to identify a general plan. According to Luisella Pejrani Baricco (2009, 120-121), the western part is similar to a single-nave building with protruding transept. In contrast, Saverio Lomartire (2007, 306) assumes a three-nave building, so that the shape of the western part of the south church of San Giovanni looks similar to a group of Carolingian churches in the Swiss canton of Grisons. Therefore, Luisella Pejrani Baricco (2009, 120-121) suggests that it is possible to date the church back to the Carolingian age – thanks to the first written mention of the church in AD 885 (Gabotto *et al.* 1913, 20-22). The erection of a north-south wall, just west of the apse, bordered on both sides by parallel burials, suggests that this building was prematurely (date unknown) abandoned.

The change from a worship-based church to one focused on baptismal functions led to an extension of the nave to the west, with the creation of a new facade wall whose position matches exactly with the present-day wall. While we cannot confirm when the baptistery underwent such a transformation, the most likely period is between the ninth and the late twelfth century, when the building was reconstructed according to the Romanesque style (Mazzilli 1980). Only a few fragments of the original

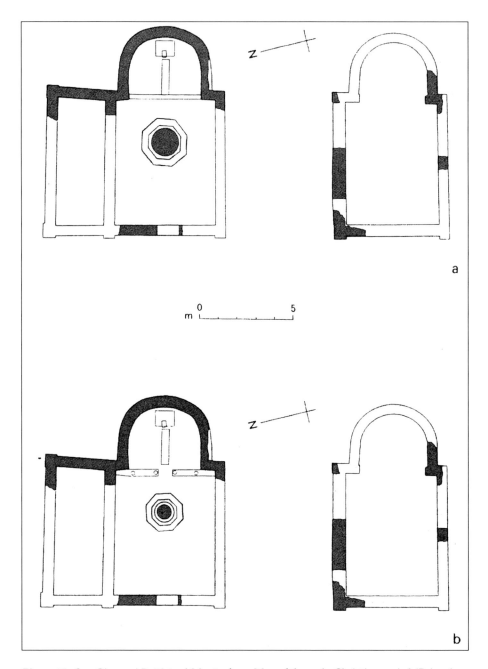

*Figure 13: San Giovanni Battista al Montorfano. Map of the early Christian period (Pejrani Baricco 1999).*

early Christian frescoes, restored and brought to light during archaeological investigations, are preserved in the baptistery (Fig. 15). The faux marble ornament consists of painted slabs alternating with vertical elements decorated with black floral branches/ ramifications on a white background. The need or wish to mimic such decoration, but with cheaper, polychrome marble slabs – very appreciated during Late Antiquity both in the most notable private locations and the most important churches – points

DEBATING RELIGIOUS SPACE AND PLACE IN THE EARLY MEDIEVAL WORLD (C. AD 300-1000)

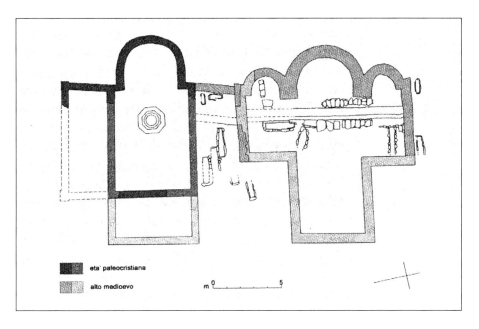

*Figure 14: San Giovanni Battista al Montorfano. Map of the early medieval period (Pejrani Baricco 2009).*

*Figure 15: San Giovanni Battista al Montorfano. Frescoes on the apsidal wall of the early Christian Baptistery (Gian Battista Garbarino).*

to elite founders. They were fully aware of the artistic trends within episcopal complexes of Northern Italy, and in particular in Milan and Novara where similar effects were achieved with the adoption of stone materials in the fifth century (Garanzini and Proverbio 2016).

### Santi Fabiano and Sebastiano

Excavation work carried out in November 2009 in the church of Santi Fabiano and Sebastiano in Verbania Suna revealed the remains of older foundations (Spagnolo and Garanzini 2011; Garanzini 2015). Despite patchy data, the prior building is commonly dated to the last quarter of the 12th century based on the analysis of the architec-

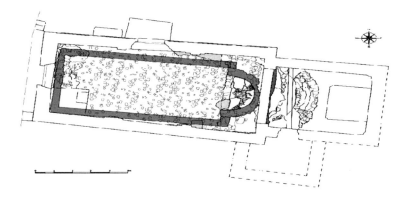

*Figure 16: Santi Fabiano and Sebastiano in Verbania Suna. Map of the early medieval phase (© Soprintendenza Archeologia, Belle Arti e Paesaggio per le province di Biella, Novara, Verbano-Cusio-Ossola e Vercelli).*

tural decoration and masonry techniques (Mazzilli 1980, 252-253). The remains of a previous church building with a single nave and a semicircular apse to the east have been discovered below a Romanesque floor (Fig. 16): they basically cover the surface of the nave of the present church. The semicircular apse (the inner span is around two meters long), separated from the nave by a structure made up of flat stone slabs connected by rather brittle mortar, was likely the base of a presbytery screen. Like in many ecclesiastical contexts across Northern Italy, the archaeological investigation of this church has not produced proven evidence for its chronology, like small findings or material remains of lithurgical vestments. Single assumptions over the church layout must take into account that it represents only one of the possible timelines, to be confirmed following a comparison with other elements (Fiocchi Nicolai and Gelichi 2001, 314-315). To some extent, the plan of the older building looks similar to the one of a wide group of small single-nave churches with a semicircular apse oriented to the east, which is typical of the period when Christianity spread into the Alps between the fifth and sixth centuries (Brogiolo *et al.* 1999; Sennhauser 2003). Not far from this site are the aforementioned church of San Giovanni Battista in Montorfano and the church of San Martino in Roccapietra (Pantò 1994; 2003, 97), a small village close to Varallo, in the district of Vercelli, but still in the Diocese of Novara. The elongated proportions of the nave are more similar to later buildings, dating from between the eighth and ninth centuries, like the church of San Tomé in Carvico (Brogiolo 1989), in the district of Bergamo, and San Martino di Serravalle in Valtellina (Brogiolo 2009).

Unfortunately, the available archaeological data from Verbania Suna and surroundings are not able to support a better knowledge of the context where the church was built; it's unclear if the early medieval church was incorporated in a nucleated village rather than segregated to service a dispersed settlement as it is unproven its functional purpose due to a lack of material evidence such as burials or a baptismal font.

### San Pietro

The village church of Gravellona Toce was first mentioned in the twelfth century by written sources mentioning the name of San Pietro (Andenna 1994). The removal

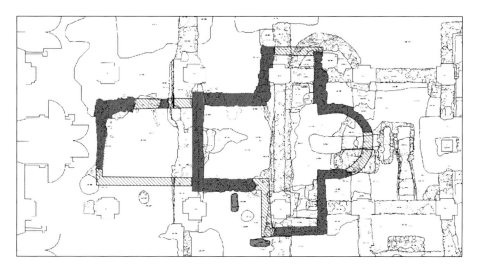

*Figure 17: San Pietro in Gravellona Toce. Map of the early medieval phase*
*(© Soprintendenza Archeologia, Belle Arti e Paesaggio per le province di Biella, Novara,*
*Verbano-Cusio-Ossola e Vercelli).*

of the floor, in the summer of 2013, shed light on a complex stratigraphic sequence comprising at least three pre-existing buildings (Garanzini 2014; 2015). The oldest building is a single-nave church with annexes on the sides and an apse with a horse-shoe-shaped inner profile, oriented to the east (Fig. 17). An atrium is placed in front of the church, although during the excavation it was not possible to verify whether it belonged to the same phase as the rest of the building due to a break in the physical relationships between the structures caused by later transformations. The nave and the atrium have a mortar floor covering almost the entire surface. A portion of the apsidal wall (for a height of not more than 28 cm!) helps to attest part of the original decoration of the baseboard that consists of red lozenges on a white background. The decorative pattern prolongs to the eastern wall of the southern annex, with black in the band below the lozenge motif. The early demolition of the church sealed this space, preserving the wall painting for which we can only offer general comparisons between Late Antiquity and the early Middle Ages. Outside the building are two cist tombs belonging to the same phase of the church: the first grave, with a north-south orientation, is close to the southern perimeter wall of the building, while the latter, with an east-west orientation, is located in the southern annex. Both the tombs are made with stone slabs fixed vertically in the ground, a type well known and widespread in the early medieval period in the district of Verbano Cusio Ossola. Churches with a cruciform plan are well documented between the fifth and seventh century, in particluar within the Alpine region (Brogiolo *et al.* 1999, 530; Cantino Wataghin and Uggè 2001); however, it is hard to deliver a real picture for this plan model (church burial, *cura animarum, etc.*), since there are not proven assumptions around the functional purpose of the side annexes that, in the case of Gravellona Toce, communicate with the nave. More recently, Paolo Piva (2010, 198) has returned to the cruciform plan, reiterating that this plan model was widespread, with all the local variations, throughout the Christian world since the fourth century.

A geographically close comparison is provided by the early Christian church of San Giulio d'Orta, dating back to the late fifth and sixth century (Pejrani Baricco 2000, 94-101). However, the church of San Giulio is quite peculiar owing to the longitudinal rooms on either side of the nave, which are absent in Gravellona Toce. Similarities have been found with the original layout of the church of San Michele in Oleggio (Pejrani Baricco 2009a, 164-166), in the province of Novara, and with the church of San Giovanni Battista in Cesano Boscone (Ceresa Mori and Righetto 2001), in the province of Milan, both of which date back to the early decades of the seventh century. The first documentary reference in the twelfth century focuses on the second phase of the church, dated to the Romanesque period (Garanzini 2014; 2015).

### San Giorgio

Few data are available in relation to the church of San Giorgio in Varzo, placed in the valley leading to the Simplon Pass. The excavation work inside the building, reported in ten surveys of very limited size, brought to light what is probably a pre-Romanesque building consisting of a single nave with an apse (Pejrani Baricco 1991). However, the pre-Romanesque chronology of the church is not unanimously accepted: more recently, Saverio Lomartire (2007, 305-306) has claimed that the sacristy of the existing church includes fragments of frescoes dating back to the 11th century (Bertelli 1993, 267-268; Segre Montel 1994, 33), the reason why he cannot exclude that the original layout could be coeval, raising doubts about its early medieval origin. That argument would require a new and extensive archaeological research to investigate the problem, still unsolved, of the origin of the church of San Giorgio in Varzo. Therefore, it is certain that the church is the oldest evidence of a permanent settlement in the Divedro valley, along the road leading to the Simplon Pass. In fact, certain archaeological statements related to permanent settlements in the Divedro valley in Roman period and in the early Middle Ages are unknown and the few references available in the literature do not seem to provide effective evidence (for a complete discussion of the topic, Garanzini in press).

### Santa Maria

In 1673, a local scholar, Giovanni Capis, mentioned an ancient church dedicated to Santa Maria in the castle of Mattarella above the town of Domodossola; yet, the real position of the building was unknown (Capis 1673 [1968], 61). A few decades later, at the beginning of the 18th century, occasional excavations in the castle identified a two-apse building, oriented to the east, with several tombs inside. The uncommon plan with two apses is documented from the early to the late Middle Ages (Piva 2001, 118-120; 2015, 66-72); in Piedmont and in the neighbouring Swiss Canton of Ticino this plan was widely adopted during the Romanesque period, between the 11th and the first half of the 12th century (Tosco 1992, 34-43; Lomartire 2007, 309; Piva 2015, 66-78). More likely it has been the chapel of the castle of the Novara bishop in the 11th and 12th centuries. Nevertheless, the accidental discovery of two bases of marble columns makes the chronology of this building more difficult. The best-preserved artefact is a square base (side about 15 cm, total conserved height 18 cm) followed by two alternating strips to a central groove, which, even if fragmentary, are reminiscent of similar single-block columns generally identified as altar supports from the early

Middle Ages. In confirmation of this argument are to be mentioned, for example, the bases of three marble columns from the church of San Ponso of Salassa (near Turin), datable to the late seventh century (Casartelli Novelli 1974, 156-158), and a marble column from Fontaneto d'Agogna (near Novara) dated, albeit with some caution, to the sixth century (Lomartire 2009, 155).

In addition, the evidence of an early medieval settlement upon the hill, then occupied by the medieval castle of the Novara bishop (Garanzini 2014a), raises doubts over the real existence of an early Christian church. However, this assumption cannot be verified due to the destruction of the building in the 18th century.


## Discussion

As mentioned in the introduction, this contribution is based on the outcome of rescue archaeological investigations of some churches within the district of Verbanio Cusio Ossola, rather than on a planned research about the early medieval architecture of local places of worship.

Therefore, the buildings assessed in the paper are not perfectly contemporary and even their chronology is sometimes far from certain, preventing any conclusion over the diachronic evolution of the Christian topography in this region. Nevertheless, the church analysis leads to some preliminary remarks about the plan model of the buildings, the relationship with local settlements and road networks and the level of possible commissioners.

First, the plan of the buildings is mostly based on the model of the single nave with an east-oriented apse. Such a plan was widespread in Northern Italy, in the Diocese of Novara and also beyond the Alps, in Switzerland, in the early Christian period and in the early Middle Ages (Brogiolo *et al.* 1999, 528; Sennhauser 2003; Colecchia 2009, 151). The type of plan was not client-specific, as attested both in some churches probably founded by the bishop and in private foundations, like the late ancient villa of Sizzano, near Novara (Pejrani Baricco 2003, 63-70). For instance, the church of San Pietro in Gravellona Toce is one of the single-nave churches with annexes on the sides, with a type of plan already documented in the Diocese of Novara (San Michele in Oleggio) and particularly widespread in the North-western Alps.

The only baptismal church among those examined in this study, San Giovanni al Montorfano near Mergozzo, seems to rely on the Diocesan models also with the octagonal shape of the font, attested during the presence of bishop Ambrogio in Milan, like the one of the Cathedral of Novara (Pejrani Baricco 1999, 72-76; Brandt 2012, 398-440). However, the plan of the building looks different, since the baptisteries identified in the dioceses are also octagonal: in addition to the Cathedral of Novara, there are also buildings in Cureggio (Pejrani Baricco 2003, 75-79), Sizzano (Pejrani Baricco 2003, 63-70) and, with many uncertainties around the chronology, Baveno (Fiocchi Nicolai and Gelichi 2001, 324-325; Cornaglia and Cornaglia 2009).

Second, as for the relationship with the ancient settlements, all the mentioned churches are placed in the valley floor at low altitudes. As far as we know, the church of San Pietro in Gravellona Toce only lies in a densely populated settlement since the Roman period, with a significant occupation in the late antique phase (Spagnolo Garzoli *et al.* 2008; Poletti Ecclesia 2015), as confirmed by the discovery of burials and residential buildings (unfortunately excavated and demolished due to a lack of control in the mid-20th century). Nearby, not far from the church, a hill is the site of the ruins of the *castrum Gravallone*, known from written sources since the eleventh century (De Vingo *et al.* 2015), although many scholars have speculated about an earlier origin (Negro Ponzi 1999, 145; Panero 2003, 272-273). Therefore, we cannot exclude the existence of a contemporary settlement phase with the oldest documented church of San Pietro in Gravellona Toce. Although little known, the church of Santa Maria is placed in a region where spare archaeological findings from Late Antiquity and the early Middle Ages seem to confirm the existence of a settlement. On the opposite, no data are known about ancient populations living around the churches of Santi Fabiano e Sebastiano in Verbania and San Giorgio in Varzo. However, there is a close relationship between the building locations and the road network, showing how important were road routes in the definition of the local Christian topography (Brogiolo and Chavarria Arnau 2005, 128-130; 2010): San Pietro lies at the intersection of the roads from the plains toward the Alpine passes, SS. Fabiano and Sebastiano is placed on the road running along the western shore of Lake Maggiore; Santa Maria was built in the middle of valleys looking beyond the Alps and San Giorgio on the road to the Simplon Pass (Bertani 2003, 247; Ardizio and Destefanis, 2016).

This relationship is even more remarkable since many authors argue that building locations along the main road routes suggest how the religious network was historically built and shaped by bishop initiative as to draw the most people into the places of worship rather than by single commissioners (Brogiolo and Chavarria Arnau 2010, 59). Actually, in case of a church excavation, when documents or inscriptions are lacking, we cannot rely on proven information to recognize a bishop initiative, but some evidence, such as a well-defined presbytery (as in San Pietro in Gravellona Toce and Santi Fabiano and Sebastiano in Verbania Suna), burials inside the same presbytery or monumental baptisteries (as in San Giovanni Battista in Montorfano), are to be considered a proof of a direct bishop intervention (Brogiolo and Chavarria Arnau 2010, 57-59). Moreover, the religious foundations subsequent to the sixth century (as with most of the cases examined in this paper) are commonly connected to the bishop initiative (Violante 1982). Also, the life continuity of the buildings, although none of the churches mentioned in this paper has ever become *caput plebis* after the Carolingian period, may disclose that they have been founded by a bishop initiative or at least following his approval. Other research contributions show how the churches in Piedmont that were indisputably privately built, such as those identified in the late ancient villas, soon (*i.e.* within the sixth century) eliminated the baptismal font, like in Centallo in Southern Piedmont (Brogiolo *et al.* 1999, 496, 532 and 536; Pejrani Baricco 2001, 560-566; Cantino Wataghin 2013, 203), or abandoned the building itself, like in Sizzano (Pejrani Baricco 2003, 63; Cantino Wataghin 2013, 203). Written sources also point out that as early as in the sixth century some bishops in North-western Italy, but also in other regions, repressed private religious foundations (Violante 1982).

The location of these churches would thus seem to indicate a function of *cura animarum* serving a vast region, whose population was sparse or at least weakly centralized. San Giovanni Battista in Mergozzo (the oldest church known in this area) is an exception, since it lies in a very remote position, on a mountain at that time completely surrounded by the water of Lake Maggiore and without convenient access roads. Therefore, it is unlikely that the church served the entire rural population, also because the *Pieve* of Mergozzo – documented in the 12th century (Gabotto *et al.* 1915, 212-214) – was located on the valley floor. In addition, we can argue that San Giovanni Battista was privately built, possibly within a *castrum* or a late ancient villa (Andenna 1989, 287). On the other hand, the presence of a monumental baptistery, the modernisation of the frescoes compared to the artistic trends in the bishop sites and the uninterrupted use of the baptismal font throughout the early Middle Ages until the Romanesque reconstruction, seem at odds with the idea of a private foundation instead of a bishop initiative (Cantino Wataghin 2006, 298; 2013). At present we cannot provide a definitive outcome about San Giovanni Battista in Mergozzo and only an extension on the investigation outside the church may clarify this question.

## Conclusions

To sum up, all the preliminary data related to the churches in the district of Verbano Cusio Ossola seem to confirm that the local religious network was built and shaped by bishop initiative rather than by private intervention. Therefore, this paper supports the evidence from the last regional contributions (Pantò and Pejrani Baricco 2001; Pantò 2003; Pejrani Baricco 2003), pointing to a higher concentration of findings of early Christian and medieval churches in the Northern Piedmont than in Southern Piedmont, especially in the Alps and Pre-Alps. In particular, this statement applies to the dioceses of Novara and Vercelli. It's no surprise that the single new findings of early medieval rural churches in Piedmont over the last few years, Santi Fabiano e Sebastiano in Verbania Suna e San Pietro in Gravellona, seem to confirm and strengthen the case. Similar to the district of Verbano Cusio Ossola, also in the district of Vercelli the distribution of the early medieval churches complies with the main road routes as if the Christian topography was shaped by bishop initiative. Second, there is no evidence of old places of worship or ancient settlements at high altitudes for the Alpine region in the district of Vercelli as well as in the district of Verbano Cusio Ossola. All the available data seem to suggest the continuing population of the Alpine region in the dioceses of Novara and Vercelli in the early Middle Ages and the likely distribution of settlements at low altitudes (Pantò 2003), whose existence is implied, in the absence of any other information, by coeval places of worship. On the other side, the low number – or even the lack in some dioceses – of early Christian and medieval rural churches in the Southern Piedmont has been related to a worse demographic crisis in this part of the region (Pejrani Baricco 2003, 58). To validate these assumptions, however, it is re-quired a more comprehensive approach as to investigate the relationship between local settlements and churches. In addition to a complete review and an updated survey of the available historical and archaeological database, a planned archaeological research on a number of representative sample sites (from site exploration to ground excavation) should lead to more in-depth analysis through rescue intervention for the protection of cultural heritage.

## Acknowledgements

I would like to thank Chantal Bielmann and Brittany Thomas for giving the opportunity to present this paper. I would also like to express my gratitude to Paolo De Vingo (University of Turin), to my friends Francesca and Andrea Daffara and to my husband, Gian Battista Garbarino, for their patient and valuable contribution to the chapter translation; possible errors in this text are solely attributable to the author.

## Bibliography

### Primary sources

An. Rav., *Ravennatis Anonymi Cosmographia et Guidonis Geographica,* in: Schnetz, J. (ed.), *Itineraria Romana* II. Lipsia 1940.

Gabotto, F., Lizier, A., Leone, A., Morandi, G.B. and Scarzello, O. 1913. *Le carte dell'Archivio Capitolare di Santa Maria di Novara*, I. Novara: Tipografia Parzini

Gabotto, F., Basso, G., Leone, A., Morandi, G.B. and Scarzello, O. 1915. *Le carte dell'Archivio Capitolare di Santa Maria di Novara*, II. Novara: Tipografia Parzini.

### Secondary Sources

Andenna, G. 1989. Riflessioni sull'ordinamento ecclesiale dell'Alto Verbano tra tarda antichità e medioevo, *Verbanus. Rassegna per la cultura, l'arte e la storia del lago* 10, 275-294.

Andenna, G. 1994. San Pietro di Gravellona tra San Gallo, i Visconti, i da Crusinallo ed i «poveri homini del loco» (sec. X-XVII). *Verbanus. Rassegna per la cultura, l'arte e la storia del lago* 15, 253-276.

Andenna, G. 2007. La diocesi di Novara in età carolingia e posta carolingia, in: Vaccaro, L. and Tuniz D. (eds), *Diocesi di Novara*. Brescia: Editrice La Scuola, 53-82.

Ardizio, G. and Destefanis, E. 2016. Organizzazione ecclesiastica e rete itineraria nell'alto Verbano, in: Garanzini, F. and Poletti Ecclesia, E. (eds), *Fana, Aedes, Ecclesiae. Forme e luoghi del culto nell'arco alpino occidentale dalla preistoria al medioevo (Atti del convegno, Mergozzo 18 ottobre 2014)*. Mergozzo: Civico Museo Archeologico, 273-292.

Bertani, A. 2003. Il *castrum* dell'isola di San Giulio d'Orta in età longobarda, in: Lusuardi Siena, S. (ed.), *Fonti archeologiche e iconografiche per la storia e la cultura materiale degli insediamenti nell'Alto Medioevo (Atti delle Giornate di Studio, Milano-Vercelli, 21-22 marzo 2002)*. Milano: Vita & Pensiero, 247-261.

Bertelli, C. 1993. Scheda 15. Frammenti di affreschi (cinque teste e un braccio), in: *Milano e la Lombardia in età comunale. Secoli XI-XIII*. Cinisello Balsamo: Silvana Editoriale, 267-268.

Brandt, O. 2012. *Battisteri oltre la pianta. Gli alzati di nove battisteri paleocristiani in Italia*. Città del Vaticano: Pontificio Istituto di Archeologia Cristiana.

Brogiolo, G.P. 1989. Lo scavo di una chiesa fortificata altomedievale: S. Tomè di Carvico. *Archeologia Medievale* XVI, 155-170.

Brogiolo, G.P. 1995. Evoluzione in età longobarda di alcuni castelli dell'Italia settentrionale, in: Boldrini, E. and Francovich, R. (eds), *Acculturazione e mutamenti: prospettive nell'archeologia medievale del Mediterraneo (VI Ciclo di Lezioni sulla Ricerca Applicata in Archeologia, Certosa di Pontignano (SI) – Museo di Montelupo (FI) 1-5 marzo 1993)*. Firenze: All'Insegna del Giglio, 191-200.

Brogiolo, G.P. 2009. San Martino di Serravalle. Gli scavi 1981-1983, in: Brogiolo, G.P. and Mariotti, V. (eds), *San Martino di Serravalle e San Bartolomeo de Castelàz. Due chiese di Valtellina: scavi e ricerche*. Cinisello Balsamo: Silvana Editoriale, 109-124.

Brogiolo, G.P. 2015. La ricostruzione della rete ecclesiatica attraverso il *corpus* europeo delle chiese altomedievali (CARE), in: Martorelli, R. and Piras, A. and Spanu, P.G. (eds), *Isole e terraferma nel primo cristianesimo. Identità locale ed interscambi culturali, religiosi e produttivi (XI Congresso Nazionale di Archeologia Cristiana, Cagliari – Sant'Antioco, 23-27 settembre 2014).* Cagliari: PFTS University Press, 273-290.

Brogiolo, G.P. and Cantino Wataghin, G. and Gelichi, S. 1999. L'Italia settentrionale, in: Pergola, P. (ed.), *Alle origini della parrocchia rurale (IV-VIII sec.), Atti della giornata tematica dei Seminari di Archeologia Cristiana (Ecole Française de Rome, 19 marzo 1998).* Città del Vaticano: Pontificio Istituto di Archeologia Cristiana, 487-540.

Brogiolo, G.P. and Chavarria Arnau, A. 2005. *Aristocrazie e campagne nell'Occidente da Costantino a Carlo Magno.* Firenze: All'Insegna del Giglio.

Brogiolo, G.P. and Chavarria Arnau, A. 2008. Chiese, territorio e dinamiche del popolamento nelle campagne tra tardo antico e alto medioevo. *Hortus artium Medievalium* 14, 7-29.

Brogiolo, G.P. and Chavarria Arnau, A. 2010. Chiese e insediamenti rurali tra V e VII secolo. Prospettiva della ricerca archeologica, in: Ebanista, C. and Rotili, M. (eds), *Ipsam Nolam barbari vastaverunt. L'Italia e il Mediterraneo occidentale tra il V secolo e la metà del VI (Atti del Convegno internazionale di studi, Cimitile – Nola – Santa Maria Capua Vetere, 18-19 giugno 2009).* Cimitile: Tavolario Edizioni, 45-62.

Cantino Wataghin, G. 1999. Gli apporti archeologici per la conoscenza delle origini della chiesa novarese, in: *Il Cristianesimo a Novara e sul territorio: le origini (Atti del Convegno, Novara 10 ottobre 1998).* Novara: Interlinea Edizioni, 55-70.

Cantino Wataghin, G. 2006. Architecture and Power: Churches in the northern Italy from the 4th to the 6th C., in: Bowden, W., Guitteridge, A. and Machado, C. (eds), *Social and Political Life in Late Antiquity.* Leiden-Boston: Brill, 287-309.

Cantino Wataghin, G. 2013. Le fondazioni ecclesiastiche nelle vicende delle aree rurali: spunti di riflessione per l'Occidente tardo antico (IV-V secolo). *Antiquité Tardive. Revue internationale d'histoire et d'archéologie (IVe-VIIIe s.)* 21, 189-204.

Cantino Wataghin, G., Fiocchi Nicolai, V. and Volpe, G. 2007. Aspetti della cristianizzazione degli agglomerati secondari, in: Carra Bonacasa, R.M. and Vitale E. (eds), *La cristianizzazione in Italia fra tardo antico e alto medioevo (Atti del IX Congresso Nazionale di Aercheologia Cristiana. agrigento 20-25 novembre 2004).* Palermo: Carlo Saladino, 85-134.

Cantino Wataghin, G. and Uggè, S. 2001. Scavi e scoperte di archeologia cristiana in Italia settentrionale (1993-1998), in: *L'edificio battesimale in Italia. Aspetti e problem (Atti dell'VIII Congresso Nazionale di Archeologia Cristiana, Genova, Sarzana, Albenga, Finale Ligure, Ventimiglia 21 – 26 settembre 1998).* Bordighera: Istituto Internazionale di Studi Liguri, 7-37.

Capis, G. 1673 [1968]. *Memorie della Corte di Mattarella o sia del Borgo di Domodossola.* Domodossola: Grossi.

Caramella, P. and De Giuli, A. 1993. *Archeologia dell'alto Novarese.* Mergozzo: Antiquarium Mergozzo.

Casartelli Novelli, S. 1974. *Corpus scultura altomedioevale. VI. La Diocesi di Torino.* Spoleto: Centro Italiano di Studi sull'alto medioevo.

Ceresa Mori, A. and Righetto, G. 2001. La chiesa di S. Giovanni Battista a Cesano Boscone, in: *L'edificio battesimale in Italia. Aspetti e problemi (Atti dell'VIII Congresso Nazionale di Archeologia Cristiana, Genova, Sarzana, Albenga, Finale Ligure, Ventimiglia 21-26 settembre 1998).* Bordighera: Istituto Internazionale di Studi Liguri, 609-629.

Cornaglia, E. and Cornaglia, S. 2009. *Il battistero di Baveno.* Verbania: Alberti.

Chavarria Arnau, A. 2009. *Archeologia della chiese. Dalle origini all'anno 1000.* Roma: Carocci.

Colecchia, A. 2009. III. Provincia di Padova. III.2. il territorio. III.2.1. Introduzione, in: Brogiolo G.P. and Ibsen M. (eds), *Corpus Architecturae Religiosae Europeae (saec. IV-X).* Vol. II. *Italia. I. Province di Belluno, Treviso, Padova, Vicenza.* Zagreb – Motovun: International research center for late antiquity and middle ages, 139-155

De Vingo, P., Garanzini, F. and Dalmasso, F. 2015. Primi dati nello studio di un castello nel Verbano Cusio Ossola: il castrum Gravallone. *Quaderni della Soprintendenza Archeologica del Piemonte* 30, 386-389.

Fiocchi Nicolai, V. and Gelichi, S. 2001. Battisteri e chiese rurali, in: *L'edificio battesimale in Italia. Aspetti e problem (Atti dell'VIII Congresso Nazionale di Archeologia Cristiana, Genova – Sarzana – Albenga – Finale Ligure – Ventimiglia, 21-26 settembre 1998).* Bordighera: Istituto Internazionale di Studi Liguri, 303-384

Garanzini, F. 2014. Gravellona Toce. Chiesa parrocchiale di San Pietro. Indagine archeologica. *Quaderni della Soprintendenza Archeologica del Piemonte* 29, 202-203.

Garanzini, F. 2014a. Il castello di Mattarella di Domodossola (Sacro Monte Calvario) alla luce dei vecchi scavi e delle più recenti indagini archeologiche. *Atti dell'Accademia Roveretana degli Agiati,* ser. IX, vol. IV, fasc. II, 77-100.

Garanzini, F. 2015. Nuovi dati dal Verbano Cusio Ossola: gli scavi della chiesa di S. Pietro a Gravellona Toce e dell'oratorio dei SS. Fabiano e Sebastiano a Verbania, in: Martorelli, R., Piras, A. and Spanu, P.G. (eds), *Isole e terraferma nel primo cristianesimo. Identità locale ed interscambi culturali, religiosi e produttivi (XI Congresso Nazionale di Archeologia Cristiana, Cagliari – Sant'Antioco, 23-27 settembre 2014).* Cagliari: PFTS University Press, 673-679.

Garanzini, F. in press. Il territorio ossolano nell'altomedioevo alla luce delle fonti archeologiche, in: Crosetto, A. (ed.), *Al tempo dei Longobardi in Piemonte. Nuove scoperte archeologiche (Atti del convegno, Asti, 11 aprile 2013).*

Garanzini, F. and Proverbio, C. 2016. Il complesso battesimale paleocristiano di San Giovanni al Montrorfano. Un aggiornamento, in: Garanzini, F. and Poletti Ecclesia, E. (eds), *Fana, Aedes, Ecclesiae. Forme e luoghi del culto nell'arco alpino occidentale dalla preistoria al medioevo (Atti del Convegno, Mergozzo, 18 ottobre 2014).* Mergozzo: Civico Museo Archeologico, 293-314.

Lieb, H. and Wüthrich, R. 1967. *Lexicon topographicum der römischen und frühmittelalterlichen Schweiz. Band I. Römische Zeit. Süd und Ostschweiz.* Bonn.

Lomartire, S. 2007. Architettura e scultura dell'alto medioevo nell'arco alpino occidentale, in: *Carlo Magno e le Alpi (Atti del XVIII Congresso internazionale di studio sull'alto medioevo, Susa, 19-20 ottobre 2006, Novalesa, 21 ottobre 2006).* Spoleto: Centro Italiano di Studi sull'alto medioevo, 299-336.

Lomartire, S. 2009. Materiali scultorei altomedioevali dall'abbazia di Fontaneto d'Agogna, in: Andenna, G. and Teruggi, I. (eds), *Fontaneto: una storia millenaria. Monastero. Concilio metropolitico. Residenza viscontea* (*Atti dei convegni, Fontaneto d'Agogna, settembre 2007 e giugno 2008*). Novara: Interlinea Edizioni, 147-168.

Mazzilli, M.T. 1980. Gli edifici di culto dell'XI e XII secolo. L'alto Verbano e le valli Ossolane, in: Gavazzoli Tomea, M.L. (ed.), *Novara e la sua terra nei secoli XI e XII. Storia, documenti, architettura*. Cinisello Balsamo: Silvana Editoriale, 231-283.

Mennella, G. 1998. La cristianizzazione rurale in Piemonte: il contributo dell'epigrafia, in: Mercando, L. and Micheletto, E. (eds), *Archeologia in Piemonte. Il Medioevo*. Torino: Allemandi, 151-160.

Micheletto, E. 1998. Forme di insediamento tra V e XIII secolo: il contributo dell'archeologia, in: Mercando, L. and Micheletto, E. (eds), *Archeologia in Piemonte. Il Medioevo*. Torino: Allemandi, 51-80.

Negro Ponzi, M.M. 1999. Romani, Bizantini e Longobardi: le fortificazioni tardo antiche e altomedievali nelle Alpi occidental, in: G.P. Brogiolo (ed.), *Le fortificazioni del Garda e i sistemi di difesa dell'Italia settentrionale tra tardo antico e alto medioevo. 2° Convegno archeologico del Garda (Gardone Riviera-Brescia 7-9 ottobre 1998)*. Mantova: SAP, 137-154.

Panero, E. 2003. *Insediamenti celtici e romani in una terra di confine. Materiali per un Sistema Informativo Territoriale nel Verbano-Cusio-Ossola tra culture padano-italiche e apporti transalpini*, Alessandria: Edizioni dell'Orso.

Pantò, G. 1994. La chiesa di san Martino a Roccapietra. L'indagine archeologica, *Bollettino Storico Vercellese* 42, 99-143.

Pantò, G. 2003. Chiese rurali nella diocesi di Vercelli, in: Brogiolo, G.P. (ed.), *Chiese e insediamenti nelle campagne tra V e VI secolo, 9° seminario sul tardo antico e l'altomedioevo (Garlate 26-28 settembre 2002)*. Mantova: SAP, 87-108

Pantò, G. and Pejrani Baricco, L. 2001. Chiese nelle campagne del Piemonte in età tardo longobarda, in: Brogiolo, G.P. (ed.), *Le chiese rurali tra VI e VII secolo in Italia settentrionale, 8° seminario sul tardo antico e l'altomedioevo (Garda 8-10 aprile 2000)*. Mantova: SAP, 17-52.

Pejrani Baricco, L. 1991. Varzo. Chiesa parrocchiale di S. Giorgio. *Quaderni della Soprintendenza Archeologica del Piemonte* 10, 170-171.

Pejrani Baricco, L. 1999. Edifici paleocristiani della diocesi di Novara: un aggiornamento, in: *Il Cristianesimo a Novara e sul territorio: le origini (Atti del Convegno, Novara 10 ottobre 1998)*. Novara: Interlinea Edizioni, 71-103.

Pejrani Baricco, L. 2000. Le fonti archeologiche per la storia dell'isola, in: *San Giulio e la sua storia del XVI centenario di San Giulio*. Novara: Interlinea Edizioni, 85-111.

Pejrani Baricco, L. 2001. Chiese battesimali in Piemonte. Scavi e scoperte, in: *L'edificio battesimale in Italia. Aspetti e problem (Atti dell'VIII Congresso Nazionale di Archeologia Cristiana, Genova – Sarzana – Albenga – Finale Ligure – Ventimiglia, 21-26 settembre 1998)*. Bordighera: Istituto Internazionale di Studi Liguri, 541-588.

Pejrani Baricco, L. 2003. Chiese rurali in Piemonte tra V e VI secolo, in: Brogiolo, G.P. (ed.), *Chiesee insediamenti nelle campagne tra V e VI secolo (9° seminario sul tardo antico e l'altomedioevo, Garlate 26-28 settembre 2002)*. Mantova: SAP, 57-86.

Pejrani Baricco, L. 2009. La chiesa abbaziale di San Sebastiano: analisi delle strutture e indagini archeologiche, in: Andenna, G. and Teruggi, I. (eds), *Fontaneto: una storia millenaria. Monastero.Concilio metropolitico. Residenza viscontea (Atti dei convegni, Fontaneto d'Agogna, settembre 2007 e giugno 2008)*. Novara: Interlinea Edizioni, 117-135.

Pejrani Baricco, L. 2009a. Scavi e scoperte intorno al San Michele, in: Venturoli, P. (ed.), *Il San Michele di Oleggio.* Torino: Editris, 161- 176.

Perotti, M. 2007. Evangelizzazione e impianto della Chiesa a Novara e nel territorio. Dalle origini al sec. VII, in: Vaccaro, L. and Tuniz D. (eds), *Diocesi di Novara.* Brescia: Editrice La Scuola, 3-52.

Piva, P. 2001. Le due chiese di San Lorenzo a Quingentole: "quadri" storici, tipologie architettoniche, contesti funzionali, in: Manicardi, A. (ed.), *San Lorenzo di Quingentole. Archeologia, storia ed antropologia.* Mantova: SAP, 115-144.

Piva, P. 2010. Edilizia di culto cristiano a Milano, Aquileia e nell'Italia settentrionale fra IV e VI secolo, in: De Blaauw, S. (ed.), *Storia dell'architettura italiana. Da Costantino a Carlo Magno.* Milano: Electa, 981-45.

Piva, P. 2015. San Pietro di Vallate, San Pietro a Bormio e il problema delle chiese a due navate, in: Mariotti, V. (ed.), *La Valtellina nei secoli. Studi e ricerche archeologiche. Volume I – Saggi.* Mantova: SAP, 49-80.

Poletti Ecclesia, E. 2015. Alla foce del Toce. Il popolamento di età romana sul golfo mediano del lago Maggiore, porto commerciale verso i passi alpini ossolani, in: Facchinetti, G. and Miedico, C. (eds), *Di città in città. Insediamenti, strade e vie d'acqua da Milano alla Svizzera lungo la Mediolanum – Verbanus.* Arona: Lavrano Editore, 101-113.

Segre Montel, C. 1994. La pittura medievale in Piemonte e Valle d'Aosta, in: Bertelli, C. (ed.), *La pittura in Italia, L'altomedioevo.* Milano: Electa, 33-46.

Sennhauser, H.R. (ed.) 2003. *Frühe Kirchen im östlichen Alpengebiet. Von der Spätantike bis in ottonische Zeit.* München: Verlag der Bayerischen Akademie der Wissenschaften.

Settia, A.A. 1993. Le fortificazioni dei Goti in Italia, in: *Teoderico il Grande e i Goti in Italia (Atti del XIII Congresso internazionale di studi sull'Alto Medioevo, Milano 2-6 novembre 1992).* Spoleto: Centro Italiano di tudi sull'Alto Medioevo, 101-131.

Spagnolo, G. and Garanzini, F. 2011.Verbania, località Suna. Oratorio dei SS. Fabiano e Sebastiano. Indagine archeologica. *Quaderni della Soprintendenza archeologica del Piemonte* 26, 324-325.

Spagnolo Garzoli, G., Ratto, S. and Deodato, A. 2008. Il centro di Gravellona Toce nell'economia degli scambi tra pianura e area alpina, in: *Une voie à travers l'Europe (Séminairede clôture, Bard, 11-12 aprile 2008).* Aosta: Imprimerie Valdotaine, 439-450.

Tosco, C. 1992. San Maurizio a Roccaforte Mondovì e il problema della chiese a due navate nell'architettura dell'età romanica. *Bollettino della Società per gli Studi Storici, Archeologici ed artistici della provincia di Cuneo* CVII/II, 5-43.

Violante, C. 1982. Le strutture organizzative della cura d'anime nelle campagne dell'Italia centrosettentrionale (secoli V-X), in: *Cristianizzazione ed organizzazione ecclesiastica delle campagne nell'alto medioevo: espansione e resistenze, XXVIII Settimana di studio del Centro Italiano di Studi sull'Alto Medioevo (Spoleto 10-16 aprile 1980).* Spoleto: Centro Italiano di Studi sull'Alto Medioevo, 963-1158.

# Space and Place

## Identifying the Anglo-Saxon Cemeteries in the Tees Valley, North-East England

*Stephen Sherlock*

## Introduction

This brief study of the Anglo-Saxon cemeteries in the Tees Valley, north-east England, seeks to find common themes that encompass a number of cemeteries that have been investigated over the last 140 years. Traditionally, the River Tees was considered to form the boundary in the sixth century between the Anglo-Saxon tribal areas of Deira (approximately the area of Yorkshire) and Bernicia (Durham and Northumberland) (Alcock 1981, 172, citing Aneirin). Recent excavations cast doubt on that suggestion based upon the distribution of artefacts and burial traditions that are commonly found on both sides of the River Tees. I examine here the published evidence for the cemeteries in the area of the Tees Valley that now forms the counties of North Yorkshire and Durham (sites referred to are in North Yorkshire unless specified otherwise). Data from the Portable Antiquities Scheme and recently excavated sites are used to examine evidence for cemeteries in the study region. Spanning the sixth to ninth centuries, this paper brings together Anglo-Saxon cemetery sites, artefacts and common burial traditions and considers the spaces and places of Anglo-Saxon cemeteries at locations within the Tees Valley.

In the process of examining the space and place of Anglo-Saxon cemeteries, the study focuses upon locations that have more than one cemetery. Examples of sites that reuse or appropriate earlier sacred sites are noted in both the sixth and seventh centuries. The establishment of a cemetery on earlier sites, for example a burial mound, an enclosure or an earlier cemetery, has been noted elsewhere (Williams 1997). Blair suggested that many religious activities would occur in the natural world and therefore the landscape was significant and locations relating to the topography would be important (Blair 2005, 182). The recognition that these locations within the landscape had a significance has been considered by Semple (2010), whilst others have argued a functional approach, that some cemeteries can be sited on boundaries (Lucy *et al.* 2009, 38)

in: Bielmann, C. and Thomas, B. (eds.) 2018: *Debating Religious Space and Place in the Early Medieval World (c. AD 300-1000)*, Sidestone Press (Leiden), pp. 93-110.

or poor-quality marginal land, for example East Mill, Norton (Sherlock and Welch 1992). Sacred sites can be natural features such as hills, woods, springs and pools or altered landscapes that have been adapted by human endeavour (Semple 2011, 743). We can therefore consider that the close proximity of certain cemeteries which appear to form clusters may relate to the significance of the immediate landscape. The Anglo-Saxon settlements and cemeteries at Hartlepool, Norton and Catterick are examples with such clusters of more than one cemetery. Furthermore, the association of some sites with Christian saints and pilgrimage can be seen at Hartlepool, Street House and Whitby (Peers and Radford 1943; Daniels 2007; Sherlock 2012). Within this context different burial traditions at the cemeteries (grave shape, form, location and grouping) suggest they could represent different social groupings or communities.

## Earlier Studies

The *Gazetteer of Anglo-Saxon Cemetery Sites* by Meaney indicated that there were seven cemeteries in Durham and 88 named in Yorkshire (1964, 83-84, 282-304). In the late 1970s a survey of sites in Bernicia by Miket focused upon 27 sites (1980, 289-305). In the latter survey, five of the sites contained Anglo-Saxon objects and remains within Roman forts, three secondary finds were within barrows, eight were stray finds of Anglo-Saxon date, five were no longer applicable following closer scrutiny and six were Anglo-Saxon cemeteries (Miket 1980, 289-305). Alcock (1981, 177) looked at the Bernician cemeteries in north-east England and suggested by and large they could be characterised as 'small in number but rich in finds'.

The discovery of a sixth-century Anglo-Saxon cemetery at Norton in 1982 and its subsequent excavation in 1984-1985 changed the prevailing view that cemeteries in the area were only small in size but rich in material culture (Sherlock and Welch 1992). Within the Tees Valley there were not many known cemeteries at that time; the site at Hob Hill, Saltburn, with 48 burials had been recorded in 1910-1912 by William Hornsby, but a full site catalogue was not published until 1987 (Gallagher 1987). In a similar vein, the cemetery at Greenbank, Darlington (Durham), discovered in 1876 when building works unearthed six skeletons and a number of Anglo-Saxon finds, was published 100 years after their discovery (Miket and Pocock 1976). What was notable about the Greenbank finds was that the brooches, particularly the Leeds (1949) type C2 great square headed brooches, were seen to have cultural links to sites to the south in Deira and Lindsey rather than those to the north (Miket and Pocock 1976, 74). These were the only early Anglo-Saxon cemeteries known from the Tees Valley. There had been stray finds, including a cremation urn from Yarm (Myres 1977, 150; Meaney 1964, 269) and other singular Anglo-Saxon objects as well as Christian burials from Hartlepool (Daniels 2007, 79), and these will be discussed later. The sixth-century East Mill cemetery and the other cemeteries at Norton are discussed in detail later as part of an exercise to examine the burial practices at the cemeteries.

## Recent Work

In the period following the publication of the East Mill, Norton cemetery (Sherlock and Welch 1992), a number of Anglo-Saxon cemeteries have been discovered by excavation, and some sites have been published, for example Catterick racecourse (Moloney *et al.* 2003) and Easington (Durham) (Hamerow and Picken 1995). These two sites have artefacts within graves that have been described by the excavators as being similar to Norton; similarly, the types of artefacts found in Yorkshire can be seen to extend north of the Tees as far as the River Wear. The implication of this is that the Tees does not seem to be a barrier because similar finds and burial and cremation practices extend from Yorkshire into Durham. Further sites are suggested by finds reported to the Portable Antiquities Scheme: for example at Dalton Percy, Grindon, Greatham, Hart and Piercebridge in Durham and Newby in North Yorkshire (Sherlock 2011, 114). A number of excavations at Catterick over many years have revealed evidence for burial practices and settlement between the fifth and seventh centuries, collated in an article in *Medieval Archaeology* (Wilson *et al.* 1996), whilst more recent discoveries at Catterick in 2015 are mentioned here. Over 150 years of work at Hartlepool was published in one volume (Daniels 2007), and these cemeteries will be considered further in this paper. Other sites are unpublished but feature in grey literature, are the subject of doctoral dissertations (Craig 2009), reported on to the Portable Antiquities Scheme in the Tees Valley (Collins 2010) and reviewed in the context of earlier monuments (Sherlock 2011).

## Tees Valley Sites

This study examines 20 sites that comprise ten sites north and ten sites south of the River Tees, commencing between 500 and 700 but with later evidence continuing into the ninth century (Fig. 18). Furthermore, these sites all have distinctive Anglo-Saxon objects, usually dress items, associated with burials or human remains. There are no fifth-century sites within the group, nor have any such sites been located. One feature of note that is examined further is that there are some locations that have more than one Anglo-Saxon cemetery, notably at Catterick, Hart, Hartlepool and Norton, although the sites at Kirkleatham and Street House will also be considered within this pattern because a second cemetery may also be located at these two sites. What is also apparent is that there are common themes in terms of burial practice that can be seen to occur on both sides of the River Tees, reinforcing the suggestion the Tees may not be the boundary between the Deiran tribe in Yorkshire and Bernicia north of the Tees.

### Catterick

The Roman town of *Cataractonium* in North Yorkshire has been subject to excavations since the 19th century (Wilson 2002; Fig. 19). In the course of this work, evidence for the town known in Anglo-Saxon times as 'Catraeth' has been uncovered on several occasions. Catraeth is recorded by Bede as the location where Paulinus baptised Christians in the River Swale on Easter Sunday in 627 (Bede *HE*, III, 14). Anglo-Saxon Catraeth has been documented (Wilson *et al.* 1996), the most recent evidence, not covered by Wilson, is mentioned here in the context of earlier discoveries. North of the Swale a *grubenhaus* (Fig. 19, no. 1) was excavated within the Roman town in 1972 (Wilson *et al. 1996*, 16), whilst Anglo-Saxon skeletons were recorded in the 1950s during roadwork near Fort Bridge (Fig. 19, no. 2) (Hildyard and Wade 1950). South of Catterick racecourse a small cemetery of 45 skeletons (Fig. 19, no. 3) was

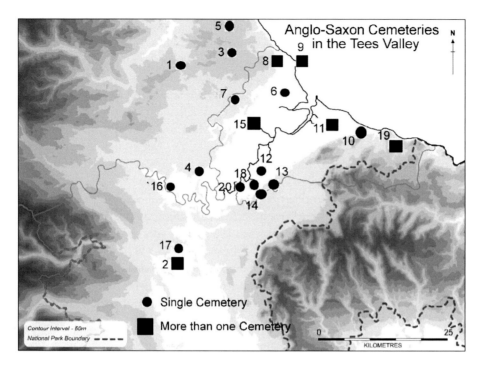

*Figure 18: Anglo-Saxon Cemeteries in the Tees Valley and environs: 1) Binchester, 2) Catterick sites, 3) Dalton Percy, 4) Greenbank Darlington, 5) Easington, 6) Greatham, 7) Grindon, 8) Hart sites, 9) Hartlepool sites, 10) Hob Hill, Saltburn, 11) Kirkleatham sites, 12) Low Lane, Ingleby Barwick, 13) Maltby, 14) Newby, 15) Norton sites, 16) Piercebridge, 17) Scorton, 18) Stainton, 19) Street House, Loftus, 20) Yarm.*

recorded within an Iron Age enclosure and dated to the sixth century based upon the finds (Moloney *et al.* 2003, 45).

Seven skeletons of probable fifth-century date were found within buildings near Dere Street at Bainesse (Fig. 19, no. 4), 4km south of Catterick (Wilson *et al.* 1996, 45). Further burials have been found within Marne Barracks. The initial discovery was made in July 1939 when skeletons were identified during excavations of a Roman building within RAF Catterick (Fig. 19, no. 5). Hildyard (1952, 241) discovered five burials and a further burial was uncovered during building works in the 1960s by Cramp (Wilson *et al.* 1996, 29-32). The burials unearthed by Hildyard and Cramp (discussed further below) have been dated to the sixth century based upon the artefacts. These artefacts comprised a florid cruciform brooch Aberg (1926) type IVa from Hildyard's excavations and Anglian jewellery including bronze sleeve clasps, amber and glass beads and a bronze swastika brooch (Cramp 1996, 30-31).

In 2015, an evaluation under the auspices of Operation Nightingale – an initiative to help rehabilitate injured soldiers by getting them involved in archaeological investigations – within Marne Barracks exposed part of the cemetery seen by Hildyard and Cramp (Sherlock 2017). Hildyard (1952) described five burials within a building and a further discovery in the 1960s recorded by Cramp brought that number to six. The recent excavations found a fragmentary bone comb and two further inhumations, both associated with a Roman stone building. The burials had both been disturbed by later

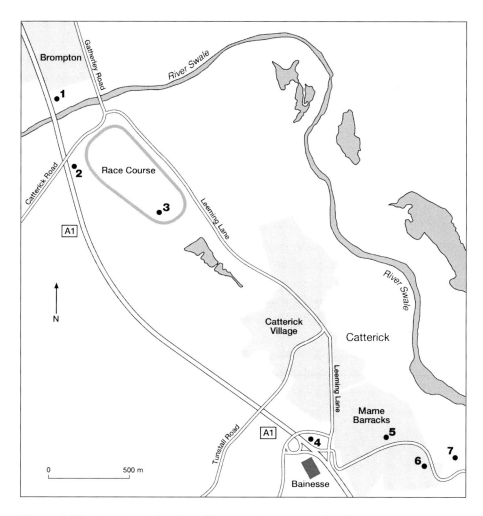

*Figure 19: Map showing the location of the seven sites mentioned at Catterick: 1) Brompton; 2) Fort Bridge; 3) Catterick racecourse; 4) Bainesse; 5) Marne Barracks; 6) Marne Barracks (1994); 7) Castle Hills.*

activity. Skeleton 7 was outside the north wall of the building and skeleton 8 was aligned north – south within the building adjacent to the threshold. Finds from grave 8, comprising an iron knife, potsherd and annular brooch, are all considered to be Anglo-Saxon in style. The limits to the site have not been defined but there is a clear trend for the reuse of Roman stone buildings as burial places in the Anglo-Saxon period at Bainesse (Fig. 19, no.4) and elsewhere in the North East (Miket 1980) on Hadrian's Wall and nearby, for example at Binchester (Coggins 1979). Excavations elsewhere within Marne Barracks in 1994 revealed a *grubenhaus* (Fig. 19, no. 6) 200m south-east of the burials with a suggestion that the building was used for weaving (Taylor-Wilson 1996, 25). Finally, at Marne, Cramp suggested that 'Castle Hills' 500m to the south of the 'cemetery' (Fig. 19, no. 7) may represent a post-Roman development that was utilised in the construction of the later motte and bailey (Wilson *et al.* 1996, 7). Cramp also argued that an Anglo-Saxon pendant cross (now lost) from 'Catterick Bridge' may have been excavated from Castle Hills in the nineteenth century (Cramp 2013, 80).

## Hartlepool and Hartness

The monastery at Hartlepool was established in AD 640 by Heiu, although it perhaps is best known for the period when St Hilda was abbess between 649 and 657 (Bede *HE*, IV, 23). Discoveries of stray finds and recent excavations have been brought together by Daniels (2007). The significant feature about the monastery 'Heruteu' at Hartlepool is that it is on a promontory known as the Headland, where the limits of the monastery and Anglo-Saxon settlement are defined, with the sea on three sides (Fig. 20) in a manner reminiscent of other early monasteries. In addition to the monastery and precinct, four distinct contemporary cemeteries have been excavated: Cross Close, Church Walk, Gladstone Street and St Helens Chapel.

The Cross Close cemetery (Fig. 20, no. 2) was first discovered in 1833 during building work at South Crescent when human remains were uncovered with namestones. These and subsequent discoveries over the next ten years were all associated with the Anglo-Saxon monastery. The burials were all aligned north – south. The total number initially found is unknown but eight namestones were recovered and other finds in-

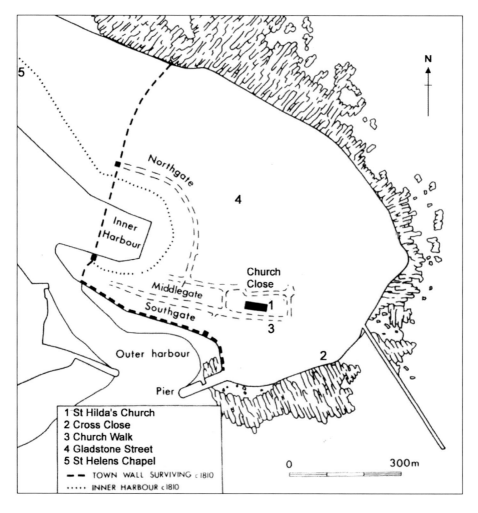

*Figure 20: Plan of Hartlepool Headland showing St Hilda's Church and the Anglo-Saxon sites.*

cluded pins and glass beads (Daniels 2007, 76). The namestones are inscribed, most with female names, and they are thought to have been placed on top of the grave. Occasionally pillow stones were found placed beneath the head. The alignment of the graves, the female gender of the deceased and the namestones have led Daniels to suggest these were 'presumably nuns from the monastery' (Daniels 2007, 80).

A further cemetery was found in 1964, during the installation of gas pipes behind Gladstone Street (Fig. 20, no. 4), when four graves and further amounts of charnel were identified, aligned north-west – south-east (Proudfoot 1979, 172). The graves had stones along the edge. There were few finds, but radiocarbon dating (cal AD 660-800, SUERC-7549, 1290±35 BP) indicates these are contemporary with the monastery and the Cross Close and South Crescent burials (Daniels 2007, 214). The north-west – south-east alignment of the burials and stone 'blocks' to mark the edges of the graves suggest that this cemetery is similar to Church Walk excavated in 1972 and 1976 (Fig. 20, no. 3). The Church Walk cemetery is significant because of the large number of graves, and a plan of the cemetery depicts boundaries to the north and east. The population of the cemetery is different to Cross Close, with adult males, females and children (Daniels 2007, 84). In terms of distribution and layout, the cemetery may have been defined for different groups, with children in one area, males (possibly monks) in a discrete area and a further area with a 'mixed population' (Daniels 2007, 93). Significantly, this cemetery had pebbles marking the edges of the graves; one burial may have had a coffin, whilst another had coffin fittings. Over the two seasons, 72 burials were noted and it was clear that this was only part of the cemetery. This cemetery is radiocarbon dated to the period of the monastery (Daniels 2007, 214-215: for Church Close, cal AD 600-900 (HAR-8599, 1320±80 BP); and for Church Walk, cal AD 630-890 (HAR-3056, 1310±70 BP)).

The final site, St Helens Chapel (Fig. 20, no. 5), was investigated in 1845 and graves were excavated in the 1960s. These were cist-like and have been compared to the burials from Gladstone Street. In summary, in Hartlepool there are four spatially distinct cemeteries with different burial practices and these are contemporary based upon the available radiocarbon dating evidence.

Hartness is centred on Hart village and was probably part of a large estate belonging to the Northumbrian royal family (Daniels 2007, 180). The name is derived from the Saxon 'Heorternesse', comprising two elements meaning an administrative area (Austin 1976, 73). Evidence for Anglo-Saxon stonework, stray finds and excavations indicate that this was a significant locale from at least the seventh century (Daniels 2012, 10). The first documentary reference to the village is found in a charter dated between 830 and 845 granted by the bishop of Lindisfarne (Hart 1975, 138).

To the west of Hart, evaluations yielded a number of structures and animal bones that are undated but are suggested by Daniels to be early medieval in origin (2012, 31-32). Within Hart church there are eight pieces of Anglo-Saxon sculpture, some showing Scandinavian influence, dating between the eighth and eleventh centuries (Daniels 2012, 14-18). East of the village an evaluation has found five graves aligned east – west, with the edges lined by pebbles, similar to Anglo-Saxon graves found on the Headland at Hartlepool. In addition, the presence of nails suggesting coffins or boxes as well as charred seaweed were further suggestions for an early medieval date (ASUD 2015, 13-14). In the adjoining field, metal detecting revealed two Anglo-

Saxon small long brooches of sixth-century date (Sherlock 2011, 114) in addition to Anglo-Saxon coins of eighth- to ninth-century date, including a silver styca dated 844-62 (Tees HER 6998) from the area (Daniels 2012, 23). To the south a geophysics survey has defined curving ditches and possible wall trenches for buildings in an area where an Anglo-Saxon cross head had previously been found. In conclusion, there is a range of evidence dating to the early medieval period around the periphery of Hart, each of which, sculpture, burials, jewellery and potential features, could be seen to represent different periods of human activity within the Anglo-Saxon period.

### Norton

Two large Anglo-Saxon cemeteries have been excavated at Norton: a sixth- to seventh-century cemetery at East Mill (Sherlock and Welch 1992) and, 200m to the south-west, an eighth- to ninth-century cemetery at Bishopsmill School (Johnson 2005). Human remains have also been found elsewhere in the area.

East Mill, Norton cemetery was excavated in 1984-1985 following the accidental discovery of human remains in 1982 in a field east of Norton mill. The site's location north of the River Tees is significant. This is still the largest Anglo-Saxon cemetery in the North East. It has both inhumations and cremations, and the artefacts have sim-

*Figure 21: East Mill, Norton – crouched burial in grave 60 with spear beside head.*

ilarities with sites to the south in East Yorkshire, Lincolnshire and East Anglia rather than with any site to the north. Later excavations in Yorkshire and Durham have found similar artefacts, such as the Leeds type C2 square headed brooch at West Heslerton (Powlesland and Haughton 1999, 253, grave 147) and at Scorton (Speed forthcoming, grave 112). Other finds recognised at East Mill, Norton, but not found further north, include scutiform pendants in graves 48 and 70, a Frankish buckle in grave 22 and silver bangles from grave 40 (Sherlock and Welch 1992). This cemetery is close to the parish boundary between Billingham and Norton. The boundaries of the cemetery itself are known; it measures 40m north – south by 75m east – west and it contained a total of 120 burials. One feature of note at this cemetery are the 32 crouched burials, including grave 60 with a spear, placed beside the head, and shield boss (Fig. 21). It is notable that the cemetery ceased to be used around the early – mid seventh century, based upon the finds.

In 1995-6 human remains were found to the west of East Mill cemetery and an excavation was undertaken in 2003 as part of a programme of building work at Bishopsmill School. Although burials were not noted when the school was built in the 1970s (R. Daniels, *pers comm*), human remains are known from the immediate area. During excavations in 2003, a total of 107 skeletons were found in 98 graves. These burials were different to the East Mill cemetery in several respects: later in date; no cremations; graves in rows; sometimes intercutting; graves aligned east – west; and few graves contained grave goods. Significantly, within some graves it appears that the burials were placed within chests or wooden caskets, based upon the iron fittings; similar fittings are known from other cemeteries of this date, for example at Ripon (Hall and Whyman 1996) and Spofforth (NAA 2002). At Bishopsmill, there was some intercutting of graves, demonstrating an amount of reuse of the site which had three phases between the seventh and tenth centuries.

There are two other cemeteries in this part of Norton, at Fernie Road and at Roseberry Road. The Fernie Road burials comprised six skeletons in stone 'coffins' (perhaps cists) and were reported to have 'swords' with them. The site was not archaeologically investigated at the time, although one of the people involved in the 1930s work was interviewed in the early 1980s (Sherlock and Welch 1992, 1). At Roseberry Road, burials were found during building works in 2007 and were recorded

| Norton sites | Skeleton no. | Radiocarbon age BP | Calibrated date range (95% confidence) |
|---|---|---|---|
| Bishopsmill | | | |
| Phase I | [190] | - | cal AD 660-790 |
| Phase III | [330] | - | cal AD 680-890 |
| Phase III | [331] | - | cal AD 650-770 |
| Phase III | [417] | - | cal AD 770-960 |
| | | | |
| Roseberry Road | | | |
| Trench 3 | [305] sk2 | 1150BP±30 | cal AD 690-750 and 760-890 |
| Trench 4 | [402] sk3 | 1140BP±30 | cal AD 690-750 and 760-890 |

*Table 1: Radiocarbon dates from Bishopsmill cemetery and Roseberry Road burials, Norton (sample numbers not available, unpublished dates courtesy of Tees Archaeology).*

by Tees Archaeology. They were radiocarbon dated and are contemporaneous with the Bishopsmill cemetery (Table 1). The Roseberry Road cemetery is 200m south-east of Bishopsmill School and further burials are noted further to the south in Roseberry Road. However, these are undated and were not archaeologically excavated. Finally, a human skull was also found 100m to the west of Bishopsmill School. The location of Anglo-Saxon settlement at Norton is unknown although the tenth- to eleventh-century St Mary's Church is further west of all the cemeteries.

At Norton it is known that there are therefore two substantial cemeteries, both with over 100 inhumations and it is thought that Bishopsmill may commence when East Mill ceases to be used. The Roseberry Road cemetery may not be linked to any other site and although contemporary with Bishopsmill it could form a burial ground for a unique group from the Norton-Billingham area who are demonstrating their uniqueness by means of a different burial location and tradition. This tradition could be reflecting the community cemeteries as described by Welch (2011, 284).

### Street House

The excavation of a conversion period (mid-seventh century) cemetery was undertaken as part of a programme of research into late prehistoric settlement in north-east Yorkshire, which took place between 2005 and 2007. The aim of the research was to assess the scale and significance of the site (Sherlock 2012). The cemetery contained 109 graves and a number of high-status burials including the only known bed burial in north-east England to date that, it is argued, served as a focus for other burials within the cemetery. There were two buildings; one is considered to be a chapel and the second is interpreted as a mortuary house (Fig. 22). This cemetery was only in use for perhaps one generation, between 640 and 665, based upon the type of artefacts found in conversion period cemeteries. Examples of these artefact types include cabochon pendants (grave 42), silver bullae (grave 43), gold wire (grave 70) and amethyst (grave 12) beads, and gold circular and triangular pendants (graves 10, 43) (Sherlock 2012, 26-43). In many cases where conversion period cemeteries have been excavated there are earlier migration period cemeteries nearby (eg, Chamberlains Barn, Beds: Hyslop 1963; Sheffields Hill, Lincs: Leahy and Williams 2001; Winnal, Hants: Meaney and Chadwick Hawkes 1970). In addition, it is suggested that in some cases settlements could be located near conversion period cemeteries (Boddington 1990, 194-196). There are not many known Anglo-Saxon cemeteries associated with settlements. At West Heslerton (Powesland and Haughton 1999) and Mucking, Essex (Hirst and Clark 2009), the cemeteries were not directly associated with the settlements. At Bloodmoor Hill, Carlton Colville (Lucy *et al.* 2009) there were burials within the settlement. In the area of this study structures are known at Hartlepool in a monastic enclosure (Daniels 2007). At Ingleby Barwick, Stockton on Tees, two sunken-featured buildings are known (Tees HER 6983), but sited over 2km to the north of a sixth-century cemetery (Tees HER 4986). At Street House, there should be a pre-conversion period cemetery and an associated settlement in the area, but these have yet to be found.

The Street House cemetery has some characteristics that are seen at other Tees Valley sites. For example, all of the burials are believed to have been crouched, based upon the size of the graves. The placement of objects within the graves by mourners is argued to be significant at this site (Sherlock 2012, 80). Examples of potsherds and finds placed

Figure 22: Reconstruction of the eastern side of the Street House cemetery showing buildings and burial mounds.

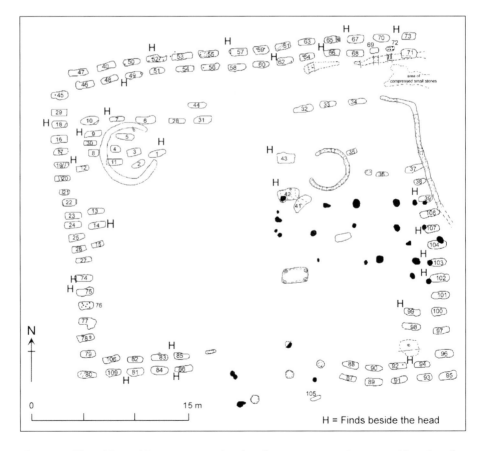

Figure 23: Plan of Street House cemetery showing the arrangement of graves and location of objects beside the head.

around the head (Fig. 23) can be seen at other sites, notably at East Mill, Norton. Also at East Mill cemetery bucket pendants were found beside the skull in graves 35 and 71 (Sherlock and Welch 1992, 44) and the wooden bucket associated with grave 120 was beside the head. It has been argued that some items within graves have been placed by mourners at the grave side, rather than being worn artefacts belonging to the deceased. Examples of funerary activity above ground, within the cemetery, can be seen at Street House. These features can be recognised in several ways: as a burial mound over graves (graves 42, 43), grave markers in stone (graves 65, 102, 103) and timber markers (graves 49, 50, 56, 62) (Sherlock 2012, 106). These are recognised by the arrangement of graves forming a rectangle and management of the use of space, pathways, grave markers, rows and mounds, all defining clear areas within the cemetery (Fig. 23).

### Kirkleatham

In 2013 an archaeological watching brief uncovered human remains on the site of Kirkleatham Hall School (Sherlock and Abramson 2015). The site is located 100m to the east of St Cuthbert's Church. The Domesday Book records for the area relate to *West Lidun* where a manor and church with a priest is recorded in the village (*Domesday Book*). The present church is considered to be on the site of the building recorded in 1066 and there is pre-Conquest stonework within the building comprising one Viking gravestone (S. Ramsdale, *pers comm*) and testimony of others now lost.

The human remains were previously disturbed during works at Kirkleatham Hall, situated at this location between 1623 (Page 1923, 371-383) and 1955 (Redcar Borough Council 1956). It was thus suggested that the burials pre-dated the hall and most probably the church, mentioned in the Domesday Book. In total 13 skeletons were recorded and the minimum number of individuals within the site was 19, suggesting there were some multiple burials in the same grave (Sherlock and Abramson 2015). The individuals were in graves aligned north – south and were considered to be similar in appearance to those excavated at the Norton cemetery (Sherlock and Welch 1992, 14). None of the graves were intact. Although artefacts were found with two burials, these could not provide a satisfactory date for the cemetery. A radiocarbon determination was obtained from a humerus recovered from skeleton 12 of 1242±28 BP (SUERC-57640) giving a date cal AD 682-875 at 95.4% probability.

The cemetery at Kirkleatham may have formed as a burial ground between the eighth and ninth centuries, similar to other rural cemeteries that may be remote from but are associated with a church.

### Discussion and Conclusions

This review of Anglo-Saxon burials within the Tees Valley has chronicled the sites in the area concentrating upon locations with more than one focus of Anglo-Saxon activity and a number of different burial traditions. Within the themes of the conference, pilgrimage to sacred places and the cult of saints is significant. I argue that the sites at Street House and Hartlepool may be linked to pilgrimage through Hilda and her contemporaries. The examples of reuse are indicative of the sacredness of the sites through time.

At Street House, a rare bed burial (grave 42) was located in one corner of the site, and it is suggested that burial mounds and two structures are associated with a possible shrine in this part of the cemetery (Fig. 22; Sherlock 2012, 128). The female buried in grave 42 was on a bed in a chamber and was interred with three gold pendants, one with a Christian motif. The reuse of this Christian motif, considered to be of Roman origin, and other reused artefacts from Street House is a further significant element in the reuse of sacred places. This has now been noted at other conversion period sites (Sherlock 2016). It is argued that the cemetery is focused around grave 42 and that the buildings, burial mounds and restricted points of access are determined to create a shrine for a high-status individual espousing Christian faith. This discrete area was defined on four sides, by a ditch to the east, graves to the north, burial mounds to the west and a structure to the south, to form an inner precinct (Sherlock 2012, 128). A similar arrangement of a building within an inner precinct, founder grave and shrine was excavated at Whithorn in south-west Scotland (Hill 1997, 90-91). This precinct and shrine was in period I, phase II dating to the sixth – seventh century. Here a circular shrine was erected in front of a 'special grave'. The shrine at times had a ditch around it and later a building was erected to the north of the shrine; a fenced enclosure, later paved, defined the inner precinct (Hill 1997, 90-91).

One aspect of commemoration of the deceased and perhaps a means to invoke familial memory is demonstrated by deposition of objects within the grave. These items are not considered dress or status items and this phenomenon has now been recognised at two sites. At Street House, it was possible to examine the placement of objects by mourners within the graves. Sherds of pottery were placed beside the head of individuals. The number and frequency of finds found beside the head suggests this was not random or coincidental (Fig. 23). In addition to pot sherds, pieces of glass vessels were found beside the head; these items may be fragments of heirlooms that are selected to be placed beside the body (Sherlock 2012, 80-81). At East Mill, Norton some of the burials were clearly crouched (as at Street House) suggesting a decision by the mourners to have the deceased buried in a particular manner, whilst some graves contained placed pendants, pot sherds, drinking vessels or, in the case of grave 120, a yew bucket beside the head. Once the deposition of objects in the grave ceases, status can be signified by coffin fittings, grave markers, and location of graves in the cemetery and erection of monuments around the grave.

Street House is an example of a cemetery that replaces an earlier site at a time of changing burial practices. The location of the earlier site and possible settlement is unknown, although a further undated burial site within 1km was excavated in the 19th century. Whilst the Street House cemetery only exists for a short period of time, it is contemporary with St Hilda becoming abbess at Whitby in 657. A distance of 18km separates the two locations linked by a road, 'Cleveland Street', argued to be Roman by Elgee (1923). Blair has proposed that the nearby village of Easington (1km south of Street House) may be the location for *Osingadun* cited as a place where Cuthbert met Aelflaed, abbess of Whitby in the 680s: they were feasting at this location 'a possession in her minster' (Blair 2005, 212). Pilgrimage and travel between Whitby, Street House and Hartlepool was possible by sea of course, but could also be followed along ancient Roman roads such as Cleveland Street.

It is suggested that within the Tees Valley burial was occurring within different cemeteries at the same location and time. This is known at ecclesiastical sites such as Ripon and Whitby, and particularly notable at Hartlepool, Norton and Catterick. At Hartlepool there are four cemeteries in use between *c.* 650 and *c.* 850. Each may have been used by a different group. Based upon the excavation evidence, there could be male and female cemeteries associated with the monastery, with the potential for a community or lay cemetery elsewhere. Once the migration period cemetery at East Mill, Norton goes out of use (*c.* 640) burial then commences at Bishopsmill, Norton, which continues in use for perhaps 300 years. The site is more extensive than the East Mill cemetery, if we accept the burials at Roseberry Road and its environs are contemporary and could be associated with Bishopsmill. It may be that Bishopsmill represents the burial ground for more than one community who buried kinfolk beside the Norton-Billingham parish boundary.

While some mid-Saxon cemeteries can be associated with monastic sites, Buckberry (2010, 11) notes that others may not be directly associated with a church before the tenth century. The cemetery at Kirkleatham perhaps fits into this tradition, where an eighth- to ninth-century burial ground is in a rural location. At a later time when a church is established, a different location is chosen (the site of the present church) and the burial rite moves to the church.

This survey of Anglo-Saxon burial data in the Tees Valley thus presents a landscape featuring a myriad of different traditions that could represent status, ethnicity, gender, race, religion and changes within a developing Anglo-Saxon society. This chapter has described an interesting range of cemeteries with different locations (*rural* – Norton and Street House; *town* – Catterick; *monastic* – Hartlepool; *royal cemetery* – Street House; *royal vill* – Catterick; *royal estate* – Hart), where the placement of human remains and association of objects in the graves change over a period of time. Thus, the Tees Valley acts as a valuable case study demonstrating the complexities of burial traditions examined across different types of sites over multiple centuries and illustrates how examination of these sites can reveal significant information with respect to the reuse of sacred space and commemoration.

## Acknowledgements

I am grateful to the editors and Neil Christie at the University of Leicester for asking me to contribute my paper to the published proceedings and for their helpful comments and those of the anonymous reviewer on an earlier draft. I was assisted by Robin Daniels, Rachel Grahame and Peter Rowe with help on local sites in the Tees Archaeology Historic Environment Record and with permission to reproduce Figs. 20 and 21. Lester Jones produced Fig. 19.

# Bibliography

## Primary Sources

Aneirin. *The Gododdin*. Translated from Welsh by K.H. Jackson (ed.). Edinburgh: Edinburgh University Press, 1969.

Bede. *Historia Ecclesiastica gentis Anglorum.* Translated from Latin by B. Colgrave and B. Mynors (eds). Oxford: Oxford University Press, 1969.

*Domesday Book.* Translated from Latin by G.H. Martin and A. Williams (eds). London: Penguin Classics, 1992.


## Secondary Sources

Aberg, N.F. 1926. *The Anglo-Saxons in England during the Centuries after Invasion.* Uppsala: Uppsala Publishing.

Alcock, L. 1981. Quantity or quality: the Anglian graves in Bernicia, in: Evison, V.I. (ed.), *Angles, Saxon and Jutes: Essays Presented to J N L Myers*. Oxford: Oxford University Press, 168-186.

ASUD, 2015. *Land East of Milbank Close, Hart, Hartlepool.* Developer Report: ASUD 3851.

Austin, D. 1976. Fieldwork and excavation at Hart, Co Durham 1965-1975. *Archaeologia Aeliana* 5/4, 69-132.

Blair, J. 2005. *The Church in Anglo-Saxon Society.* Oxford: Oxford University Press.

Boddington, A. 1990. Models of burial settlement and worship: the final phase reviewed, in: Southworth, E (ed.), *Anglo-Saxon Cemeteries: A Reappraisal*. Stroud: Sutton, 177-199.

Buckberry, J. 2010. Cemetery diversity in the mid to late Anglo-Saxon period in Lincolnshire and Yorkshire, in: Buckberry, J. and Cherryson, A. (eds), *Burial in Later Anglo-Saxon England c. 650-110 AD*. Oxford: Oxbrow Books, 1-25.

Coggins, D. 1979. Durham: Binchester. *Medieval Archaeology* 23, 236.

Collins, R. 2010. Recent discoveries of Anglian material in North East England. *Medieval Archaeology* 54, 386-390.

Craig, F.E. 2009. *Burial Practices in Northern England c. 640-850 AD: A Bio-Cultural Approach*. Thesis submitted for the degree of Doctor of Philosophy, University of Sheffield.

Cramp, R. 1996. RAF Catterick 1966, in: Wilson, P.R., Cardwell, P., Cramp, R.J., Evans, J., Taylor-Wilson, R., Thompson, A. and Wacher, J.S., Early Anglian Catterick and Catreath. *Medieval Archaeology* 40, 29-32.

Cramp, R. 2013. A lost pendant from near Catterick bridge, Yorkshire, in: Reynolds, A. and Webster, L. (eds), *Early Medieval Art and Archaeology in the Northern World: Studies in Honour of James Graham-Campbell*. Leiden: Brill, 73-86.

Daniels, R. 2007. *Anglo-Saxon Hartlepool and the Foundation of English Christianity*. Tees Archaeology Monograph 3. Oxford: Oxbow Brooks.

Daniels, R. 2012. *Heritage of Hart: Anglo-Saxon Hart.* Tees Archaeology Report TA12/03. Hartlepool: Tees Archaeology.

Elgee, F. 1923. *The Romans in Cleveland.* Princeton: Hood Publishing.

Gallagher, D.B. 1987. The Anglo-Saxon cemetery at Hob Hill, Saltburn. *Yorkshire Archaeological Journal* 59, 9-27.

Hall, R.A. and Whyman, M. 1996. Settlement and monasticism in Ripon, North Yorkshire, from 7th – 11th centuries AD. *Medieval Archaeology* 40, 62-150.

Hamerow, H. and Picken, J. 1995. An Early Anglo-Saxon cemetery at Andrews Hill, Easington, County Durham. *Durham Archaeological Journal* 11, 35-66.

Hamerow, H., Hinton, D.A. and Crawford, S. 2011. *The Oxford Handbook of Anglo-Saxon Archaeology*. Oxford: Oxford University Press.

Hart, C.R. 1975. *The Early Charters of Northern England and the North Midlands*. Leicester: Leicester University Press.

Hill, P. 1997. *Whithorn and St Ninian: the Excavation of a Monastic Town 1984-1991*. Stroud: Sutton Publishing.

Hildyard, E.J.W. 1952. A Roman and Saxon site at Catterick. *Yorkshire Archaeological Journal* 150, 241-245.

Hildyard, E.J.W. and Wade, W.V. 1950. Trail Excavations at Catterick. *Yorkshire Archaeological Journal* 37, 402-419.

Hirst, S. and Clark, D. 2009. *Excavations at Mucking: Vol 3, The Anglo-Saxon Cemeteries*. London: Museum of London Archaeology.

Hyslop, M. 1963. Two Anglo-Saxon cemeteries at Chamberlains Barn, Leighton Buzzard. *Bedfordshire Archaeological Journal* 120, 161-200.

Johnson, P.G. 2005. Cemetery excavations at Bishopsmill School, Norton. Unpublished assessment and analysis, Tees Archaeology Archive Report.

Leahy, K. and Williams, J. 2001. Sheffield's Hill, two Anglo-Saxon cemeteries. *Current Archaeology* 175, 310-313.

Leeds, E.T. 1949. *A Corpus of Early Anglo-Saxon Great Square Headed Brooches*. Oxford: Clarendon Press.

Lucy, S., Tipper, J. and Dickens, A. 2009. *The Anglo-Saxon Settlement and Cemetery at Bloodmoor Hill, Carlton Colville, Suffolk*. East Anglian Archaeology 131. Cambridge: East Anglian Archaeology.

Meaney, A.L. 1964. *A Gazetteer of Early Anglo-Saxon Burial Sites*. London: George Allen and Unwin.

Meaney, A.L. and Chadwick Hawkes, S. 1970. *Two Anglo-Saxon Cemeteries at Winnal*. Society of Medieval Archaeology Monograph 4. London: Society of Medieval Archaeology.

Miket, R. 1980. A restatement for the evidence from Bernician Anglo-Saxon burials, in: Rahtz, P., Dickinson, T. and Watts, L. (eds), *Anglo-Saxon cemeteries 1979*. British Archaeological Reports 82. Oxford: British Archaeological Reports, 289-305.

Miket, R. and Pocock, M. 1976. An Anglo-Saxon cemetery at Greenbank, Darlington. *Medieval Archaeology* 20, 62-74.

Moloney, C., Holbrey, R., Wheelhouse, P. and Roberts, I. 2003. *Catterick Racecourse, North Yorkshire: The Reuse and Adoption of a Monument from Prehistoric to Anglian Times*. West Yorkshire Archaeological Services 4. Leeds: West Yorkshire Archaeological Services.

Myres, J.N.L. 1977. *A Corpus of Anglo-Saxon Pottery of the Pagan Period*. Cambridge: Cambridge University Press.

Northern Archaeological Associates 2002. *Cemetery Excavations at Village Farm, Spofforth, North Yorkshire. Archaeological post-excavation assessment*. Unpublished report for Northern Archaeological Associates.

Page, W. 1923. *Victoria County History: Yorkshire North Riding Volume II*. London: Boydell and Brewer.

Peers, C.R. and Radford, C.A.R. 1943. The Saxon monastery of Whitby. *Archaeologia* 89, 27-88.

Powlesland, D. and Haughton, C. 1999. *West Heslerton: The Anglian Cemetery*. Yedingham: Landscape Research Centre.

Proudfoot, E. 1979. A note on some burials from Back Gladstone Street, Hartlepool. *Archaeologia Aeliana Series* 5/7, 169-177.

Redcar Borough Council, 1956. *Minutes of Finances and General Purposes Committee, 2nd July 1956*, Redcar.

Semple, S. 2010. In the open air, in: Carver, M., Sanmark, A. and Semple, S. (eds), *Signals of Belief in Early England*. Oxford: Oxbow Books, 21-48.

Semple, S. 2011. Sacred spaces and places in pre-Christian and conversion period Anglo-Saxon England, in: Hamerow, H., Hinton, D.A. and Crawford, S. (eds), *The Oxford Handbook of Anglo-Saxon Archaeology*. Oxford: Oxford University Press, 742-763.

Sherlock, S.J. 2011. Anglo-Saxon cemeteries in the Tees Valley and their association with Neolithic and later monuments, in: Brooks, S., Harrington, S. and Reynolds, A. (eds), *Studies in Early Anglo-Saxon Art and Archaeology Papers in Honour of Martin G Welch*. British Archaeological Reports British Series 527. Oxford: BAR Publishing, 112-120.

Sherlock, S.J. 2012. *A Royal Anglo-Saxon Cemetery at Street House, Loftus, North East Yorkshire*. Tees Archaeology Monograph 6. Hartlepool: Tees Archaeology.

Sherlock, S.J. 2016. The reuse of "antiques" in conversion period cemeteries. *Medieval Archaeology* 60/2, 242-265.

Sherlock, S.J. 2017. Excavations at Marne 2015: Operation Nightingale-Marne Explorer. *Yorkshire Archaeological Journal* 89, 75-98.

Sherlock, S.J. and Abramson, P. 2015. The discovery of an Anglo-Saxon cemetery at Kirkleatham, near Redcar in Cleveland. *The Archaeological Forum Journal, CBA Yorkshire* 3, 21-34.

Sherlock, S.J. and Welch, M.G. 1992. *An Anglo-Saxon Cemetery at Norton, Cleveland*. Council for British Archaeology Research Report 82. London: Council for British Archaeology.

Speed, G. forthcoming. *Excavations at Hollow Banks Quarry, Scorton, North Yorkshire: The Romano-British and Anglian Cemeteries*.

Taylor-Wilson, R. 1996. RAF Catterick, 1994, in: Wilson, P.R., Cardwell, P., Cramp, R.J., Evans, J., Taylor-Wilson, R., Thompson, A. and Wacher, J.S., *Early Anglian Catterick and Catreath. Medieval Archaeology* 40, 22-29.

Welch, M.G. 2011. The Mid Saxon 'Final Phase', in: Hamerow, H., Hinton, D.A. and Crawford, S. (eds), *The Oxford Handbook of Anglo-Saxon Archaeology*. Oxford: Oxford University Press, 266-287.

Williams, H. 1997. Ancient landscapes and the dead: the reuse of Prehistoric and Roman monuments as Early Anglo-Saxon burial sites. *Medieval Archaeology* 41, 1-32.

Wilson, P.R. 2002. *Cataractonium: Roman Catterick and its Hinterland, Excavation and Research 1958-1997*. Council for British Archaeology Research Report 102. York: Council for British Archaeology.

Wilson, P.R., Cardwell, P., Cramp, R.J., Evans, J., Taylor-Wilson, R., Thompson, A. and Wacher, J.S. 1996. Early Anglian Catterick and Catreath. *Medieval Archaeology* 40, 1-61.

# Religious Change vs Cultural Change

## The Case of Islamisation in the Early Medieval Period

*Jose Carvajal Lopez*

## Introduction

The concepts of religion and culture belong to that sphere of social knowledge where definitions are imprecise by necessity and where boundaries between different elements are blurred. No one is surprised to see concepts like Christianity or Islam used at the same time as religious and cultural markers, with more emphasis on one or the other meaning depending on the particular circumstances of the mention. However, that does not mean that we should not try to keep an awareness of the differences between religion and culture, because they are certainly different spheres of life. In other words, while a certain overlap between the two concepts is understandable (and necessary, as I explain below), the lack of a critical approach to try to keep them separate may produce major misinterpretations or underplay of historical and archaeological evidence. This does not mean, however, that we should not consider religion as a part of culture; rather the opposite: I argue that once the concept of religion is analysed in relation to material culture, its connections to other aspects of culture and society become evident. In this chapter I offer an example of how this conceptual separation contributes to refining our interpretation of the process of Islamisation in the early Islamic period (that is, during the first expansion of Islam (*c.* AD 622-1000), which roughly is contemporaneous to the early medieval period in Europe). I look at some examples of the transformation and creation of sacred spaces by Muslims in the Near East and in Iberia, highlighting the common and specific intricacies of each one of them, to finally extract some conclusions. My aim is to question the idea of Islamisation as a process that can be described only as a religious change and to suggest instead that the only way in which we can really understand it is considering a more transcendental cultural transformation in which changes in religious beliefs need to be tied to historical changes that encompass the material world and the ways in which people engage with it. The

in: Bielmann, C. and Thomas, B. (eds.) 2018: *Debating Religious Space and Place in the Early Medieval World (c. AD 300-1000)*, Sidestone Press (Leiden), pp. 111-126.

case that I will make in this chapter is that of the construction of sacred spaces and people's entanglement with them in daily life.

An interesting example of this would be one of the *muṣallā*/s in the north-western desert of Qatar (Fig. 24). A *muṣallā* is a small space for prayer, similar to a mosque, but much smaller in size. The structure is basically a *qibla* (that is, a wall facing Mecca) and a *miḥrāb*, a small apse in the centre of the wall. The structure in the picture has no archaeological context and it is not properly dated, but it very likely belonged to the tribe of Al-Naʿīm of Qatar, the most recent owners of this territory. The Meleiha well is one of the water reservoirs around which the Al- Naʿīm used to establish their summer camps and it is still nowadays in the heart of their tribal lands. The well itself may have been older, as well as the *muṣallā*. However, this example is not unique in Qatar nor in the deserts of the Middle East (King 1980, 268-270, for pre-Islamic and Islamic *muṣallā*/s in the Arabian Peninsula and Avni 1994 for early Islamic examples in the Negev desert). It has been suggested that these structures may have pre-Islamic roots (Johns 1999, 83-85). The interesting point that I want to make with this *muṣallā*, however, is to show how different the conception of sacred space is for a Bedouin in the desert in comparison with the perception of sacred space of Muslims of the towns. In the desert, a simple row of stones or even a line in the sand can be used to delimitate a temporary sacred space; in a town, this space needs to be permanent and clearly marked with architectonical elements. There is not a doctrinal difference in between the two types of spaces. Also, the differences described above are not necessarily more important than a number of common elements that will be discussed below. However, they are enough to make Muslims from the city to wonder at the way in which Bedoin *muṣallā*s work. For example, when I showed the *muṣallā* to one of my Egyptian students, she found it hard to believe that she was in front of a sacred space. This is due

*Figure 24: An example of muṣallā found in Qatar (Image: Crowded Desert Project).*

DEBATING RELIGIOUS SPACE AND PLACE IN THE EARLY MEDIEVAL WORLD (C. AD 300-1000)

to the fact that even within the same religion, even when the same ritual is followed, cultural differences are evident.

## The Transformation of the pre-Islamic into the Islamic World

The foundation of Islam in Arabia and its subsequent expansion through Eurasia and Africa brought about many changes. The nature of these changes and their speed is archaeologically more or less well known in some areas (*e.g.* Whitcomb 1995; Boone 2007; Walmsley 2007; Avni 2014 for Levant; Glick 1995; García Moreno 2011 for al-Andalus; Kennet 2004; 2005; 2007; 2012; Priestman 2013 for the Persian Gulf; Power 2012 for the Red Sea; Elzein 2004; Fenwick 2013; Horton and Middleton 2000 and Insoll 2003 for reviews of evidence in Sudan, North Africa, the Swahili Coast and Subsaharan Africa respectively), but due to lack of information is still a matter of discussion in most territories (*e.g.* most of North Africa, including Egypt, and Central Asia, the Indian Ocean, and much of Subsaharan and East Africa). However, change in itself has not been explained so well, probably because a single narrative is considered. In this narrative, change is triggered by the arrival of a foreign army that conquers the territory and puts it under the control of a distant, Islamic policy (the Caliphate or any of its surrogate states). This is a narrative that has not been made explicit outside of the academic and non-academic circles of those who hold the extreme position that Islam expanded only because it was imposed by the sword, a point of view which is untenable in the light of the evidence that we have available nowadays. However, the narrative of transformation as a direct consequence of conquest has not yet been criticised, and as such it is still taken for granted (a good example is the way in which Bulliet 1979 considers the way in which Islamic conversion and politics intermingle). While this narrative apparently works in most of the studied cases, those where the Muslim armies conquered a land before its Islamisation (and which are usually narrated with more or less detail in the written sources), it would be difficult to explain how the process worked in areas that were not conquered, as in large areas of Subsaharan Africa (*cf.* the Gao region in Mali as studied by Insoll 1996; 2000; for Tadmakka, also in Mali, see Nixon 2009; for the area of current Sudan, see Elzein 2004), the East African Coast (*cf.* Horton and Middleton 2000) and South Asia (*e.g.* see Eaton 1993 for the Islamisation of the Indian Subcontinent, and of Bangladesh in particular or Geertz 1971 for Indonesia). We still lack comprehensive approximations to the Islamisation in Central Asia and in wide territories in China and around the Indian Ocean. Even in the case of the areas that were conquered and brought under the control of an Islamic polity, the question remains on how the change occurred. Archaeological studies tend to focus on the intervention of the state as the main promoter of the religion by way of building infrastructures, like mosques, madrasas, and so on (Milwright 2010, 125-131), and look at the change in burial rituals as a way to calibrate the process of Islamisation (Milwright 2010, 131-135). Historical studies based on sources can also pinpoint at the role of pious individuals in fostering the religion with their living example, their peregrination, *etc.* (*e.g.* Fierro and Marín 1998 for the case of al-Andalus). These types of studies are very valuable, but in focusing on state intervention or on religious developments they offer a very partial vision of the cultural and social change that marks the separation between pre-Islamic and Islamic societies. An unchallenged focus on state intervention in the promotion and protection of the religion leaves aside many relevant (probably the most relevant) agents of change, by downplaying their own motivations which are tied to ongoing social dynamics in a way that the state – dominated by its own internal logics – is not. Equally, focus on belief and ritual changes brings the risk of isolating the field of religion from the wider social process (*cf.* Insoll 2004). In my opinion, a study of Islamisation needs to be tied down to very particular historical and geographical circumstances in order to be understood from the point of view of the individuals affected by it (*cf.* Horton 1991; Eaton 1993; Insoll 1996; 2000; Carvajal López 2008; 2009; 2013; Carvajal López and Day 2013; 2015; Carvajal López, Hein *et al.* 2017; Molera *et al.* 2017). This allows to consider the 'Umma paradox' (Marranci 2008, 103-114), that is, the diversity within the unity of Islam (see also Insoll 1999, 9-11), as the result of the historical process of the expansion and definition of Islam itself during its first centuries of existence, and not as a simple matter of allowance and flexibility of Islamic traditions (although they are related to it, of course). The above mentioned historical complexity of Islam from its beginning has to be taken into account when reflecting about the creation of sacred spaces: not only are there several perspectives taken by scholars, but there are also several plausible possibilities within a variety of Islamic traditions and we should consider them separately.

## Creation of Sacred Spaces: Perspectives of Change

When the first Muslims were creating their sacred spaces, they were inspired by the traditions inherited from their (mostly) Arab background, but they also had at their reach the local example, experience and possibilities developed in the areas that they had conquered, including the traditions of the Byzantine and Sassanian empires. These different backgrounds include spaces, architectural elements and configurations, decorative elements that enhance aspects of ritual, *etc*. They include the particular relations of these spaces with the surrounding, non-religious contexts as well, as we will see below. The way in which all these elements intermingled has been a matter of interest for scholars, who have proposed different ideas to explain this. In my opinion, these ideas can be summarized in four different points of view which underline different aspect of the process, yet are not mutually exclusive:

1. Adoption: It consist in taking an element of a different tradition with little or no changes at all. It is the case, for example, of the seizing of sacred spaces that had previously been used for other beliefs in conquered towns in Levant or in al-Andalus (*cf.* Guidetti 2014).

2. Adaptation: It is a similar process as the one described above, but the taken element undergoes some substantial changes in order to be admissible to the Islamic tradition. This is a fundamental process in the creation of Islamic art as Oleg Grabar saw it (Grabar 1973).

3. Resilience: While adoption and adaptation are parallel processes, resilience is their reverse, because it explains the resistance of the Muslims to drop their original Arab background. Resilience of Arab traditions is a quite evident feature of the devel-

opment of early Islam if one looks for it. It is quite visible, for example, in some examples of urbanism like in Fusṭāṭ (Akbar 1989; Whitcomb 2012) or in the shape of the first mosques (Johns 1999). In spite of that, scholars have tended to overlook it, focusing more on the processes of adoption and adaptation.

4. Change of structuring principles as a result of production and reproduction of practices: Although it is a much more complex elaboration than any of the processes outlined above, I would like to present this alternative as one in which all of the above-mentioned ideas are included and, what is more, can only be understood in relation to the others. This idea is a development of the ideas of Bourdieu (1977; 1990) and Giddens (1984) applied directly to the question here. More development of this proposal is offered below.

### Adoption and Adaptation

The jump of the Muslim Arabs from a group of desert tribes to the elite of a world empire was possible, or at least facilitated, by the assimilation of the traditions and expertise found in the Byzantine and Sassanian empires. Therefore, the emphasis that scholarship has laid upon the processes of adoption and adaptation, particularly in the fields where state power and its cosmological representation are important, is somehow justified. This emphasis is evident in the processes of interpretation of cultural elements related to the creation of sacred spaces as well, in particular when these sacred spaces are important scenarios for the representation of power.

A clear example of a case of adoption and adaptation would be the construction of the Dome of the Rock in Jerusalem by the Umayyad caliph ʿAbd al-Mālik ibn Marwān (r. AD 685-705) in AD 691 (Fig 25). The building erected in the Temple Mound (or the *Ḥaram al-Sharīf*, the Noble Sanctuary) has been interpreted as an attempt to claim (and therefore to adopt) the whole of the sacred space and to make a clear statement about the superiority of Islam over the other two monotheistic religions. The layout of the building, the decoration techniques and the use of Arabic as an imperial language in the inscriptions, all elements clearly modelled after Byzantine traditions, show clearly adoption and adaptation of former traditions in support of an imperial idea of Islam

*Figure 25: The Dome of the Rock in the Ḥaram al-Sharīf (Image: Meunierd/Shutterstock).*

(Grabar 1973; Elad 1992; Johns 2003). It is important to take into account that 'Abd al-Mālik was the same caliph that carried out the monetary reform that created the gold-silver and copper pattern that was going to last for centuries (Johns 2003) and the same one that put an end to the second *fitna* (the internal strife for power that opposed the Marwānids, the second branch of the Umayyads, with other rival candidates to the caliphate; *cf.* Kennedy 1986, 82-122; Cobb 2010). He was certainly the paradigm of an imperial caliph (Johns 2003; but *cf.* Hoyland 2006 for a nuanced, yet not altogether different view on the role of this ruler).

However, there are also traditions that suggest that the Dome of the Rock was built in order to give a building to the Muslims that were already praying in the area, along with members of other religions. The object of their adoration was the *Ṣakhra*, the foundation stone of the Dome, which is also the rock from which Muhammad is believed to have ascended to heaven with the Archangel Gabriel and where he stood to pray with Abraham, Moses and Jesus (Elad 1992). Whether the account of the adoration by Muslims before the erection of the building is true or not (and as we will see below, there is no reason to consider it false), the fact is that it was used to justify the creation of the Dome and the claiming of the *Ḥaram al-Sharīf* for Islam. This is therefore an interesting case of a relationship with the past of an event – the erection of the Dome of the Rock – for which both a break pattern – the consolidation of a new policy – and a continuity pattern – the fostering of an ongoing tradition – can be argued.

The Dome of the Rock and the *Ḥaram al-Sharīf* are quite exceptional, but not the unique example of this pattern of adoption and adaptation. It is well known that early Muslims used to take over sacred spaces of other religions. Mosques were built in the spaces that had been previously occupied by churches in cities all over the Mediterranean, from Damascus to Cordoba (*cf.* Guidetti 2014), and the same phenomenon occurred in the more eastern lands that Muslims conquered, in temples of other religions. A recent work by Guidetti (2014) has shed some light on the narrative of the reuse of the sacred space of cathedrals for congregational mosques in several Syrian cities: Damascus, Hims, Aleppo, Diyarbakir, Urfa, and Amman where churches were in use, mosques do not seem to have been initially built to substitute the pre-existing temples, but to co-exist in parallel with them, or, sometimes, even inside them. To be sure, Muslims claimed only parts of the sacred grounds and built their mosques respecting the churches. It is only several decades, or even centuries, after the conquest that things changed: mosques were then rebuilt as more central buildings and the sacred spaces dedicated to other religious communities were not always respected (see Table 2 for the different chronologies of this process in the different cities). Guidetti suggests that the change of attitudes may have been caused by the loss of power of negotiations of the religious communities in front of the Muslims authorities. These communities had worked as intermediaries between the people of the cities and the Muslims in the time of the conquest, but after a period of time they would no longer be in a position to protect any privileges. As a possible second reason, Guidetti admits that there might have been relevant changes in the perception that Muslims had of themselves between the period of the conquests of Syria, which roughly covers the 630s, and the period in which different dynasties, starting with the Umayyads at the beginning of the eighth century, consolidated a vision of Islam as a religion intimately linked to state power.

| Town | Date of Islamic conquest | Date of building of congregational mosque |
| --- | --- | --- |
| Damascus | 635 | 705 |
| Ḥimṣ | 636 | 12th century |
| Aleppo | 637 | 715 |
| Diyarbakir | 639 | After 11th century |
| Urfa | 637 | 825 |
| Amman | 636 | Mosque and cathedral coexisted during the whole early Islamic period |

*Table 2: Dates of conquest of Syrian towns and the date of building of their mosques (according to Guidetti 2014).*

This chronology of erection of the Umayyad congregational mosques, for example in Damascus and in Aleppo, certainly fits well with the idea developed around the Dome of the Rock and the policies of 'Abd al-Mālik (whose son and successor al-Walīd I [*r.* AD 705-715] was the patron of these mosques). These mosques were conceived as a manifestation of the growing power of the state. At the same time, they were not built on the bases of the rights of the conquerors over the vanquished, since that could have only happened when the generation of the conquerors was still in power. Rather, the state took over the sacred space and sought legitimation of this fact by linking it with the past of the sites. One way of doing this was claiming the relevance of the site for Muslims (as it occurred in the *Ḥaram al-Sharīf*). Another one was purchasing the land to the rightful owners (as in the relevant case of Damascus). Of course, there is very little here that tells us how the different religious communities of the time, including the Muslims, reacted towards these policies. This double pattern of break and continuity in relation to the past is telling more about politics than about society.

### Sacred Spaces and the Resilience of Arab Traditions

This contribution has focused so far on sites that were relevant for a pre-Islamic religious community and that were transformed after the Muslim conquest. However, there are also mosques founded *ex novo* from the Muslims. One of the most notable of them is in Kūfā (Iraq), which constitutes one the earliest foundation of a mosque. It was founded on the command of the second of the four *Rāshidūn* Caliphs, 'Umar ibn al-Khattāb (*r.* AD 634-644), in AD 637, only five years after the death of the Prophet. The building, studied by Creswell (1969, 48-58), already shows most elements of the basic structure of a mosque: a walled square layout divided in between a hypostyle roofed space (the praying hall, or *muṣallā or ẓulla*) and an open courtyard (*ṣaḥn*), the whole complex orientated towards Mecca; the only significant exceptions in this pattern are the absences of the *miḥrāb* in the *qibla* wall and of the portico (*riwāq*) lining up the courtyard. Almost every single mosque built from this period onwards shows those same basic elements. The tradition establishes that this basic design is inspired in the house of the Prophet in Madina, which contained some structural elements (courtyard, house and roofed area in the courtyard) that later on would become the different key parts of the hypostyle mosque (*ṣaḥn*, *muṣallā* and *riwāq* respectively) (Creswell 1969, 48-58; Johns 1999). Johns (1999) has criticised these traditions and the interpretations that take them for granted and has instead argued that the first mosques seem to have been a purposeful creation of the period. Their design would include the basic design of temples of the long-standing pre-Islamic tradition (what Johns calls the hypaethral mosques, or open-air spaces for pray), influences from other models of temples taken from religions in the Middle East and some elements of the Mosque of the Prophet, which would have already filtered many of the pre-Islamic traditions and made them acceptable for the Islamic faith. The key point to bear in mind is that the mosque was a model created on purpose to highlight a new ritual and a new religion. Johns suggests that the figure of 'Umar ibn al-Khattāb could be the actual mind behind the creation of the successful model of mosque, because of the dates, the information provided by the written sources and the well-known policy of this caliph of building mosques (Johns 1999, 109-110). Whether Johns' theory is right or not, it is unquestionable that the design of mosque as a sacred space is quite different from the models of temples found in the area at the time of the expansion of Islam (churches, synagogues, fire temples, *etc.*) and that they must be considered intimately linked to Arab traditions or developments from those traditions. A very attractive point of Johns' suggestion is precisely the link that he is able to establish between the pre-Islamic traditions and the modest Bedouin structures, which are widely attested archaeologically, as we have seen above.

I must be very clear when linking the hypaethral mosques of Johns (which include the examples of the Negev collected in Avni 1994 and those of Western Arabia reported by King 1980, 268-270) with the presentation of the Bedouin structures documented in Qatar. They are all clearly coming from the same tradition of pre-Islamic open-air temples, but the way I use them in my argument is quite different to the way in which Johns does it in his. He emphasizes that his proposal of establishing a line of influence between the hypaethral temples and the model of mosque established in the early Islamic period is yet to be shown, since there are no archaeological data that can

*Figure 26: Mosque in abandoned village of al-Jumail, Qatar (19ᵗʰ-20ᵗʰ centuries) (Image: Alizada/Shutterstock).*

DEBATING RELIGIOUS SPACE AND PLACE IN THE EARLY MEDIEVAL WORLD (C. AD 300-1000)

be used to link both of them directly. From my perspective this is a minor question, because I am interested in the use of the hypaethral structures as Muslim sacred spaces, independently of their relationship to a model of worship and ritual established by the state. My point here is that one of the resilient elements of the Arab tradition is the legitimacy of any Muslim to establish a sacred space without the concourse of any established state or religious authority. If the early Islamic political power was successful in creating a model of mosque, it was never able to monopolize the creation of sacred space itself. In contrast to religions like Christianity, the temples of Islam are not places to connect directly with the Heavens, but with an ancestral place on the Earth: Mecca. Therefore, any space is potentially sacred as long as it allows a Muslim to find the right direction to this focal point. Since the structure of the religion of Islam lacks a formal hierarchy, there is no power that can claim the sole authority to build mosques and any believer can create their own place to pray (Fig. 26). This only means that there is not a doctrinal need for a believer to pray and follow the rituals in a particular place, but of course other factors, like social pressure or manifestations of political allegiance, may be decisive in this sense. The consequences of this will be discussed below.

### The Problems of Adoption, Adaptation and Resilience as Considered Separately

The concepts of adoption, adaptation and resilience can be very informative in relation to particular issues considered in isolation, but when applied to a complex question like the creation of sacred spaces in early Islam they are confusing. The reason for this confusion is related on the one hand to the complementarity of the concepts, which are related to one another (as noted above). On the other hand, and in relation to the first reason, the separate use of the concepts forces us to think in terms of continuity or break between the pre-Islamic and the Islamic period, because the timeframe for the adoption, adaptation or resistance of any element requires to consider a moment before and a moment after the process under consideration, and the differences in between those moments. However, considering all the processes together in the same social dynamics allows us to escape a confusing and unproductive dichotomy between continuity and change.

In the particular case of Islamisation, the dichotomy between continuity and break that this way of thinking produces leads to consider the expansion of Islam as a religious change rather than as a more complex cultural change. From a strictly theological point of view, change cannot be gradual, contradictory and problematized: it is a matter of accepting dogmata. This is of course not necessarily the view of the people involved in the change (which is rather more complicated), but it is the change that we are assuming to have happened from the exclusive perspective of religion. There are two main problems with this perspective. The first one is that it forces us to consider the existence of longer or shorter transitions, that is, periods of time when we have to acknowledge that the change is still incomplete. In those periods of time we can only guess what is going on aided by the more or less scarce data that we may have and what our own idea about the change itself is. This occurs, for example, in the crucial decades that go from the conquest of the Syrian cities and the building of the Umayyad congregational mosques. The second problem is derived from the first one: in the absence of questions about the process that it is driving change, we tend to consider change itself as self-explanatory. This is why the process of Islamisation is so scarcely understood from the point of view of social change: it is usually conceived that everything changed with the arrival of Muslims and with their establishment of a state. But in missing the complexities of this process, we are unable to understand the role that different people, different communities, played in it.

## A Proposal to Consider Sacred Space from the Perspective of Practice

Is there another possible approach? Rather than using separately the concepts of adoption, adaptation and resilience and thus to be trapped by the dichotomy of continuity and break to explain the phenomena described before, my suggestion is to plan the study of sacred spaces from the perspective of an integral approach to the material space by looking for the ways in which a harmonious combination of the three concepts and the physical evidence points to socially and historically consistent scenarios. In other words, we should change our focus of study from the physical to the social and historically contingent space. The physical space is simply a location, but the social space is a construction made on the basis of very particular references of the group of people that engage historically with the location and with everything that it contains. In making this shift, we no longer speak about the transformation of space, but rather about the social process of the creation of that space as sacred. From this point of view, the different cultural and social dimensions can be brought together in a common explanatory framework.

A good example of that type of approach to sacred space is that of the mosque area of Ilbīra, a town in the Iberian Peninsula, near Granada (South East Spain). Ilbīra is one of the earliest towns of the Muslims in Iberia, but its congregational mosque was not build until the year AD 864, in the context of an expansion of the Umayyad power from Cordoba. In particular, in the area of Ilbīra, this expansion of state power became contested, and conflict arose with different sectors of society which the sources identify respectively as Arabs, Renegades (non-Muslims, or apostates) and the *Ahl Ilbīra*, or the People of Ilbīra (presumably Muslims, and presumably non-Arabs). Arabs and Renegades would clash amongst themselves and in some cases also with the forces of the state, while the People of Ilbīra, directly threatened by the other parties, would look for an alliance sometimes with the Renegades and eventually with the Cordoban government. This period of revolt ended when the state put down the Renegades and managed to reach advantageous agreements with the Arabs and the People of Ilbīra (for more information on these groups and conflict, see Carvajal López 2008; 2013; Carvajal López, Román Punzón *et al.* 2014). According to the written sources, the mosque of Ilbīra was built in the place where an earlier temple had been erected by a certain Hanash ibn 'Abd Allāh al-San'ānī, a mythical character associated to the conquest of Iberia (Simonet 1982 [1896], 22-25 and Fig. 5; on the character of Hanash al-San'ānī, see Fierro 1988 and Fierro and Marín 1998). Thus, as the Damascene Umayyads claimed the relationship of Muhammad with the *Ṣakhra* in order to have the legitimacy to overtake the *Ḥaram al-Sharīf*, so the Cordoban Umayyads, presumably with the acquiescence of the People of Ilbīra and the Arabs, seemed to have use the figure of Ibn al-San'ānī when claiming the space to erect the congregational mosque. The mosque served as a space of representation of the power of the Umayyads, underlining

*Figure 27: Miḥrāb of the Mosque of Cordoba, erected in 961 by order of the Caliph Al-Ḥakam II. The grandeur of the building and of this particular part were designed to link religion and the power of the Umayyad dynasty (Image: Toni Genes/Shutterstock).*

the success of Cordoba in the region, and also perhaps as a material commemoration of the agreement between the Umayyad government, the Arabs and the People of Ilbīra.

The mosque of Ilbīra was found more than 100 years ago (Gómez Moreno 1986 [1898]), but its location has been lost again. The excavations that took place in 2007 in the area in search of the building have not been successful, but they have documented an Islamic cemetery that can be dated at around the same time than the foundation of the mosque. The tombs were dug in the soil and covered with tiles, but, interestingly, one of them stood out. It was clearly monumental, made in roughly shaped ashlar stones. However, its excavation showed that the tomb had been originally very similar to the rest that is, covered with tiles, and that at some point it was reopened and re-made with the ashlar stones (Malpica *et al.* 2008). The refurbishment of the tomb as a focal point clearly implied a transformation of the sacred space of the cemetery. The radiocarbon dates of the body and the dates of some pottery sherds around the tomb suggest that the transformation of the burial space is roughly contemporaneous to the process of the creation of the congregational mosque nearby. I have suggested, on the bases of this and other evidence of the period that what we are documenting is the establishment of a 'cultural standardisation' in the area of Granada by the Umayyad dynasty of Cordoba. In other words, the Umayyads set themselves as the legitimate driving force of the expansion of Islam by merging ritual and political aspects, and in this way they were successfully influencing the way in which Islam (and Islamic culture in general) should be manifested all over al-Andalus (Carvajal López 2013). Before the erection of the congregational mosque in Ilbīra and the refurbishment of the tomb, the sacred space (whatever its physical form and elements were) would have been used for the representation of local powers, the powers of a Muslim society which had a different language to express their authority in terms of material culture. The construction of the mosque implied the takeover of this sacred space by the Umayyads from Cordoba, who would transform it into a space of representation of their own power, with their own language. As documented, this process consists in the creation of a sacred space not only as a representation of a religion, but, more importantly in social terms, as the issue of an statement of power in which religion and belief play a fundamental but well delimited role, as it still be seen in the Mosque of Cordoba nowadays (Fig. 27).

While the adoption and adaptation of spaces and historical elements is obvious in the choice of the place for the congregational mosque in Ilbīra, a factor of resilience of the Arab tradition must be considered in relation to this case: the legitimacy for any Muslim individual to create a sacred space beyond any constraints from state or religious authority. This capacity places a strong stress in the fabric of the political power itself. Sacred spaces can in fact become foci of concentration of symbolic capital, with the consequent emergence of alternative centres of power to those of the recognized authorities. For this reason, it is only logical that at some point the development of the early Islamic polity would require the creation of central sacred places that, beyond their function as spaces for pray, would be understood also as spaces for the representation of the political power of the state. In this perspective, sacred spaces were also spaces for contesting or reaffirming established political structures. In order to find more examples, we can return to the Dome of the Rock: it must not be forgotten that one of the alleged motives for its construction was 'Abd al-Mālik's plan to substitute the centrality of Mecca, at that time in the hands of a political anti-caliph, 'Abd Allāh ibn al-Zubayr (r. AD 680-692), for that one of Jerusalem (Elad 1992, but see Johns 2003, 425-426 for a criticism of this point). Although this is not a confirmed account, it shows how the location of the sacred spaces was conceived as a tension between religious symbolism and political power. The end of the coexistence of sacred spaces for different religions in the Syrian towns that Guidetti has documented (2014) can perhaps be related to similar processes of power representation.

## Conclusion

In the introduction I argued for the necessity of keeping an awareness of the differences between religion and culture. The aim of this is not to establish a full separation of the two concepts (which is impossible), but to put them in a perspective that allows appreciation of their relationship and the effects of it in the case of Islamisation, or more precisely, in particular cases of creation of sacred space during the early Islamic period. These examples show that it is actually more productive to try to understand the creation of sacred space in the context of a historically contextualized culture than in that of its transformation from one religion to another. I have particularly focused on the use of sacred space as a scenario for the contest between alternative conceptions of power, but I believe that this discussion can and indeed needs to be taken to other grounds as well. Particularly, and always in my experience, changes in craft production and object consumption offer a very promising field for the nuanced understanding of cultural change with relevant religious implications.

As a final thought, I would like to revisit the concept of Islamisation considering all the above. If we understand Islamisation as the way in which Islam is transmitted in the form of a set not only of beliefs, but also of practices and structuring principles, then we cannot limit it to the process of conversion: it is a social and cultural process. In other words, Islamisation is a matter of cultural change and continuity, whether we are considering the inhabitants of an area recently brought under the influence of Islam or whether we are talking about the process of socialisation of individuals born and raised within an Islamic society. The point of my statement is not to underplay the obvious differences between the two situations, but rather to highlight the common ground which allows us to study both under the same paradigm. The advantages of this conception of Islamisation are very important. The aim of historical and archaeological research is now the particular and specific circumstances of cultural transmission of religious practices. This perspective allows room for many different conceptions of the transcendental content of a religion (as there are as many as believers), and therefore not only doctrinal and theological aspects of the religion should be considered when making interpretations of the available evidence. Religious practices are historically situated in a material world, and therefore they are affected by possibilities and constraints coming from different dimensions of life. Sacred spaces such as the ones presented in this chapter are material and social spaces, and therefore they play a role beyond religion. It will be interesting to explore in the future the religious implications of segments of material culture that current interpretations place outside the religious sphere. The reflections of Insoll (2004) about the connections religion with other spheres of life open a very exciting avenue of research.

## Acknowledgements

I wish to thank Brittany Thomas and Chantal Bielmann for their kind invitation to contribute to this edited volume. This article was made possible by the NPRP Grant 7-551-6-018 from the Qatar National Research Fund (a member of Qatar Foundation). The statements made herein are solely the responsibility of the author.

## Bibliography

Akbar, J. 1989. Khatta and the Territorial Structure of Early Muslim Towns. *Muqarnas* 6, 23-32.

Avni, G. 1994. Early Mosques in the Negev Highlands: New Archaeological Evidence on Islamic Penetration of Southern Palestine. *Bulletin of the American Schools of Oriental Research* 294, 83-100.

Avni, G. 2014. *The Byzantine-Islamic Transition in Palestine: An Archaeological Approach.* Oxford: Oxford University Press.

Boone, J. 2009. *Lost civilisation: the contested Islamic past in Spain and Portugal.* London: Duckworth.

Bourdieu, P. 1977. *Outline of a Theory of Practice.* Cambridge: Cambridge University Press.

Bourdieu, P. 1990. *The Logic of Practice.* Cambridge: Polity Press.

Bulliet, R. 1979. *Conversion to Islam in the Medieval Period: an essay in quantitative history*. Harvard: Harvard University Press.

Carvajal López, J.C. 2008. *La cerámica de Madinat Ilbīra y el poblamiento altomedieval de la Vega de Granada (siglos VIII-XI)*. Granada: THARG.

Carvajal López, J.C. 2009. Pottery production and Islam in south-east Spain: a social model. *Antiquity* 83/320, 388-398.

Carvajal López, J.C. 2013. Islamicisation or Islamicisations? Expansion of Islam and social practice in the Vega of Granada (south-east Spain). *World Archaeology* 45/1, 56-70.

Carvajal López, J.C. and Day, P.M. 2013. Cooking pots and Islamicisation in the early medieval Vega of Granada (Al-Andalus, sixth to twelfth centuries). *Oxford Journal of Archaeology* 32/4, 433-451.

Carvajal López, J.C. and Day, P.M. 2015. The production and distribution of cooking pots in two towns of South East Spain in the 6th – 11th centuries. *Journal of Archaeological Science. Reports* 2, 282-290.

Carvajal López, J.C., Hein, A., Glascock, M.D. and Day, P.M. 2017. Combined petrographic and chemical analysis of water containers and glazed wares in the Early Medieval Vega of Granada (south east Spain, 6th to 12th centuries CE). *Journal of Archaeological Science. Reports (https://doi.org/10.1016/j.jasrep.2017.09.016)*.

Carvajal López, J.C., Román Punzón, J.M., Jiménez Puertas, M. and García García, M. *In press. The Islamisation of the Vega of Granada*. Brepols: Turnhout.

Cobb, P. 2010. The empire in Syria, 705-763, in: Robinson, C. (ed.), *The New Cambridge History of Islam. Vol. 1: The Formation of the Islamic World. Sixth to Eleventh Centuries*. Cambridge: Cambridge University Press, 226-268.

Creswell, K.A.C. 1969. *Early Muslim Architecture*. Oxford: Oxford University Press.

Eaton, R.M. 1993. *The Rise of Islam and the Bengal Frontier, 1204-1760*. Berkeley: University of California Press.

Elad, A. 1992. Why Did 'Abd al-Malik Build the Dome of the Rock? A Re-Examination of the Muslim Sources, in: Raby, J. and Johns, J. (eds), *Bayt al-Maqdis. 'Abd al-Malik's Jerusalem*. Oxford: Oxford University Press, 33-58.

Fenwick, C. 2013. From Africa to Ifriqīya: Settlement and Society in Early Medieval North Africa (650-800). *Al-Masāq* 25/1, 9-33.

Fierro, M. 1988. The introduction of hadith in al-Andalus (2nd/8th-3rd/9th centuries). *Der Islam* 66, 68-93.

Fierro, M. and Marín, M. 1998. La Islamización de las ciudades andalusíes a través de sus ulemas (s. II/VIII-comienzos del siglo IV/X), in: Cressier, P. and García-Arenal, M. (eds), *Genèse de la ville islamique en al-Andalus et au Maghreb occidental*. Madrid: Casa de Velázquez-CSIC, 65-97.

García Moreno, L. (ed.) 2011. *711. Arqueología e Historia Entre Dos Mundos*. Madrid: Comunidad Autónoma de Madrid. Servicio de Documentación y Publicación.

Geertz, C. 1971. *Islam Observed. Religious Development in Morocco and Indonesia*. Chicago: University of Chicago Press.

Giddens, A. 1984. *The constitution of society: outline of the theory of structuration*. Berkeley: The University of California Press.

Glick, T.F. 1995. *From Muslim fortress to Christian castle: social and cultural change in Medieval Spain*. Manchester: Manchester University Press.

Gómez Moreno, M. 1986 [1888]. *Medina Elvira*. Granada: Grupo de Autores Unidos.

Grabar, O. 1973. *The Formation of Islamic Art*. London: Yale University Press.

Guidetti, M. 2014. The contiguity between churches and mosques in early Islamic Bilād al-Shām. *Bulletin of the School of Oriental and African Studies* 76/2, 229-258.

Horton, M. 1991. Primitive Islam and Architecture in East Africa. *Muqarnas* 8, 103-116.

Horton, M. and Middleton, J. 2000. *The Swahili: The Social Landscape of a Mercantile Society*. London: Blackwell.

Hoyland, R. 2006. New Documentary Texts and the Early Islamic State. *Bulletin of School for Oriental and African Studies* 69/3, 395-416.

Insoll, T. 1996. *Islam, Archaeology and History. Gao Region (Mali) c. AD 900-1250*. British Archaeological Report (International Series) 647. Oxford: Tempus Reparatum.

Insoll, T. 1999. *The Archaeology of Islam*. London: Blackwell.

Insoll, T. 2000. *Urbanism, Archaeology and Trade. Further Observations on the Gao Region (Mali). The 1996 Field Season Results*. British Archaeological Report (International Series) 829. Oxford: Tempus Reparatum.

Insoll, T. 2003. *The Archaeology of Islam in Sub-Saharan Africa*. Cambridge: Cambridge University Press.

Insoll, T. 2004. *Archaeology, Ritual, Religion*. London: Routledge.

Johns, J. 1999. The 'House of the Prophet' and the Concept of the Mosque, in: Johns, J. (ed.), *Bayt al-Maqdis: Jerusalem and Early Islam*. Oxford: Oxford University Press, 59-112.

Johns, J. 2003. Archaeology and the History of Early Islam: The First Seventy Years of Islam. *Journal of the Economic and Social History of the Orient* 46/4, 411-436.

Kennedy, H. 1986. *The prophet and the age of Caliphates: the Islamic Near East from the sixth to the eleventh century*. London: Longman.

Kennet, D. 2004. *Sasanian and Islamic Pottery from Ra's al-Khaimah: classification, chronology and analysis of trade in the Western Indian Ocean*. British Archaeological Report (International Series) 1248. Oxford: Archaeopress.

Kennet, D. 2005. On the eve of Islam: archaeological evidence from Eastern Arabia. *Antiquity* 79/303, 107-118.

Kennet, D. 2007. The decline of Eastern Arabia in the Sasanian period. *Arab Archaeology and Epigraphy* 18/1, 86-122.

Kennet, D. 2012. Archaeological history of the Northern Emirates in the Islamic period: an outline, in: Potts, D. and Hellyer, P. (eds), *Fifty Years of Emirates Archaeology*. Abu Dhabi – Dubai – London: Motivate Publishing, 189-201.

King, G. 1980. Notes on Some Mosques in Eastern and Western Saudi Arabia. *Bulletin of the School of Oriental and African Studies* 43/2, 251-276.

Malpica Cuello, A., García Porras, A., Carvajal López, J.C., Mattei, L., Ruiz Jiménez, A., Narváez Sánchez, J.A., González Escudero, A., García-Contreras Ruiz, G. and Koffler Urbano, T. 2008. Informe de la II Campaña de Excavación Sistemática dentro del Proyecto «La ciudad de Madinat Ilbira». *http://www.medinaelvira.org/doc/completo07.pdf* (accessed: 23 Dec 2015).

Marranci, G. 2008. *The Anthropology of Islam*. Oxford-New York: Berg.

Molera, J., Carvajal López, J.C., Molina, G. and Pradell, T. 2017. Glazes, colorants and decorations in early Islamic glazed ceramics from la Vega de Granada (9th to 12th centuries AD). *Journal of Archaeological Science. Reports (https://doi.org/10.1016/j. jasrep.2017.05.017).*

Nixon, S. 2009. Excavating Essouk-Tadmakka (Mali): new archaeological investigations of early Islamic trans-Saharan trade. *Azania: Archaeological Research in Africa* 44/2, 217-255.

Power, T. 2012. *The Red Sea from Byzantium to the Caliphate: AD 500-1000.* Cairo: American University in Cairo Press.

Priestman, S. 2013. *A Quantitative Archaeological Analysis of Ceramic Exchange in the Persian Gulf and Western Indian Ocean, AD c. 400 – 1275.* Unpublished PhD dissertation, University of Southampton.

Simonet, F. J. 1982 [1896]. *Cuadros Históricos y Descriptivos de Granada. Coleccionados con motivo del cuarto centenario de su memorable conquista.* Madrid: Atlas.

Walmsley, A. 2007. *Early Islamic Syria: an archaeological assessment.* London: Duckworth.

Whitcomb, D. 1995. Islam and the socio-cultural transition of Palestine – early Islamic period (638-1099 CE), in: Levy, T.E. (ed.), *The Archaeology of Society in the Holy Land.* London: Leicester University, 488-501.

Whitcomb, D. 2012. Formation of the Islamic city. A second archaeological period of urban transition, in: Matthews, R. and Curtis, J. (eds), *Proceedings of the 7th International Congress on the Archaeology of the Ancient Near East (12-16 April the British Museum and UCL, London), Vol 2.* Wiesbaden: Harrassowitz Verlag, 619-631.

# Interactions between the Clerical Enclosure and the Extra-Claustral Clergy in Carolingian Francia

## A Sacred Space with Porous Walls

*Stephen Ling*

## Introduction

Perceptions and attitudes towards sacred space used by the clergy in Carolingian Francia have attracted much scholarly attention in recent years (Czock 2015; Collins 2012; de Jong 1996 and 1998; Claussen 2004 and 2006; Meens 1996 and 2007). The work of de Jong (1995, 1996, and 1998) in particular has demonstrated the important role of the cloister, which served as a sacred space where the purity of the clergy could be maintained and reproduced through the education of young oblates. The education received within the enclosure would prepare trainee clerics for their future careers, either as members of the enclosed canonical clergy, or as extra-claustral clerics entrusted with serving the pastoral needs of the laity. Letters, such as those between Alcuin and his former pupils, show that such pastoral clerics often remained in touch with their former communities, seeking guidance from those who continued to live enclosed lives. These links between the cloister and the extra-claustral clergy were also emphasised by episcopal writers such as Chrodegang of Metz (d. 766) and Theodulf of Orléans (d. 821), both of whom sought to incorporate the extra-claustral clergy in the life of their cathedral communities. As Claussen (2004; 2006) has shown, Chrodegang's Rule (*c.* 750) included all clergy in the ritual life of the cloister, and the extra-claustral clergy were expected to join their enclosed brethren on Sundays and key feast days. Likewise, in his first episcopal statute (*c.* 798) Theodulf of Orléans involved the extra-claustral clergy in the rituals that surrounded the celebration of feast days within the cathedral close. Despite this the walls of the cloister are often seen as a cleavage point within the ordering of the Frankish Church. Monks and canons, are defined by the fact they lived

in: Bielmann, C. and Thomas, B. (eds.) 2018: *Debating Religious Space and Place in the Early Medieval World (c. AD 300-1000)*, Sidestone Press (Leiden), pp. 127-142.

contemplative lives within the enclosure. By comparison those diocesan priests, tasked with pastoral care, are defined by the fact they engaged with the secular world and slept beyond the walls of the enclosure (van Rhijn 2007, 6-8).

This chapter will examine the central role of the cloister to the life of all clerics. It will focus on the role of the enclosure as a physical space central to the life of the urban and sub-urban clergy and as an ideological crutch within the thought-world of rural clerics, who lived well beyond the bounds of the clerical enclosure. It will argue that Carolingian Churchmen perceived the clerical enclosure as a sacred space with porous walls, a space that was foundation of the life of all clerics whether they were professed canons, or whether they served as pastoral extra-claustral clerics.

## The Importance of the Cloister: Defining the Claustrum in a Clerical Setting

Before undertaking this analysis, a discussion of the role and purpose of the claustrum (Cloister) and how Frankish Churchmen conceived of this holy and exclusive space is essential. The word cloister is commonly associated with the colonnaded quadrangle that became a defining archetype of monastic architecture, yet the term *claustrum* should not automatically be associated with this specific space, often late antique and Early Medieval writers used this term to denote the entire monastery (Dey 2004, 362-363). The noun *claustrum* means a barrier, bolt, door or gate and it is closely linked with the word *clavis,* meaning a door-key, a fact not lost on Isidore of Seville who stated: 'claustrum are so called because they are closed [claudere]' (Barney and Hall 2006, 311; Dey 2004, 363). Throughout the period the word also maintained its classical association with a military fortification (Dey 2004, 363). This notion of a physically and spiritually fortified enclosure and separated space was a defining feature of monastic life from the sixth century onwards (Dey 2004, 362-369). Those who lived the enclosed life were locked away to separate them from the profanity of the secular world and enforce mutual discipline within the community (Dey 2004, 370-371). Within these secured spaces three common buildings defined the daily life of the community: the church, the dormitory, and the refectory. These functional buildings were spaces that ensured the purity of the enclosed life. A common dormitory with separate beds ensured individuals would avoid the sinful temptations of the flesh. The young, who were more prone to sexual activity, were supervised by more senior members of the community who slept amongst them. Dining together in community guaranteed that all ate a humble diet and avoided 'illicit things from which they ought to abstain' (Gundlach 1892, 480-481). The oversight of the abbot or bishop, and the reading of sacred texts during the meal, meant the refectory avoided the licentious behaviour that accompanied lay feasting. Humility and reverence were the ideological orders of the day ensuring the purity of the monks and priests tasked with mediating between man and God (de Jong 1995, 629).

While clerics had undoubtedly been cloistered prior to the mid-eighth century, from this time onwards there was an increasing focus on establishing *claustra* exclusively for clerics, particularly those within cities where the profane and impure lay close at hand. As Paul the Deacon recounted, Chrodegang of Metz, 'brought the clergy together and made them live within the confines of a cloister in the image of a monastery [*Instar cenobii intra claustrorum*] (Kempf 2013, 86-87). This focus on clerical communities mirroring monastic practices was re-emphasised throughout the eighth and ninth centuries as the council of Tours (813) put it:

> *We considered that the canonical clergy of the city, who dwell in the bishop's household. As they live in the cloister, where they will easily be able to perform the canonical hours. Likewise may they all sleep in one dormitory, and similarly may they dine in one refectory… In a similar manner also the abbots of the monasteries in which the canonical life has existed from antiquity or can now be seen. May they with anxious care provide for their canons, so that they may live in the cloister and dormitory, in which they also sleep and also eat. May they keep canonical hours.* (Werminghoff 1906, 289)

Such statements neatly summarise the key features and purpose of the enclosed life for the canonical clergy. Like their monastic brethren these buildings acted to maintain the purity of the canonical clergy. For clerics whose role was defined by their sacramental duties, the purity, discipline and supervision of the enclosure, meant the essential sacraments they performed were unpolluted by worldly sinful actions. As such living an enclosed life increasingly became a desirable trait amongst the clergy (de Jong 1998, 49-55). While the pastoral nature of the clerical life made it impossible for all clerics to live disciplined and supervised within the cloister, as will be discussed below, extra-claustral clerics, who lived and slept beyond the perimeter of the clerical enclosure remained intimately tied to these prominent sacred spaces.

## The Enclosure and Clerical Education

The fact that oblates educated within both monasteries and houses of canons were destined to undertake pastoral work outside the enclosure is made clear by the documents used to regulate and train them. From the 780s onwards capitularies and admonitions issued by the Carolingian court consistently emphasised the importance of monastic and canonical cloister schools. The purpose of these schools appears to have been twofold; namely to ensure that those who lived the enclosed life were able to perform the liturgy of the Divine Office in the correct manner, and that those tasked with spreading the word of God to the laity were able to understand and explain scripture. Thus, whilst Charlemagne's letter to Bagulf of Fulda (784) (Boretius 1883, 79-80; Loyn and Percival 1975, 63-64) focused on the importance of 'reading and chanting' within the enclosure, chapter 17 of the council of Tours (813) requested that homilies given by the bishop should be translated into the vernacular, 'so that all may more easily understand things which are said'[1] (Werminghoff 1906, 288). This clause suggests a close link between extra-claustral clerics and the school within the cathedral close, where such translations were likely compiled. The circulation of such texts implies

---

1    Here the council is quoting directly from the English Legatine Council (786). (Hadden and Stubbs 1871, 460, trans., Carela 2006, 118-119.) This likely represents the posthumous influence of Alcuin, who had been present at the Legatine Council and had served as abbot of St. Martin's, Tours (796-804) (Wright 1983, 353-359).

that extra-claustral clerics were to be included in aspects of life within the cathedral close. The discussion of schools within Theodulf of Orléans' First Episcopal Statute (*c.* 798) certainly supports this notion. This text was likely composed in response to the *Admonitio Generalis* (789) and chapter 19 of the statute enforced the Admonitio's command (*c.* 70)[2] for schools 'to be created in every monastery and episcopal residence' (van Rhijn 2007, 33-49; Mordek *et al.*, 2013, 222-225; Boretius 1883, 59-60; trans., King 1987, 217). Interestingly, Theodulf not only established such a school at Orléans, but also encouraged the extra-claustral clergy to send their relatives to the various cloister schools established within his diocese:

> '*If any of the presbyters wishes to send his nephew or other relative to school in the church of the Holy Cross, or in the monastery of Saint Aignam, or of Saint Benedict, or of Saint Lifard, or in others of those monasteries which it has been granted us to rule, we grant him permission to do so.*' (Brommer 1984, 115-116; trans., Dutton 2004, 110)

Some of these boys would likely go on to fulfill their clerical office as extra-claustral clerics serving the pastoral needs of the laity in their villages and towns. Alongside the cloister schools Theodulf (c. 20) also ordered that the extra-claustral clergy should establish their own schools, mirroring the practices of the sacred space of the cathedral close:

> '*Let Presbyters keep schools in the villages and hamlets, and if any of the faithful desire to entrust his small children to them to be taught their letters, let them not refuse to receive them and teach them, but let them teach them with the greatest love, noticing what is written: 'They, however, who shall be learned shall shine as the splendor of the firmament, and they who instruct many to righteousness shall shine as stars forever and ever.' When therefore they teach them, let them demand no fee for this instruction, nor take anything from them, except what the parents shall offer them freely through zeal for love.*' (Brommer 1984, 116; trans., Dutton 2004, 110)

These parochial schools should be viewed as complementing the cloister school, serving as part of a wider system that both ensured clerical purity and discipline, while also offering local boys a route into the clergy. Some of the boys trained by the local priest within these extra-claustral schools may well have been sent to the cathedral close to continue their education and join the ranks of the enclosed clergy. (van Rhijn 2006, 128). That such low-ranking boys could attain high office is demonstrated by the career of Walafrid Strabo (d. 849). Walafrid was born in humble circumstances in Alemannia, yet rose to become the tutor of Charles the Bald, moving in the highest circles of Frankish society. This meritocratic rise was the result of Walafrid's education within the cloister schools of Reichenau and Fulda and the

---

2    It should be noted that Mordek's new transcription reordered some of the chapters of the Admonitio Generalis. This provision is numbered as c. 72 in King's translation, which drew on Boretius's older transcription (Boretius 1883).

DEBATING RELIGIOUS SPACE AND PLACE IN THE EARLY MEDIEVAL WORLD (C. AD 300-1000)

patronage he received from his tutor, Hrabanus Maurus (d. 856) (Nelson 1992, 82-88; Stone 2011, 149; Stevens 1995, 13-20).

The schoolbooks created for use within the cloister schools provided the knowledge clerics would need to serve both in the cloister and outside it. Hrabanus Maurus' influential 'On Clerical Training', compiled for use at Fulda, is a prime example (Knöpfler 1900). This manual was divided into three sections. The first discussed grades of cleric and the different types of sacraments, with a particular focus on the role of the Eucharist and the rite of baptism (Contreni 1995, 109). The second contained summaries of: the Divine Office; the liturgical year; feast days; hymns; heresies; prayers and blessings. Meanwhile the third addressed grammar, rhetoric, and mathematics. This third book was compiled from various authoritative texts including: Augustine's 'On Christian Doctrine'; Gregory the Great's 'Pastoral Care'; Cassiodorus's 'Institutes of Divine and Secular Learning'; and Isidore of Seville's 'Etymologies' (Knöpfler 1900; Contreni 1995, 109). The description of the Divine Office contained within the second book of this text would have been of use in an enclosed setting, while the provisions of the first and third sections would have proved useful to those who were involved in pastoral care. In particular, Gregory the Great's 'Pastoral Care' offered guidance to those who served outside the enclosure, helping them to understand their duties and the role of a preacher. Within the manual Hrabanus Maurus gave specific advice on preaching, emphasising that those who give sermons should modify the style of their message to meet the needs of their audience. (Contreni 1995, 109).

Other schoolbooks were also created to prepare oblates for ecclesiastical careers both within the cloister and outside it. Paxton (1990) has identified a late ninth century manuscript (Rome, BAV, Pal. lat. 485) used explicitly for this purpose. This codex is made up of 16 quires written in a variety of hands dated between *c.* 860 and *c.* 880 but nonetheless represents a coherently planned manual, compiled either by Bishop Adalbero of Augsberg (d. 910), or Bishop Haito of Mainz (d. 913), both of whom served as abbots of Lorsch (Paxton 1990, 28). The content of the first quire of this codex is particularly salient as it provides instructions for the performance of penance in two settings and in two languages. The first section consists of a Latin letter written by a 'certain wise man', likely to be Othmar (d. 759), an eighth century abbot of St Gall. The letter contains a typical formula for confession within the cloister, namely: 'an invocation followed by catalogues of sins in thought and deed and of neglect of Christian duties, a second invocation, and a prayer for forgiveness' (Paxton 1990, 9). The Old High German text that forms the second section of the quire is radically different to Othmar's letter, this vernacular tract is overtly aimed at the laity and refers to sins against: 'one's parents; lord; neighbours; children; and to the failure to pay the tithe' (Paxton 1990, 9). The penitential contents of this quire therefore offered training for life within the cloister and outside it. Key texts from the rest of the codex would have proved most useful to those training to minister in the secular world, in particular the thirteenth quire contained a copy of Theodulf's First Episcopal Statute with discreet and fully rubricated chapter titles (Paxton 1990, 14; 21-22; 27). Although Theodulf's Statute may well have been used within the cloister, its contents were primarily addressed to the extra-claustral clergy, and sought to expand the discipline of the enclosed life to those who lived beyond the sacred space of the cloister (Ling 2015, 22-64).

## Clerical Networks

Hrabanus Maurus' 'On Clerical Training', and the training manual identified by Paxton (1990), illustrate that by the end of ninth century clerics trained within monastic and clerical enclosures were prepared to serve both in secular world, and in enclosed communities. Once an oblate completed their training, whether they remained within their motherhouses, moved to another community, or undertook pastoral work in the parishes, it is clear that links were maintained with their old masters and communities. As de Jong (1998, 58-61) points out, the priests trained within enclosed communities formed members of an old boy network based on a shared upbringing in the cloister. Both abbots Bagulf (779-802) and Hrabanus Maurus (822-842) compiled registers of the brothers who formed part of the Fulda congregation. These lists included those who lived within the bounds of the monastery, and those who lived in the dependent *cellae* that were owned and operated by the house. Over two thirds of those listed by Hrabanus Maurus were priests, deacons, or clerics (Raaijmakers 2006, 308; 2012, 187-189). Although many of these clerics would have served functions within the abbey church, others would likely have been involved in the provision of pastoral care, working from the *cellae* that formed part of Fulda's family of churches. The community of Fulda was also keen to commemorate their dead brethren and the *Annales Necrologici* list the deceased brothers who were prayed for during the liturgical rituals of the Daily Office (de Jong 1996, 242-245; Raaijmakers 2006, 308-312; Raaijmakers 2012, 181-189). The majority of those brothers listed by Bagulf and Hrabanus Maurus in their registers are also listed in the *Annales Necrologici* (posthumously); even if the brother had long since left the confines of the cloister to pursue an ecclesiastical career elsewhere, his home community remembered him in both life and death (Raaijmakers 2006, 308).

The 'old boy networks' formed between the masters of the cloister school and their former pupils can also be detected within the vast letter collection of Alcuin. The deacon's letters to his pupils recalled their shared experience within the sacred space of the enclosure, and emphasised the spiritual union shared by master and pupil despite their physical separation. In 801 Alcuin wrote to some of his former pupils stating:

> 'What a happy time it was when 'we diced together' by my fireside. Now all is changed. The old man is left behind, begetting other sons and lamenting the scattering of his old boys. But 'what does the damnable hunger for gold not do?' Let use be together in spirit while separated in body.' (Dümmler 1895, 359; trans., Allot 1974, 129)

These epistles were imbued with a parental tone and Alcuin often reminded his students of the lessons they had learnt in the classroom. Significantly, Alcuin not only corresponded with other members of the enclosed clergy, but also wrote to extra-claustral clerics undertaking pastoral work. His letter to the priest Odwin (MGH 134), demonstrates this point (Dümmler 1895, 202-203; trans., Allot 1974, 136-137). Odwin undertook pastoral work in Septimania and during the 790s, and appears to have been part of the anti-Adoptionist preaching campaign coordinated by Alcuin and Benedict of Aniane (Page 1909; Chandler 2002; Cabaniss 2008, 36-40). In his letter Alcuin began by renewing his ties with Odwin and reminding him of his training within the cloister:

*'As by divine grace and long labour I enabled you to qualify for the priesthood, I hope you will carry out your duty in the house of God with a distinction worthy of the care I took to instruct you so that you would understand the order of holy baptism. So I would like to write to you briefly on the inner meaning of the whole service, that you may know how important it is to omit nothing that has been put in the service by the holy fathers.'* (Dümmler 1895, 202; trans., Allot 1974, 136)

Once these ties had been renewed, Alcuin moved on to discuss the rite of baptism and how it should be performed. In particular he argued against the Spanish practice of a single emersion:

*'His nostrils are touched so that he may stand by the faith he has received as long as they draw breath. His breast also is anointed with same oil, that the devil's entry may be blocked by the sign of the cross. His shoulders also are marked to give him protection on all sides. The anointing of the breast and shoulders also marks firm faith and persistence in good works. So he is baptised three times in the name of the Holy Trinity. Man who was made in the image of the Trinity is rightly renewed to that image by calling upon the Trinity, and he who has fallen into death in the third degree of sin, that is, by free will, should rise to life by grace being raised three times from the font.'* (Dümmler 1895, 202; trans., Allot 1974, 137)

Although not explicitly anti-Adoptionist, this section of the letter no doubt provided guidance to a cleric working in the field, offering him both a practical reminder of the manner in which baptism should be conducted, and an explanation of the rite in firm trinitarian terms. As such the contents of this letter could also be used by Odwin in his preaching campaign. Even though Odwin had left the enclosed life to undertake pastoral work, he remained closely tied to the sacred space of the cloister, and was guided by the principles espoused by his master who remained within its bounds.

In another letter to an un-named priest (MGH 294) Alcuin exhorted his former pupil to remember the purity of his cloistered upbringing and his education, reminding him to live his life according to these virtues:

*'What is this I hear about you, my son, not from one person whispering in a corner but from crowds of people laughing at the story that you are still addicted to the filthy practices of boys and have never been willing to give up what you should never have done. Where is your fine education? Your brilliant work on the scriptures? Your good character? Your courageous spirit? Your fear of hell? Your hope of glory? How is it you do not shrink from doing what you should forbid others to do?'* (Dümmler 1895, 451-452; trans., Allot 1974, 133-134)

Whether the cleric addressed was a member of an enclosed community, or whether they ministered in the secular world, what worried Alcuin was his former pupil's lack of purity and how this might impede his ministry. As Czock has recently highlighted such sin was not simply a 'personal misdeed' but a stain on the entire church congregation. (Czock 2015, 35). The cleric's implied sexual misdemeanours were a serious concern and a betrayal of the purity of his office and his enclosed upbringing.

These letters illustrate how clerical networks generated within the cloister school created conduits through which the ideals and regulations and discipline of the enclosed life could percolate from the cloister to the extra-claustral clergy. For all clerics life within the sacred space of the cloister served as both an ideological and practical model to guide their lives. They looked to the cloister for guidance and, as the registers and *Annales Necrologici* of Fulda demonstrate, clerics remained spiritually linked to their old foundations.

## Sundays, Feasts and Festivals: Relations between the Enclosure and the Extra-Claustral Clergy

As well as the networks and bonds created within the schoolroom, there were clear attempts to include the extra-claustral clergy in the ritual life of both houses of monks and canons. Such involvement illustrates the permeability of the clerical cloister and offered a route by which ideals could spread from the cloister to those clerics who ministered to the secular world. Chrodegang's Rule (Bertram 2005) provides the best witness to these attempts (Claussen, 2004, 206-248; 2006, 119-147). Chapters 8, 20, 21, 30, 31 and 33 of Chrodegang's Rule all directly discuss the involvement of the extra-claustral clergy in the life of the cloister, those clerics who lived in and around Metz were to enter the cloister on Sundays and feast days. Chapter 8: 'That they should come to chapter every day' summarises the inclusive attitude taken by Chrodegang. The rule emphasised the important educational and disciplinary role played by the chapter, placing this meeting at the centre of the life of the community:

> '*We have said that all should come to Chapter every day, both that the soul may hear the Word of God, and also that the bishop, archdeacon or whoever is in charge may give whatever commands he has to command, may correct what needs correction and ensure what needs to be done is done.*' (Bertram 2005, 33, trans., 60)

For Chrodegang it was important to include the extra-claustral clergy in this key gathering of the congregation of canons, and the second half of chapter 8 focuses exclusively on this group:

> '*Any clergy who are outside the enclosure, and live in the city, should come to Chapter every Sunday, vested in chasubles and the usual vestments as is found in the Roman order. On these Sundays and principal feasts of saints, all the clergy who live outside the enclosure, as we have said, should come to Vigils and to Lauds. On these days they should remain vested in their proper rank, and each one should stand according to his rank until Mass has been celebrated. If anyone acts differently, he shall be excommunicated by the archdeacon or primicerius, or even, if need be, subjected to corporal punishment. And on Sundays and the principal feasts of saints, as we have said, they should all eat in the refectory together with the rest of the clergy, at the tables allotted to them.*' (Bertram 2005, 34; trans., 61)

Here the extra-claustral clergy were subjected to the canonical discipline of the bishop, joining with the enclosed community to receive spiritual instruction and correction. This instruction was tempered to meet the needs of those who lived outside of the cloister. While the Rule of Chrodegang was to be read on most days, at the Sunday Chapter Chrodegang ordered the reading of 'tracts and other homilies or whatever may edify the hearers' (Bertram 2005, 33; trans., 60). The Sunday Chapter therefore offered a method of delivering pastoral messages to the extra-claustral clergy and their congregations. It also provided a conduit by which the discipline, norms and purity of the enclosed life could be carried outside the enclosure (Claussen 2004, 248-290). The final clause of chapter 8 commanded the extra-claustral clergy to remain in the cloister and dine with their brethren. Chapters 20 and 21 provide further details of the dining arrangements within the cloister on Sundays and feast days. Chapter 20: 'Of the observance of Lent' (Bertram 2005, 38-39; trans., 66-67), prescribes the diet and behaviour expected to be followed by all clerics during Lent:

> *'Let them* [the clergy] *be sparing in the amount of food and drink they take to the extent that God gives them strength: specifically every day except Sundays from the beginning of Lent until Easter they should eat in the refectory after saying Vespers, and they should abstain from certain foods and drinks according to what the bishop thinks reasonable. They should not eat anywhere else during those forty days, neither in the city, nor in monasteries, nor in any place at all, even their own homes, unless they happen to be so far off that they are unable to be with their brothers to take their meal at the proper time. Then they have permission, in such a case of necessity, to eat the same ration as the other clergy have, and they are to be careful not to anticipate the proper times.'* (Bertram 2005, 38-39; trans., 66)

Once again the extra-claustral clergy joined the cathedral community, sharing in their meal and also their fast. Those who ministered far from the cathedral, and could not physically join with the community, were expected to copy the practices of the enclosure in their locality and were dine at the same time as those in the cloister. As will be discussed below, by mid-ninth century it is clear that at *conviva* extra-claustral clerics were copying the dining practices of their enclosed brothers, reproducing the rituals of the enclosure at their meetings. These conventions emphasised the spiritual bond between the extra-claustral and enclosed clerics and also reinforced notions of their purity.

Chapter 21 of Chrodegang's Rule: 'Of the arrangement of tables in the Refectory', builds upon the provisions of chapter 8 and chapter 20, providing the details of the mealtime interactions between the extra-claustral clergy and those who slept within the Cathedral close. The tables in refectory were to be hierarchically arranged and those clerics who served in the secular world are given their own place within Chrodegang's order:

> *'The first table is for the bishop and his guests and whoever the bishop bids. The second table is for priests; the third for deacons; the fourth for sub-deacons; the fifth for the remaining orders; the sixth is for abbots and whoever the superior bids; at the seventh the canons who live outside the outside the canonical close should eat on Sundays and festivals.'*

The image of seven tables united in one community harked back to the portrayal of the early Church described in the Acts of the Apostles (Classen 2004 80-81; 2006, 135-138). This biblical model of the Christian community provided much inspiration to Chrodegang when writing his Rule, indeed in Claussen's (2006) view the creation of an Christian community encompassing both the cathedral clergy and the wider population of Metz was Chrodegang's primary aim. Alongside this ideological image of the Church as an apostolic community, feasting together also served a key social function, creating and reinforcing bonds of confraternity and spiritual brotherhood that transcended the bounds of the enclosure (Effros 2002; Meerseman 1977).

Such themes of confraternity recur in chapters 30 and 33 of the rule. Chapter 30: 'of the feasts of Saints', lists the key feasts to be celebrated in the diocese, namely: Christmas; Easter; the Epiphany; the Ascension; Pentecost; the Purification and the Assumption of St Mary; the Twelve Apostles; St. John the Baptist; and St. Remi (Bertram 2005, 45-46; trans., 75-76). These feasts were to be commemorated by meals either in the bishop's house or in the refectory. After the meal the clergy were to, 'have two or three drinks together in the recreation room, enough to celebrate, but to avoid drunkenness' (Bertram 2005, 45-46, trans., 75-76). On these occasions both the enclosed and extra-claustral clergy could join together toasting the saint whose life they were celebrating. Such celebrations would also emphasise the brotherly love and charity that bound all ecclesiastical members of the diocese together (Meerseman 1977, 157-160).

Significantly, Chrodegang commanded that: 'the custom which has existed of giving a dinner for the clergy on these festivals in the abbeys which we have in or near this city, should not be maintained if at all possible' (Bertram 2005, 46; trans., 76). Chrodegang wished to ensure that the bishop or his representative could directly oversee the celebrations and feasting, thus preventing and correcting licentious behaviour. This clause also shows that it was common to include the extra-claustral clergy in monastic feasts on key saints days, although Chrodegang seemed unhappy about the practice preferring his clergy to dine in the cathedral close.

Chapter 33 of Chrodegang's Rule provided more detail of the rituals that would accompany the celebration of feasts. Here there was a focus on all clergy gathering together in the cathedral dressed in the correct vestment and attending the chapter and Mass with the bishop:

> 'On Sundays or the feasts of saints or when the pontiff or his deputies determine, all the officials should put on their vestments in the morning after Prime has been sung, including their chasubles, as church law requires. Once properly vested, they may hurry to their duties with no delay. When the first bell is heard they should all go to Chapter, and hear a reading there; then they should go together to church, and when bell has rung the second time they should wait for the pontiff, as the custom is in the church of Rome. No shall leave his place afterwards until everything is finished, except for those who follow and serve the pontiff, or those who are occupied in some necessary duty if it be such that it cannot possibly be deferred; and they should inform the bishop or his delegates about this.' (Bertram 2005, 49; trans., 79-80)

Chrodegang was not alone in involving the extra-claustral clergy in the celebration of major feast days. The concluding chapter of Theodulf of Orléans' first episcopal statute focused on the central role of the cathedral close and the bishop. It instructed that on public occasions as many clerics as possible should attend Mass in cathedral:

> 'On account of which care must be taken that all come together in public to the holy mother church to hear the solemnization of Masses and preaching. Likewise it is decreed that in the city in which a bishop has been established all the presbyters and people, both of the city and of its environs in vestments, should stand with devout hearts at the Mass itself until the benediction of the bishop and Communion, and afterwards if they wish they may with permission revert back to their own rank, after the benediction and Communion have been received. And priests should diligently watch out that neither in the oratories nor the suburban monasteries, nor in the suburban churches, should they presume to celebrate masses before the second hour except with great caution, and with the doors locked, so that the people may not at all be able to absent themselves from the public solemnities, from the Mass or preaching of the bishop, but all of them, the priests of the suburbs as well as those assigned to the city, and all the people, as we said above, may come together with them for the public celebration of Masses'.[3]

The inclusion of the extra-claustral clergy in the rituals of the cathedral close gave them an opportunity to renew their spiritual bonds with their mother church and with the bishop. These rituals would also have served to both reinforce the social networks created within the cloister schoolroom and reaffirm the common identity of all clergy, whether they slept in the enclosure or not. The congruence between chapter 46 of Theodulf's first statute, and chapter 33 of Chrodegang's Rule, may indicate that in the eighth and ninth centuries it was common practice to include the extra-claustral clergy of city and its environs in the life of the cathedral community. In particular Chrodegang's rule explicitly sought to create bonds of confraternity between those in the enclosure and those who ministered and lived outside its walls. More importantly by involving the extra-claustral clerics in the ritual life of the community, both Chrodegang and Theodulf offered a means by which the norms of the enclosed life could be spread and copied by those who lived outside the enclosure. These authors explicitly stated that the practices of the cathedral close should be spread beyond its

---

3    The final chapter of Theodulf's first episcopal statute survives in several versions and different editors have dealt with this precept in different ways. The version quoted above comes from the *Patrologia Latina* 105, 208 and preserves the text found in the *Codex Suessionicus*. For translation and commentary see: McCracken and Cabiniss (1957, 398). The *Monumenta Germaniae Historica* preserves a different version of the precept which unifies c. 45 and c. 46 (Brommer 1984, 141-142). Although this lacks the detail of the *Codex Suessionicus,* it preserves the reference to the city, and to the mother church. It also states that with the exception of nuns, all must come together to hear the bishop's preaching: *Admonendus est populus, ut ante publicum peractum officium ad cibum non accedat, et omnes ad publicam* **sanctam matrem ecclesiam** *missarum sollemniaet* **praedicationem audituri conveniant, et sacerdotes per oratoria** *nequaquammissas nisi tam caute ante secundam horam celebrent, ut populus a publicis sollemnibus non abstrahatur .* **Sed sive sacerdotes, qui in circuitu urbis aut in eadem urbe sunt, sive populus, ut praediximus, in unum ad publicam missarum celebrationem conveniant** *exceptis deo sacratis feminis, quibus mos est ad publicum non egredi, sed claustris monasterii contineri.*

walls. For Chrodegang (c. 27) the extra-claustral clergy were to lock their churches after Compline, mirroring the practices of Porter within the cathedral close. Once these doors were locked the parochial priests were to behave in a similar manner to their enclosed brothers:

> 'The custodians of the churches, who sleep therein, or in the houses next to them, should preserve silence as far as possible, like the rest of the clergy, and after Compline they should not eat or drink. They must not allow those who have stayed outside the gate after Compline to come in.' (Bertram 2005, 43-44, trans., 73)

It is highly significant that chapter 144 of the Canonical Institute maintained and expanded upon this tradition. Local churches were to become miniature cloisters, once the doors were locked the public space of the church became a more exclusive and spiritual site.

In a similar vein in his First Episcopal Statute Theodulf ordered village schools to be established by his diocesan priests, mirroring the cathedral school. (Brommer 1984, 116; trans., Dutton 2004, 110). Theodulf's emphasis on clerical purity also stemmed from the practices of the enclosure, his extra-claustral clergy were to live in the world, but set themselves apart from secular practices. They were to follow the principles of the enclosed life beyond the bounds of the cloister. Following the Benedictine tradition, priests were exhorted 'to be continually reading' (Brommer 1984, 113; trans., Dutton 2004, 110; Vernarde 2011, 160-163). More explicitly in chapter 21 Theodulf quoted extensively from chapter 4 of the Rule of Benedict, making this chapter a foundation for the life of all clerics (Vernarde 2011, 32-37):

> 'It has pleased us to insert into this our prescript the opinion of a certain father about the instruments of good works which contains with great brevity what ought to be done and what avoided.' (Brommer 1984, 117-119; trans., Dutton 2004, 111)

In his First Statute (852), Hincmar of Rheims, demonstrated that he too sought to spread the norms of the enclosure to the extra-claustral clergy. (Pokorny and Stratmann 1995, 34-45). This text focused on the regulation of the rural clergy through the bishop's representative, the dean (Meriaux 2008, 129-136). Chapter 14 discussed clerical feasting at the *convivium* and how clerics were to behave on such occasions (Pokorny and Stratmann 1995, 41-42). Mirroring the practices of both the Rule of Benedict (c. 38), (Venarde 2011, 134-137) and perhaps also Chrodegang's Rule, (c. 21) (Bertram 2005, 40; trans., 68-69) the dean was instructed to bless the food and one of the clerics was to recite a passage of holy reading whilst the clergy dined. After the meal the group were to sing and perform the liturgy together, in a similar fashion to their enclosed brethren (Pokorny and Stratmann 1995, 41-42). Hincmar therefore imposed the customs of the enclosure on the extra-claustral clergy of his diocese, and his rural deans fulfilled the role of the bishop, leading the *convivium* and regulating the behaviour of those who gathered together. The regulation of such meetings allowed the clergy to renew their bonds of spiritual brotherhood by reproducing the practices of those clerics who inhabited the sacred space of the cloister. It should be noted that in Fourth Episcopal

Statute (874) Hincmar of Rheims censured extra-claustral clerics who directly attached themselves to enclosed communities as it interfered with the provision of pastoral care (Pokorny and Stratmann 1995, 80-81; van Rhijn 2007, 6-8 and 139-145). However, this criticism was likely a response to the problems of providing for the needs of laity in rural areas. Hincmar did not wish for all clerics to involve themselves directly in the life of the enclosure as this was impractical. Nonetheless, he still expected extra-claustral clerics to govern themselves and their meetings by the principles of the cloister, with the dean offering spiritual correction to his priests.

## Conclusion

The enclosure was clearly central to the life of all clerics, whether they were canonical clergy, or extra-claustral clerics tasked with serving the needs of laity. The practicalities of pastoral care meant that extra-claustral clerics could not live enclosed lives, defined by the sharing of a dormitory and property, communal meals and the performance of the divine office in congregation. Nonetheless the *claustrum* clearly remained at the heart of their thought-world. Networks and bonds of friendship created within the cloister schoolroom were undoubtedly important to young priests tasked with undertaking pastoral care. Clerics such as Odwin maintained links with their former communities, seeking guidance and advice to assist them in their pastoral missions. The inclusion of such extra-claustral priests in the ritual life of the enclosure, particularly on feast days, presented an opportunity for spiritual renewal and correction. Such occasions also served a practical purpose allowing the bishop to discipline, correct, and instruct his diocesan clergy, while also acknowledging their membership of the wider clerical order. When outside the bounds of the enclosure pastoral clergy were encouraged to mirror the practices of the cloister and thus share in spirit the purity of that sacred space. Extra-claustral clerics may have been separated geographically from their enclosed brothers, but by enacting shared rituals they expressed bonds confraternity and unity with those who inhabited the sacred space of the cloister.

## Bibliography

*Primary Sources*
Allott, S. 1974. (trans.) *Alcuin of York: His Life and Letters.* York: William Sessions.
Bertram, J. 2005. (ed. and trans.) *The Chrodegang Rules: The Rules for the Common Life of the Secular Clergy from the Eighth and Ninth Centuries.* Aldershot: Ashgate.
Barney, S., and Hall, M., 2006. (eds.) *The Etymologies of Isidore of Seville,* Cambridge, Cambridge University Press.
Boretius, A. 1883. (ed.). *Capitularia Regum Francorum I,* MGH, *Leges.* Hannover: MGH.
Brommer, P. 1984. (ed.) *Capitula Episcoporum,* I, MGH, *Leges.* Hannover: Hahnsche Buchhandlung.
Dümmler, E. 1895. (ed.) *Epistolae Karolini Aevi,* II, MGH, *Epistolae.* Berlin: MGH.
Dutton, P.E. 2004 (ed.) *Carolingian Civilization.* Toronto: University of Toronto Press.

Gundlach, W., 1892.(ed.), *Codex Carolinus, Epistolae Merovingi et Karolini aevi I* (Epp. III), Berlin, MGH, 476-657

Hadden, A.W. and Stubbs, W. 1871. (ed.) *Councils and Ecclesiastical Documents Relating to Great Britain and Ireland,* vol. III. Oxford: Clarendon Press

King, P.D. 1987. (trans.) *Charlemagne: Translated Sources.* Kendal: King.

Knöpfler, A. 1900 (ed.) *Rabani Mauri de Institutione Clericorum Libri Tres.* Munich: Lentner

Loyn, H.R., and Percival, J., 1975 (ed.). *The Reign of Charlemagne: Documents on Carolingian Government and Administration.* London, Edward Arnold.

McCracken G. and Cabaniss, A. 1957. (eds.) *Early Medieval Theology* Philadelphia: Westmenster Press.

Mordek, H., Zechiel-Eckes, K., and Glatthaar, M., 2013 (eds.) *Die Admonitio Generalis Karls des Großßen , MGH, Fontes Iuris Germanici Antiqui in Usum Scholarum Separatim Editi,* XVI. Wisebaden: Hahnsche Buchhandlung.

Pokorny, R. & Stratmann, M. 1995 (eds.) *Capitula Episcoporum,* II, MGH, *Leges.* Hannover: Hahnsche Buchhandlung.

Vernarde, B.L. 2011. (ed. and trans.) *The Rule of Saint Benedict.* London: Harvard University Press.

Werminghoff, A. 1906. (ed.) *Concilia Aevi Karolini,* I, MGH, *Leges.* Hannover: MGH.


### Secondary Sources

Cabaniss, A. 2008. Translator Introduction, in: Grabowsky and Radl (eds.). *Benedict of Aniane: The Emperor's Monk.* Kalamazoo: Cistercian Studies, 27-53.

Carela, B., 2006. *Alcuin and Alfred: Two Anglo-Saxon Legal Reformers,* Unpublished PhD Thesis, Unvierstiy of North Carolina.

Chandler, C.J. 2002. Heresy and Empire: 'The Role of the Adoptionist Controversy in Charlemagne's Conquest of the Spanish March. *The International History Review* 24/3, 505-527.

Claussen, M.A. 2004. *Reform of the Frankish Church: Chrodegang of Metz and the Regula Canonicorum in the Eighth Century.* Cambridge: Cambridge University Press.

Claussen, M.A. 2006. Practical Exegesis: The Acts of the Apostles, Chrodegang's 'Regula Canonicorum' and Early Carolingian Reform, in: Blanks, D., Frassetto, M., Livingstone, A., (eds.). *Medieval Monks and their World: Ideas and Realities.* Leiden: Brill, 119-147.

Collins, S. 2012. *The Carolingian Debate Over Sacred Space.* Basingstoke: Palgrave Macmillan.

Contreni, J.J. 1995. The Pursuit of Knowledge in Carolingian Europe, in: Sullivan, R. E. (ed.). *The Gentle Voices of Teachers: Aspects of Learning in the Carolingian age.* Columbus: Ohio State University Press, 106-142.

Czock, M. 2015. Early Medieval Churches as Cultic Space between Material and Ethical Purity', in M. Bley, N. Jaspert, and S. Köck (eds.), *Discourses of Purity in a Transcultural Perspective* (300-1600), Leiden, Brill, 23-42.

Dargen, C. 1905. *A History of Preaching.* New York: Hodder & Stoughton.

de Jong, M., 1995. Carolingian Monasticism: The Power of Prayer, in R. McKitterick (ed.) *New Cambridge Medieval History,* Vol. II, (Cambridge, 1995), 622-653

de Jong, M. 1996. *In Samuel's Image: Child Oblation in the Early Medieval West.* Leiden: Brill.

de Jong, M. 1998. '*Imitatio Morum*': The Cloister and Clerical Purity in the Carolingian World', in: Frassetto, M. (ed.). *Medieval Purity and Piety: Essays on Medieval Clerical Celibacy and Religious Reform.* London: Routledge, 49-80.

Dey, H. 2004. Building Worlds Apart and the Construction of Communal Monasticism From Augustine Through Benedict, *Antique Tardive,* 11, 357-371.

Effros, B. 2002. *Creating Community with Food and Drink in Merovingian Gaul.* Houndmills: Palgrave Macmillan.

Kempf, 2013 *Paul the Deacon: Liber de Episcopis Mettensibus: Edition, Translation and Introduction* (Paris, 2013).

Ling, S. 2015. *The Cloister and Beyond: Regulating the Life of the Canonical Clergy in Francia from Pippin III to Louis the Pious.* Unpublished PhD Thesis, University of Leicester.

Meens, R. 1996. Ritual Purity and the Influence of Gregory the Great in the Early Middle Ages, in: Swanson, R.N. (ed.). *Unity and Diversity in the Church,* Studies in Church History 32. Cambridge, Mass: Blackwell, 31-45.

Meens, R. 2007. Sanctuary, Penance, and Dispute Settlement under Charlemagne: The Conflict between Alcuin and Theodulf of Orleans over a Sinful Cleric. *Speculum* 82, 277-300.

Nelson, J.L. 1992. *Charles the Bald.* London: Longman.

Meersseman, G. and Pacini, G.P. 1977. *Ordo Fraternitatis, Vol. 1, Italia Sacra: Studi E Documenti Di Storia Ecclesiastica.* Rome: Herder.

Mériaux, C. 2008 Orde et Hiérarchie au Sein du Clergé Rural Pendant Le Haut Moyen Âge, in: Bougard, F., Iogna-Prat, D., and Le Jan, R. (eds.). *Hierarchie et Stratification Sociale Dans L'Occident Medieval (400-1100).* Turnhout: Brepols, 117-136.

Page, R.B. 1909. *The Letters of Alcuin*, PhD Thesis, University of Columba.

Paxton, F.S. 1990. *Bonus Liber:* A Late Carolingian Clerical Manual from Lorsch (Bibliotheca Vaticana MS. Pal. Lat. 485), in: Mayali, L. and Tibbets, S.A.J.(eds.). *The Two Laws: Studies in Medieval Legal History Dedicated to Stephan Kuttner.* Washington, D. C.: Catholic University of America Press, 1-30.

Raaijmakers, J. 2006. Memory and identity: the *Annales necrologici* of Fulda, in: Corradini, R., Meens, R., and Possel, C., (eds.). *Texts and Identities in the Early Middle Ages.* Vienna: Verlag der Österreichischen Akademie der Wissenschaften, 303-321.

Raaijmakers, J. 2012. *The Making of the Monastic Community at Fulda,* c. 744-c.900. Cambridge: Cambridge University Press.

Stevens, M. 1995. Walahfrid Strabo a student at Fulda, in: Stevens, W. M. (ed.). *Cycles of Time and Scientific Learning in Medieval Europe.* Aldershot: Ashgate, 13-20.

Stone, R. 2011. *Morality and Masculinity in the Carolingian empire.* Cambridge: Cambridge University Press.

van Rhijn, C. 2006. Priests and the Carolingian reforms: The Bottlenecks of Local *Correctio*, in: Corradini, R., Meens, R., and Possel, C., (eds.). *Texts and Identities in the Early Middle Ages.* Vienna: Verlag der Österreichischen Akademie der Wissenschaften, 219-237.

van Rhijn, C. 2007. *Shepherds of the Lord: Priests and Episcopal Statutes in the Carolingian Period.* Turnhout: Brepols.

Wright, R. 1981. Late Latin and Early Romance: Alcuin's *De Orthographia* and the Council of Tours (AD 813), in: Cairns, F. (ed.). *Papers of the Liverpool Latin Seminar,* Vol. 3. Liverpool: Francis Cairns, 343-363.

# The monastery of Saint Maurice of Agaune (Switzerland) in the first millennium

*Alessandra Antonini*

*Translated by Chantal Bielmann*

## Introduction

Nestled between the cliffs of the Rhone, the history of Agaune (now known as Saint-Maurice) began during the Roman colonisation around 15 BC. The settlement was set up as a minor tax post – a decision likely made by its proximity to the Great Saint Bernard Pass – where traders travelling to and from the Italian peninsula were levied import and export taxes. Centuries later it became the setting of a dispute between Emperor Maximian (286-305) and a group of soldiers known as the Theban Legion. According to Bishop Eucherius of Lyon (*Passion of the Martyrs of Agaune*, written after 435), the Theban Legion, led by Maurice, refused to sacrifice to the emperor as part of the imperial cult while en route to Gaul. As a result of their refusal, the Legion was killed near Agaune around AD 300. While the veracity of this event remains in question (see Woods 1994), it is the subsequent events that propelled Agaune into a major religious centre. Specifically, the alleged discovery of the martyrs' bones by Bishop Theodore, the first known bishop of Valais, around AD 380, which prompted the building of a basilica to house their relics. It is this event that provides the basis for the cult, which spread rapidly and thus profoundly changing the fate of the community.

Indeed, by the middle of the fifth century, Agaune was already one of the main religious centres of the Burgundian kingdom. It was the conversion of King Sigismund (516-524) from Arianism to the Catholic Faith which saw the growth of the site. Following a council with bishops Maximus of Geneva and Avitus of Vienne, the Burgundian ruler turned the sanctuary of Agaune into a 'national' monastery for his kingdom in AD 515. The monks, guided by their abbot Hymnemode and inspired by Eastern traditions, practiced *laus perrenis*, effectively 'a chant without interruption'.

in: Bielmann, C. and Thomas, B. (eds.) 2018: *Debating Religious Space and Place in the Early Medieval World (c. AD 300-1000)*, Sidestone Press (Leiden), pp. 143-158.

*Figure 28: The abbey complex seen to the southwest. In front of the basilica, a grey paving draws ground the church's location Parvis and the Aula (left). On the back of the tower, a suspended roof the rock protects the remains of the Martolet court (Archéotech SA, 2014).*

The abbey of Saint Maurice, solemnly inaugurated on September 22 with many bishops and dignitaries in attendance, is the oldest monastery in Europe that has never known a period of neglect (Wood and Shanzer 2002: 22-23; Fig. 28).

Considering this rich past of the Saint-Maurice abbey, it is not surprising that the settlement was of interest to archaeologists. How was the monastery organised? How have past and current archaeologists dated the various building phases and interpreted excavated remains? These questions are explored in the remainder of this chapter which, following a recent season of excavation, updates our understanding of the monastic site.

## History of the Excavations at Saint Maurice

The first major excavations at the abbey of Saint Maurice took place in 1896. Conducted with the approval of the then Father-Abbot Paccolat, the excavations focused on a courtyard located next to a cliff later known as the 'Martolet'. Led by Canon Peter Bourban (professor and archivist of the Abbey), the initial goal of

*Figure 29: Excavations of Canon Bourban in the courtyard of Martolet (summer 1903). In the foreground, the eastern apse of the martyrial church.*

these early excavations was to unearth the first churches by Bishop Theodore and King Sigismund. In 1899, the trenches revealed two apses and a crypt at the foot of the bell tower and further work between 1902 and 1903 brought to light a series of tombs, including sarcophagi. The collection was described by Canon Peter Bourban as being the most interesting collection of sarcophagi in the country (Michelet 1988, 224). The following year saw the early excavators unearth a western choir and a crypt and, indeed, the alleged tomb-shrine of Saint Maurice himself. Canon Bourban, assisted by engineer Jules Michel, recorded most of these excavations, including photographssuch as the one in Fig. 29.

The excavators, in their hopes to learn more about the first foundations of the monastery, also unearthed evidence that the monastic site contained burial spaces. Alongside evidence of two apses, a crypt on the east side of the nave, and a crypt within a choir on the west side were established through these early excavations. The presence of crypts is of note – these liturgical features denote a change in the use of space and the intention to give access to the space, presumably so that the holy relics could venerated.

The excavated remains garnered great interest in both Switzerland and abroad. However, enthusiasm was mixed on the side of the resident local monks: Bourban had to fight to achieve his desire to revive the pilgrimage to the tomb of the saint. As early as 1897, he made the tomb accessible to visitors, although women were regrettably excluded as the cloister prohibited their presence in the monastic community. Eventually access was changed due to falling rocks from the cliff in 1909 and in 1916 the Canon inaugurated the tomb in honour of Saint Maurice.

The next period of excavation occurred between 1944 and 1948, led by cantonal archaeologist Louis Blondel and art historian Pierre Bouffard. The primary focus of the renewed excavations was to establish a plan of the remains of the Martolet, which was accomplished in 1946. Further excavations began after 1947, when the expansion of the abbey church presented an opportunity to extend the research to the spaces surrounding the Martolet (Blondel 1948). This resulted in the discovery of a large cemetery north-east of the bell tower, featuring graves found at ten different levels, the oldest including a tomb with a painted arcosolium. To the south, in the cloister, a baptistery was unearthed in 1948 (Blondel 1949). By 1967, Blondel had published numerous articles tracing the history of the convent including a summary of the different stages of constructions based on the findings of the excavations (see Blondel 1948; 1949; 1951; 1957; 1966; 1967). These hypothetical conclusions, including the interpretation that the first church built at the site was indeed Theodore's fourth-century construction, were not challenged until Eggenberger and Stöckli (1975, 22-32). Their examination of the previous excavations resulted in questions of Blondel's outline of the architectural developments as well as recommendations to work to conserve the remains which had already begun to degrade. A similar inquiry was raised by Hans-Jörg Lehner from 1994 to 1996, who examined the damage caused by roots from nearby large trees and a rockslide to the site (Lehner 1995).

Despite these post-excavation investigations and inquiries, the next major period of archaeological excavation occurred between 2001 and 2013. Led by the TERA office based in Sion, the project initially focused on determining the multiple construction phases of the church in the courtyard of the Martolet. However, soon after the work expanded to evaluate the growth and transformation of the town and the abbey over time – a systematic survey which can considerably enrich the history of the monastery. Recent discoveries made during repairs in the courtyard and the redevelopment of an avenue in 2012 and 2013 have particularly revolutionised our knowledge of the origins of the abbey. In particular, the remains indicate that a major religious centre was already established in the fourth century, likely by Bishop Theodore. The centre was then further enriched by the patronage of King Sigismund in the sixth century (Fig. 30). The monumental plan shows that the royal foundation of 515 was an expansion project which included not only the church at the foot of the cliff (*e.g.* the Martolet) but also a second church (*e.g.* the Parvis), aligned with the first church, and a palace with a reception hall. These three large buildings were arranged around the baptistery, the symbolic centre of the religious and spatial complex: it is here that the porticos converged with the funerary aisles. The sanctuary of the Martolet, however, was placed at a higher elevation than the other spaces, emphasising its protective role over the relics of the martyrs. The church of Saint-Sigismund located south of the town was similarly set up on a small hill. This former funerary basilica, likely dedicated to Saint John, was

*Figure 30: Saint-Maurice, layout remains the abbey district in the first millennium (Tera 2014). A: Necropolis and the Martolet church; B: Parvis church; C: Baptistery; D: Palace with reception (an aula); E – F: Large and small buildings with hypocaust; G: St. Sigismund church (now known as Church of St. John); H: Building with hypocaust; I: Ancient road.*

also a place of pilgrimage due to the presence of relics of the Burgundian king and his children (Antonini 2015).

The history of the excavations thus demonstrates a regular emphasis on understanding the phasing of the architectural developments of the monastery, with more recent work beginning to expand this to understand the settlement as a whole. This long focus on the walls, apses, graves, and other liturgical features, however, present an opportunity to better understand the interior space and its organisation over time. The remainder of this chapter thus examine different parts of the monastery and related structures.

## The Remains in the Martolet courtyard

### From Venerated Tomb to Church

The Martolet is the best-known area of the archaeological site (Fig. 30A). The earliest phase of human activity is a late second-century AD Roman necropolis near a sacred spring. Indeed, the discovery of an altar dedicated to the Nymphs illustrates that the site had been previously used for a religion. Within the necropolis, a tomb was placed in the centre of an elevated area at the foot of the cliff. It was deep and marked by a funerary monument, making it different to other burials – thus probably the tomb of an important person (Fig. 31A). The monument would have been visible from the nearby route. The feature experienced another period of building with the construction of a simple square mausoleum on top of the tomb, likely around AD 350. Subsequent burials arranged next to the mausoleum suggests that the feature acted as a point of veneration (Fig. 32A). This hypothesis is further substantiated by the transformation of the mausoleum into a small oratory in AD 380 (Antonini 2015, 92). This was accomplished by adding a room to the east (perhaps for worship?) and a terrace on the opposite side. These small rooms indicate that a group of people used to gather in this place to commemorate the dead, buried next to a possibly venerated tomb.

Thus, Agaune was already a space for religious worship – whether if one looks back to the altar dedicated to the Nymphs or the fourth-century mausoleum seemingly acting as a point of veneration – when Bishop Theodore, around 380, replaced the oratory with a church built in honour of the Theban martyrs (Fig. 32B). This fourth-century church was then periodically expanded, possibly the work of abbots perpetuating the memory of the fame and glory of the martyrs. Circa 400, the sanctuary was completely rebuilt with a slightly more developed apse (Fig. 32C). The many graves placed near the relics of the Theban martyrs (*ad sanctos*) as well as the presence of a baptistery and the porticos surrounding the various buildings of the religious complex testify to the existence of a rapidly growing pilgrimage.

### An early medieval monastic complex (AD 515- AD 999)

In the sixth century, the apse of Theodore's church was replaced by polygonal apse with a slightly larger interior (Fig. 32D). This expansion of the choir is associated with the work of King Sigismund in AD 515, who according to historical records was officially announcing the creation of a monastery (see Wood and Shanzer 2002). If this marks a new monastic organisation, it represents the culmination of work resulting in a monu-

*Figure 31 (above): The privileged tomb of ancient necropolis, with the remains of its mark (a). Three tombs with north-south orientations (b, c, d) are next to him; they are partially covered by the paved floor of the churches.*

*Figure 32 (right): The Court of Martolet, looking West (2009). The mausoleum (A) is built on the privileged tomb of ancient necropolis (\*). It will be replaced by a church rebuilt several times. The succession of apses first semi-circular (B, C) and Polygon (D, E) and, finally, facing west (F), shows the expansion of the sanctuary. Left, the entrance corridor of the first three churches.*

mental architectural complex with the following features: a primary church based next to the cliff, a second church with a similar orientation with the older church in the Martolet, a baptistery, and a palace with a reception room (Fig. 30B and D).

From the start, the church of the Martolet was characterised by an architectural style which adapted at each reconstruction of the building. The portico that ran along its south and west facades is one of these elements: it housed the path, with a staircase that allowed visitors and members of the monastic community to reach the threshold of the nave. This portico was built to be part of a network of protected corridors through which passed processions and also created privileged burial spaces. The mortuary chapel built between the apse and the cliff is a second element of the complex. This chapel retained its function until the construction of the actual church in the 17th century. The implication of a network of corridors demonstrates plans by the leaders of the monastery regarding access around the complex as well as how monks and presumably guests would be able to access to key burial spaces.

The rising status of the abbey with its steady influx of pilgrims brought about profound change to the monastic community. Perhaps most evident of this observation is the rebuilding of the Martolet church in the late sixth century into a larger structure (Fig. 32, E). Its organisation was relatively similar: a long, vaulted corridor, moved south in relation to the earlier building, served as the substructure of the floor of the new sanctuary (Fig. 33). Moreover, the funerary chapel at the foot of the cliff was raised. The reuse of the architectural layout and the many Roman stones found in the masonry served as a reminder to the visitors of the ancient origins of the place. Furthermore, the continued need for a long, vaulted corridor brings to mind an intentional plan of how pilgrims and visitors of the abbey would visit the church and the relics (Antonini 2015).

In the eighth century, the apse of the sanctuary was rebuilt in order to make room for a corridor crypt decorated with imitation marble slabs and with painted plaster on its walls (Fig. 34). This crypt may have preserved the relics of the martyrs around with which the pilgrims could gather during processions. Then, by the ninth century, a new building was set up. The nave was made wider and was subdivided into three by two rows of pillars with the entrance now found where the old apse once was. The choir with a new corridor crypt was raised at the west end of the nave (Fig. 32 F).

By the end of the first millennium, this sanctuary was the only abbey church. It was made larger during the Romanesque period with the construction of the bell tower which was subsequently flanked by side chapels (Fig. 35). In the 17th century, it was replaced by the current basilica while integrating the old bell tower, a current symbol of the town of Saint-Maurice.

### The Baptistery

Discovered in 1948, the baptistery was the subject of a brief study due to its importance as a place of conversion (Fig. 30C). Currently located in the basement of the St Catherine courtyard, west of the present church, the only physical remains of the baptistery include a baptismal pool (Fig. 36). The circular tank (diameter, 1.50m; depth, 1.70m) with 80-100cm wide masonry is accessible from two symmetrical staircases arranged in a north-south axis. Two steps and the beginning of a third are preserved on the north side; on the south side, the first and part of the second are preserved. The

*Figure 33: The vaulted corridor of the fourth building. The entry consists of an ancient arc in replacement. At the other end, a monumental staircase dating back to the church of the Martolet.*

*Figure 34: The eastern crypt Martolet (fifth building). The pictorial decoration of the walls imitates marble coating. Looking west, around 1907.*

*Figure 35: The court of Martolet looking east. In the foreground, the Western bedside sixth church with its crypt. The tomb-reliquary is fitted into the central corridor.*

vessel was adapted to the liturgical changes first by reducing its size, then filled and replaced by a baptismal font. These changes reflect how the baptismal rite transitioned from full immersion or infusion to sprinkling or infant baptism, possibly around the sixth century.

The building housing the baptismal pool is known by surviving masonry sections. Likely rectangular (12.70 x 9.70m) on an east-west orientation, it was located on a slight hill. A square apse was added in a later building phase as well as annexes to the

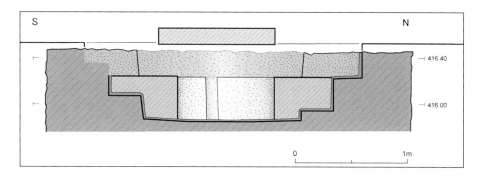

*Figure 36: Schematic section of the pool (north-south, west view). The primitive cell (red), first narrowed by a circular masonry (dimmed), was then backfilled and covered with a slab (blue).*

north and south with a courtyard in the west. The choice to place the baptismal pool in an elevated building emphasises the importance of the baptistery as a symbolic centre of the whole architectural complex. Considering the circular form, the dating of the pool to the early fifth century, contemporaneous to the second phase of the Martolet church, seems plausible. The presence of a baptistery during this period has a number of implications: the space acting as a place of conversion, the likely need for an episcopal presence to conduct the ceremony, and more (Davies 1962).

### The Parvis Church

The second church in the eastern part of the Martolet church is not mentioned by any sources: several partial excavations were needed in order to understand the extent and importance of the building (Fig. 30B). In 1947, Louis Blondel identified the northwest annexes, including the tomb topped by a painted recess (arcosolium). Between 1974 and 1975, Werner Stöckli discovered the north wall of the nave, with the start of the apse and the north-east funerary annexes. The western façade was located within the current basilica in 2004, which allowed for an estimation of size of this building. A geophysical survey confirmed in 2005 the preserved remains under the Parvis church – it was only between 2012 and 2013 when part of the monastery was being restored that archaeologists were able to uncover the apse and southern sector of the early medieval complex (Antonini 2015). During these recent excavations, no remains were destroyed in order to study the earlier phases; new pipelines were even diverted to best preserve the ancient walls, floors, and numerous tombs.

The Parvis church also includes a wide nave and a polygonal apse with at least one buttress. The walls of the nave formed a large bench 1 metre above the floor. A mortar floor featuring an intense red surface, perfectly smooth without joints or steps, covered the first arranged burials in the building. The re-treading observed in the nave indicates that many of the funerary coffins were reused during the mid-seventh and eighth centuries for new burials.

The dimensions of the sanctuary, 30 x 16m, were similar to those of the third church of the Martolet, built in the sixth century. The typology of the burials also seems to confirm the existence of the Parvis church around the same time. The building, however, was not built in one piece: a partial analysis showed that the choir is newer than the nave. Several chancels (low architectural barriers) subdivided the nave and reflected certain ritual changes. One, built prior to the mortar floor, separated the liturgical choir from the nave; another narrower chancel, contemporary to the mortar floor, separated the front of the apse – the space reserved for the clergy and undoubtedly containing the altar.

The Parvis church is also surrounded by annexes. A chapel can be found north of the apse, accessible from the presbytery. The entrance features four columns whose bases and 'negative drums' are preserved. On the chapel's south wall, 15cm from the ground, a jeweled and painted red cross surrounded by a black double line appears to mark the location of a grave.

A funerary annex is attested in the north-east. Accessible from the rectory, the room featured analogous paint as that found at the arcosolium near the northwest corner of the nave. To the south, an annex with a mortar floor covering graves is situated in the extension of an apsed chapel. The western façade of the chapel was probably bordered by a portico.

By the eighth century, the funerary use of the building becomes redundant. A new floor was installed above the older one and in front of the presbytery's chancel, a wide path lined with thick masonry (suggesting an extra function) was added. In the ninth century, the mortar in the ground was still covered by a wooden floor, before the building was destroyed by fire.

### The ancillary buildings

The church built by Theodore was not an isolated monument. From the fourth century, a religious community developed around the church. The importance of pilgrimage is obvious. However, a baptistery placed at the centre of the architectural complex during the early medieval period, in the corridor leading to the tombs of the Theban martyrs, also suggests the community acted as space for conversion. This is particularly interesting and feeds into the debate about accessibility of monastic spaces. Who had access to these sites? What spaces were 'open' and which were closed? We can see that porticos and corridors connected the various buildings, suggesting that there were multiple routes to gain access to the tombs within the monastic complex.

Burial space is also prominent throughout the monastic complex. *Ad sanctos* burials are attested even at the foot of the Martolet church. And it was not just in and around the Martolet church where we see burials – the Parvis church, built east of the Martolet, the church of Saint-Sigismund and the basilica 'Condemines', found near the Rhone were funerary basilicas as well. Furthermore, the recent excavations have brought to light the existence of a 'palace'. This huge assembly hall was arranged between the baptistery to the west and the public road to the east. The presence of such a large space attests to the importance of Agaune and the monastic complex. Alongside conversion space and burial space, we see an element of royal or elite space at the monastery.

Some of the buildings have been under extensive investigation. Others are known only by a few elements preserved in a small area or in narrow trenches. The data for these new spaces is patchy. Thus, any new excavations within the perimeter of the abbey and its surrounding areas can thus change the overall plan of the religious community.

## The Palace and its Reception Room

Discovered south of the Parvis church, the building covers an area of approximately 22m by at least 30m (Fig. 30D). Its eastern façade is located near the main road; its western façade near the baptistery. A portico is observed along the south side of the structure whereas a cobble path is featured near the north side. The interior is divided into at least two large spaces. The eastern shape, trapezoidal in form, appears to have served as a ceremonial room (eg. an aula): a podium (height one step) placed against the western wall is interpreted as the location of the *cathedra* – the seat upon which the spiritual and political leader of the abbey and region sat (Fig. 37). At a later date, the wall behind the platform is replaced by an apse indicating a monumentalisation of the space. The level of the great hall's walkway, made up of 20cm-thick screed mortar, was tinged red and was solid with no cracks. It covers a network of interconnected channels (hypocaust system) which allow heating the floor. This layer is the last of five superimposed levels observed on 1.10m high.

The shape of the western room, in its final form, was large (21 x 10m) and accessible by a door in its northern side. Not far away, two steps leaning against the north-east corner of the room led to a staircase to the second floor. A second door located in the apse creates another passageway. In the south, the building is bordered by a corridor or

*Figure 37: The remains of the palace discovered in Agaune. Orthogonal view taken with a drone. (Archéotech SA, 2013).*

a portico where the floor has been disturbed several times to lay pipes in the hollowed tree trunks in order to allow the flow of wastewater to the east.

Overall the remains suggest a high-quality building, renovated several times. The radiocarbon dating derived from organic material associated with the last levels suggests the building was still in use between the second half of the seventh century and the first half of the eighth century. A plank found under the apse (c. AD 550) and fibres of a post supporting the ceiling of the western room (c. AD 400) however deliver earlier dates. The five superimposed floors of the aula, all established before adding the apse, allow for the hypothesis that the large building existed at the beginning of the sixth century. Its location near the road and the monastic space suggests the room was used as a residence for an abbot or bishop or even a king when visiting the monastery.

A second large building was also discovered further south near the college (Fig. 30E). It includes several small rooms alongside one large room of approximately 12.50m wide and at least the same in its length. On the south side, the walls separating the rooms lean against another long wall that seems to define the abbey complex. The secondary rooms featured either earth or mortared floors, while the floor of the hall comprises a hypocaust system similar to that found in the aula. This building was ravaged by fire, like the Parvis church and the aula; the grave of a child, discovered in the demolition, is dated to the tenth century.

A small dwelling, perhaps a house, was found between the two large buildings. It comprises a room with floor heating and, in the north, a small kitchen with two foyers. The heated mortar floor covered an elevated pavement supported by tiles (both whole and piecemeal). An arched opening in the eastern wall allowed the necessary access to heat the hypocaust (*praefurnium*). This house was without a doubt another part of the monastic complex, as it was developed inside the enclosure but it was arranged more freely in comparison to the sanctuaries and the large reception rooms, connected by porticoes and built along the same axes marked by the baptistery and the church of the Martolet. This free organisation of ancillary buildings is indeed the rule in monastic settlements during the High Middle Ages.

## Discussion and Conclusion

What do all these structures and phases tell us about religious space? The first, perhaps, the most obvious observation is that the monastery of Saint-Maurice was (and arguably still is) the site of considerable investment. The regular construction between the fourth and sixth century alone demonstrates how bishops, abbots, and even kings developed the site. But developed it into what? The initial structures of the fourth and early fifth century suggest a burial church with some evidence of veneration; thus the interpretation that the first church was meant to emulate a 'martyrial' church. But we should not forget the presence of the baptistery! This liturgical feature provides added complications: namely that the site acted as a place of conversion, which could indicate that the church was a place where catechism took place.

The space changed again in the sixth century – a result of the actions of King Sigismund transforming the site into a monastic complex. This adds another level of complication regarding access: Were only men allowed? Were parts of the complex 'closed' to the public? The network of corridors suggests there was an attempt to 'control' access to different parts of the abbey, with emphasis being placed on specific graves. The change to the baptistery in the sixth century would suggest that the monastery still acted as a centre of conversion and thus, arguably, 'open' to lay people. Furthermore, the presence of a palace and a reception room used possibly as late c. AD 750 indicates that Agaune began to act as not just a centre of worship but as a centre of power – whether royal or episcopal remains the question.

Thus, the abbey of Saint-Maurice presents us with an intriguing study with respect space. First, we have an excellent example 'transformation'. The site itself experienced extensive periods of building throughout the first millennium as outlined above, ranging from the transition of the site from a Roman necropolis to a church and finally from a church to a monastic complex. Second, the abbey of Saint-Maurice presents a case study for how space can be experienced by different people: to a non-Christian, a space for conversion; to a Christian, a space of worship and veneration; to an abbot and monk, a space of solitude and prayer; to a bishop and a king, a space of power. Finally, it also demonstrates the power of place and the permanence of religious space. Today, the old Abbey recently celebrated 1500 years of its continued existence. The effort devoted to archaeological research in recent years has gone hand in hand with restoration, conservation, and a new presentation of the remains (2008-2014). These archaeological remains act as witness to its ancient past that has its beginnings even before the martyrdom of Saint Maurice and his companions.

## Bibliography

### Primary Sources

Eucherius, *Passio Acaunensium Martyrum*, ed. B. Krusch, *Monumenta Germaniae Historica Scriptores rerum Merovingicarum 3* (Hanover 1896).

### Secondary Sources

Antonini, A. 2015. Archéologie du site abbatial (des origines au Xe siècle), in: Andenmatten, B., and Ripart, L. (eds), *L'abbaye de Saint-Maurice d'Agaune 515-2015 Volume 1 – Histoire et archéologie*. Gollion: Infolio Editions, 59-110.

Blondel, L. 1948. Les anciennes basiliques d'Agaune. *Vallesia* 3, 9-57.

Blondel, L. 1949. Le baptistère et les anciens édifices conventuels de l'Abbaye d'Agaune. *Vallesia* 4, 15-28.

Blondel, L. 1951. Les anciennes basiliques (de St-Maurice). *Echos de Saint-Maurice* 49, 15-52.

Blondel, L. 1957. Le martyrium de St-Maurice d'Agaune. *Vallesia* 12, 283-292.

Blondel, L. 1966. Plan et inventaire des tombes des basiliques d'Agaune. *Vallesia* 21, 29-34.

Blondel, L. 1967. La rampe d'accès à la basilique d'Agaune: une rectification. *Vallesia* 22, 1-3.

Davies, J.G., 1962. *The Architectural Setting of Baptism*. London: Barrie and Rockliff.

Eggenberger, P. and Stöckli, W. 1975. La découverte en l'abbaye de Saint-Maurice d'une épitaphe dédiée au moine Rusticus. *Helvetia archaeologica* 6, 22-32.

Lehner, H-J. 1996. Saint-Maurice. *Vallesia* 51, 341-344.

Michelet, H. 1988. Saint-Maurice: aperçu sur le site archéologique du Martolet. *Echos de Saint-Maurice* 84, 221-245.

Wood, I. and Shanzer, D. 2002. *Avitus of Vienne: Selected Letters and Prose* (Translated Texts for Historians 38). Liverpool: Liverpool University Press.

Woods, D. 1994. The origin of the cult of St. Maurice. *Journal of Ecclesiastical History* 45, 385-395.

# Exploring Monastic Space and Place in the Swiss Alps

*Chantal Bielmann*

## Introduction: Religious Space and Place

Within archaeology and history alike, scholarship has examined the significance of spaces and places in relation to power dynamics, economies, ritual and belief, and so on. Importantly distinctions remain in how we regard and interpret places and spaces, especially within a historical framework. Lefebvre (1991, 234-235), for example, noted how churches and monasteries can have fixed topographical attributes (*e.g.* a specific place) but also represent relationships between the living and the dead, ritual and belief, power and authority, production and market economies and so on. Furthermore, if one follows de Certeau (1984, 117), 'place' and 'space' are fundamentally different things: a place is a location and thus stable; a space only exists when you are moving from one place to another ('intersections of mobile elements'). Elements of both de Certeau and Lefebvre can be seen in more recent studies examining in particular the relationship between religions and the spaces and places they inhabit. Geographic analyses like Stump's (2008) book on *The Geography of Religion: Faith, Place and Space,* contemporary archaeological studies, such as the University of Leicester's *Mapping Faith and Place Project*, and discussions within environmental psychology in relation to place-attachment theory on religious sites (*e.g.* Mazumdar and Mazumdar 2004) are just a few examples of our fascination with places of worship and their spaces. These studies explore how religious centres were perceived and valued, eventually becoming centres of cultural worth and significance to both local and foreign communities. Cassidy-Welch's (2001) introduction to *Monastic Spaces and their Meanings* rightly demonstrates the many ways in which one can examine spatial concepts, noting key themes such as the production of space, the meanings given to spaces and places, and the distinction between place and space. Cassidy-Welch (2001, 8) also observes that theories of space and approaches to space and place have rarely been applied to monastic sites with notable exceptions (*e.g.* the work of Gilchrist on gendered spaces in monastic sites and Biddick on the rural space of the medieval peasant), a view I share today – despite her work being published over 10 years ago!

in: Bielmann, C. and Thomas, B. (eds.) 2018: *Debating Religious Space and Place in the Early Medieval World (c. AD 300-1000)*, Sidestone Press (Leiden), pp. 159-174.

It is puzzling when one explores why this gap exists, especially considering that the significance of space and monastic sites was written about by many hagiographers. References to the 'desert', the foundation of monasteries in relation to a holy man retreating to solitude life, and more are all themes found within most hagiographic texts. For example, this passage from Sulpicius Severus' Life of Saint Martin (*Vit.Mart.*X) not only describes the fixed placement of Martin's monastery but also how one would approach the site:

> 'He [Martin] *established a monastery for himself about two miles outside the city. This spot was so secret and retired that he enjoyed in it the solitude of a hermit. For, on the one side, it was surrounded by precipitous rock of a lofty mountain, while the river Loire had shut in the rest of the plain by a bay extending back for a little distance; and the place could be approached only by one, and that a very narrow passage.*'

Other hagiographies follow similar patterns when describing places for ascetic or monastic worship. Of course, discussions on the 'retreat from society' have been outlined. Lawrence (1984, 2), his book on medieval monasticism still valuable today, outlines how the 'retreat' is an essential component to understanding Christian monasticism. Indeed, to be fair, there has been a resurgence of scholars exploring monasticism with more emphasis on place and space. Pratich (2004, 423), for example, described how monasteries left a 'decisive imprint on the landscape', ranging from not only the construction of the monastic houses, cells, and walls, but also their manipulation and control of water-ways and agriculture. Other researchers, including Rosenwein (2001, 282-284) and Sennhauser (2008, 43), discuss the significance of monastic spaces in relation to power, noting the 'strategic placement' of many alpine monasteries in relation to key passes. The problem, however, with both Rosenwein and Sennhauser is that their arguments rely predominantly on the politico-historical events around which the monasteries were founded, not upon the actual spaces and places in which they inhabit. Thus, I argue that there is considerable scope to explore monastic space and place within a spatial archaeology framework. This particular framework considers the individual building and settlements within their geographic environment, placing emphasis on the position and arrangement of the settlement (Ashmore 2002, 1173). Moreover, with the advancements made with Geographic Information Systems (GIS), there is more scope to explore in detail specific questions regarding monastic place, notably about their visibility within the natural landscape.

Indeed, these types of studies already exist within other archaeological contexts. For example, Eve and Crema (2014) utilised visibility analysis and point-process modelling to explore the reasons behind Bronze Age settlement pattern of Leskernick Hill in Cornwall, UK. The visibility analysis here contributed to their conclusion that the site was chosen to 'optimise the visibility of nearby tin-extraction areas' (Eve and Crema 2014, 267). Their study equally points out that their model is 'closest to the truth' recognising future work could create a better model (Eve and Crema 2014, 275-276). An older paper by Gillings (2009) similarly adopts the viewshed methodology to explore the visibility as a factor in past settlement placement. Here Gillings (2009, 335-339, 343) uses the megalithic structures of Alderney (a Channel island) as his dataset and uses a question-based approach to this dataset: what locational factors (sea-views, visual exposure, *etc.*) apply to the Alderney monuments? Another element of Gillings work that should be considered is that he chose to use an affordance-viewshed – essentially a theoretical framework that stresses how animal-environment relations are intertwined *not* separated (Gillings 2009, 340, 344). Utilising this framework, the results of analyses on both sea-view visibility and prominence argue 'that adherence to a prescriptive set of topographic or visual criteria is difficult to sustain' (Gillings 2009, 351). The main benefit of evaluating Gillings work, despite its prehistoric framework, relates to his analysis of limitations with regard to visibility analyses. Poor datasets in particular appear to be one of the main limitations – the quality of the geodata will greatly influence the accuracy and validity of a model.

Considering these case studies, in particular their discussion of limitations, this paper explores monastic space and place using ArcGIS as a means to explore the spatiality, focusing on the visibility, of monastic settlements located in the Swiss Alps. As noted above, the first monasteries were established in remote places to promote and support their ascetic life by avoiding all forms of indulgences. Are monasteries in the Alps trying to follow a similar model? ArcGIS provides a useful method to evaluate the question of visibility by creating a virtual representation of the landscape and querying whether the sites were indeed visible or not. While these questions have been evaluated by historians and archaeologists, ArcGIS provides an objective manner in which to evaluate site choice – why did people choose this location? Here, the use of spatial software also allows us to query whether the choice of settlement was linked to visibility and thus have strategic value for the monarchs involved in their construction. It also allows the user to consider other variables, such as height and viewing angle, when determining the visibility of a location. However, it should be noted immediately that ArcGIS outputs, including the results of the viewshed analysis performed here, are models, a representation of reality, rather than reality itself. Limitations will always exist within a modelling environment and I examine these accordingly in the paper. Despite this, I agree with Wheatley and Gillings (2002) that the modelling capacity of ArcGIS is a strength rather than a weakness as it allows us to generate possible outcomes and to test different theories by changing the variables.

The Alps in particular make an interesting region. From poets to historians, the Alps have often been described as desolate and inaccessible. Woodsworth (1836, 15) described the Alps (specifically Wetterhorn and Schrekhorn, two mountains near Bern) as the 'Pikes of Darkness named, of Fear and Storm'. Emily Dickinson's (1924, 80) poem 'Our lives are Swiss' focuses on the Alps as a border:

> *Italy stands the other side,*
> *While, like a guard between*
> *The solemn Alps,*
> *The siren Alps,*
> *Forever intervene!*

Perhaps most relevant here is John de Bremble, a twelfth-century English monk, who provides this colourful juxtaposition during a visit to the Great Saint Bernard Pass near Martigny (*Epi.Cant.* CXCVII, 181):

*'I have been on the Mount of Jove; on the one hand looking up to the heaven of the mountains, on the other shuddering at the hell of the valleys, feeling myself so much nearer heaven that I was more sure my prayers would be heard.'*

While all these descriptions of the Alps provide a small glimpse of the fascination people have had with these mountains over time, it is de Bremble's account that is of note. Namely, his description of the 'hellish valleys' in contrast with the 'heaven of the mountains' further presents the Alps as a place where holy men might be able to confront demons, a common trope found within the hagiographic lives associated with these places.

This chapter explores the question of monastic space and place utilising a spatial archaeology framework using three Alpine case studies: The Abbey of Saint Maurice d'Agaune located in the Valais Alps, Disentis Abbey, and St John's Benedictine Convent in Müstair, both in the Rhaetian Alps. These particular sites serve as excellent case studies due to their location in Alpine locations and their rich material culture, including structural remains dating to the early medieval period (*c.* AD 500-800). Each provides a case study for different placement settings: Müstair built on 'new ground', Saint-Maurice built above a possible Roman Nymphaeum, and Disentis built above the supposed remains of two local saints. Furthermore, research on all three sites has placed considerable emphasis on the importance of their locations, even to the point to suggest their geographic location was a fundamental part of their foundation: Sennhauser (2008, 42) on the strategic locations of Müstair and Disentis; Rosenwein (2001, 282) on the power implications of the placement of Saint Maurice d'Agaune near the Saint-Bernard Pass. Thus these sites present us with an interesting juxtaposition: hagiographic and traditional perspectives suggesting these sites as monasteries should be described as remote and inaccessible whereas modern scholarly literature describes them in terms of their political and seemingly important locations. I thus ask the following questions: how visible were these monasteries within their respective landscapes? In terms of their fixed locations, their 'place', what attributes can we assign to them?

I first explore the context in which these particular sites arose, namely early medieval monasticism in Switzerland. Within this section, I then delve into more detail on the geographic location and historical context of the three particular sites. This is then followed by a discussion of the methodology, namely viewshed analysis, evaluating the function and success as spatial analyses but also the inherent assumptions associated with them. I follow this with a discussion on the results and the significance of these findings.

## Early Medieval Monasticism in Switzerland

Between the fourth and ninth centuries, approximately 16 monastic houses were built up across Switzerland (Fig. 38). These communities, many still monasteries today, were placed in a variety of places: forested places, near major roads, islands, and in Alpine valleys. This number, while based on hagiographical, historical, and archaeological evidence, illustrates the popularity of monastic building across the period. While Pauli (1984, 188) saw the influx of monks and the ascetic life in the Alps as a direct influence of the first monasteries set up in France by St Honorat and in Austria

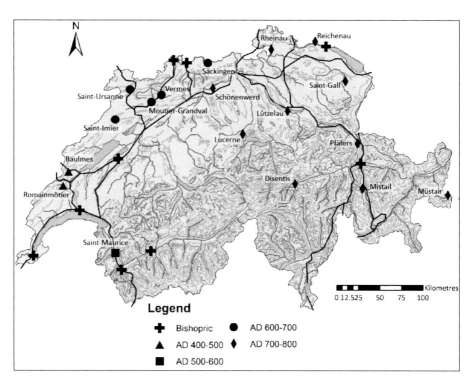

*Figure 38: Map of Switzerland depicting the monasteries building between AD 300 and 800 (Image by author).*

| Period (AD) | Administration | Monastic Communities | Potential Noble/Royal Founder |
|---|---|---|---|
| 400-550 | Burgundian | Saint Maurice | King Sigismund with Bishop Maximus |
| 550-750 | Merovingian | Moutier-Grandval | Duke Gundoin via Saint Germanus |
| | | Vermes | Duke Gundoin via Saint Germanus |
| | | St Ursanne | Duke Gundoin via Saint Germanus |
| | | Romainmotier | Duke Ramelen in Jura via wife |
| | | Baulmes | Duke Ramelen in Jura via wife |
| | | Sackingen | Unknown Founder |
| 700-800 | Alamanni (?) | Lutzelau | Noble Landolt via his wife Beata |
| | | Rheinau Abbey | Unknown Founder |
| 750-850 | Carolingian | St Gallen (?) | Carloman via Saint Gall (?) |
| | | Disentis | Charles Martel via Saint Pirmin |
| | | Reichenau | Charles Martel via Saint Pirmin |
| | | Pfafers | Charles Martel via Saint Pirmin |
| | | St Leodegar Monastery (?) | Pepin the Short (?) |
| | | Müstair | Charlemagne (?) |
| | | Mistail | Louis the Pious |

*Table 3: Monasteries and their noble founders (Author's work).*

by Severin, the spread of monasticism has been more recently linked to three particular impetuses (Bielmann 2014): fifth-century influences from French ascetics and Italian ecclesiastical support for monasticism; influence from Ireland via St Columbanus and Merovingian politics in the seventh century; and encouragement from Carolingians to build monasteries in the Alps *c.* AD 750.

While this paper does not explore in detail the various historic and administrative factors that impacted monastic building in the Alps, it should be highlighted that a recent analysis of monasticism in Switzerland found that the majority of monasteries built in Switzerland had a noble founder rather than an ascetic one (Bielmann 2014, 214; Table 3). This observation thus raises another question: would a monastery built with support from a layman still attempt to set up the religious community in a remote and isolated place? Further exploration of this question alongside more insight into the historical and archaeological setting of the three case studies is examined below.

### The Abbey of Saint Maurice

The abbey of Saint Maurice is perhaps the most famous of the three monasteries discussed here. The monastery recently celebrated its 1500-year anniversary, producing a new substantial text detailing its historical, cultural, and archaeological significance. A visit to the abbey from the region of Lake Geneva (*e.g.* heading towards Martigny in the south-east) revealed how the community is actually concealed by the local geography. Despite its location in a town near a major Roman route to the Great Saint Bernard Pass (2469m), the monastery could only be seen until one manoeuvred through the valley between the two bluffs and crossed the River Rhone. However, the exact opposite observation can be noted when travelling to Saint-Maurice from the pass. The wide and relatively flat landscape of the town made it easier to see the abbey's clock tower. The visibility of the monastery during the late Roman and early medieval periods, however, remains another question and depends greatly on our understanding of the site's archaeology and settlement history.

Established as a minor post along the *Via Claudia*, one of the main routes connecting Italy to Gaul, our understanding of Saint-Maurice's (formerly named *Agaunum*) settlement history is largely skewed towards the area in which the monastery was built. In particular, excavations have been able to determine that a second-century necropolis stood at the future site of the monastery, near a water source dedicated to the Nymphs. Between 325 and 350 a mausoleum is added to the area and subsequently expanded to feature an oratory. It is around 375-400 that archaeologists propose that the first hall church was constructed and later modified with fifth-century sacristies on either side of the apse. This new interpretation of the archaeology adds some validation to Bishop Eucherius' (*c.* 380-449; *MGH SS rer. Merov. 3*, 20-41; Bielmann 2014, 125-126) account on how Bishop Theodorus of Martigny built up the first church dedicated to Saint Maurice and the Theban Martyrs following the discovery of the martyrs' relics (Woods 1999, 388-390). While this basilica was unlikely constructed initially as a monastic house, subsequent accounts suggest the place was visited and revered. Gregory of Tours (*Glory of the Martyrs* 74, p. 69) wrote about the 'power' of the tombs of Theban martyrs and an excerpt from the Life of the Jura Fathers recounts how Romanus sought the basilica of the martyrs (*Lives of the Jura Fathers* 44). Thus we can suggest that Roman settlement of *Agaunum* and the future site of the monastery were at least known and visited during the fourth century. Undoubtedly locals visited the site for use of the necropolis and the church with some early pilgrims visiting the church.

It is in AD 515, with the foundation of the monastery by King Sigismund, that the monastery experiences further building. Antonini's reinterpretation of the archaeology and the significance of the changes can be read in the subsequent chapter. While Sigismund's expansion lacked extensive building, Avitus of Vienne's Homily 25 emphasises the significance of the location, recalling the story of the death of the Thebans, and even comments on the new-found monastery's accessibility (Shanzer and Wood 2002, 379-380):

> '...whose entry is not shut at night, because it has no night; whose doors are always wide open to the just, but inaccessible to the impious.'

The monastic site saw continued building throughout the sixth century, with the addition of ancillary buildings, a baptistery, and a widening of the nave of the church. As a place of power, its prestige grew throughout the Carolingian and post-Carolingian period. Not only do can we make note of Pope Stephen's visit to the monastery in 754 but also the coronation of King Rudolf in 888 (Vischer *et al.* 1995, 32; Rosenwein 1998, 273). Other monasteries were founded with Saint-Maurice acting as the model, such as King Guntram's Saint-Marcel de Chalon in 584 (Rosenwein 1998, 282). As a place of pilgrimage, we can make note of the popularity of relics of St Maurice, which by the time of the 13th century had even been acquired by Henry III (Dupont Lachenal 1956, 393-444). Furthermore, the presence of a font indicates that people came to the monastery to be baptised. Finally, the many reliquary boxes, ranging from the early medieval to medieval period, as well as historical accounts of pilgrims visiting the monastery suggest that the monastery was highly accessible.

### The Benedictine Abbey of Disentis

Located in the Surselva region in eastern Switzerland, the Benedictine Abbey of Disentis is the least well-known of the three monasteries examined here. Unlike Saint-Maurice. Disentis abbey can be reached from three directions: from the west (Chur), the south (Lukmanier Pass; 1915m), and the east (Oberalp Pass; 2044m). My own visit was perhaps the most straightforward: from Chur, I drove 61.5km westward through the Rhine valley. From this particular direction, the abbey is visible from a moderate distance due to its elevated position to the road as well as its imposing appearance, a product of renovations from 1692 to 1712. If one chose to visit the abbey via the Oberalp pass (*e.g.* Andermatt to Disentis), however, the monastery remains hidden in the local terrain – including various small hills obscuring the view from higher elevations. Based on this observation, it could be argued that the building was established in a location that would make it visible from a distance travelling from the Pass but locally, somewhat invisible. A counter to this observation, however, is the question whether Oberalp pass would have been used during the early medieval period – indeed today, the pass is regularly closed in the winter. Finally, from the Lukmanier Pass (*e.g.* Blenio to Disentis), a well-used pass during the early and later medieval periods, the monastery is only visible from 2 kilometres.

The history and archaeology of Disentis abbey is less exact and has had less exploration in comparison to Saint Maurice and the convent of St John in Müstair. Indeed, we do not know whether there was a pre-existing settlement at Disentis prior to the foundation of the monastery. Furthermore, its foundation date remains difficult to pinpoint. One account alleges the monastery was established *c.* AD 720 after the martyrdom of two local ascetics, Sigisbert and Placidus, by Victor of Chur in the late seventh century (Kaiser 1998, 48). Another account alleges the monastery was established by Saint Pirmin with the support of Charles Martel in AD 711 (Jerris 2002, 99-100). Despite the conflicting accounts, the well-studied Will of Tello corroborates the existence of Disentis Abbey in AD 765 (Jerris 2002, 100; Sennhauser 2008, 45; Bielmann 2014, 129). While the abbey fell into disarray after its destruction in AD 940 by raiding Saracens, it was shortly rebuilt by Ottoman rulers. Sennhauser (2008, 45-46) argues that the reason for the abbey's reconstruction was in order to better safeguard the Lukmanier Pass. Indeed, the monks of Disentis Abbey became known 'Guardians of the Lukmanier Pass' and the site became a major hospice for Ottoman rulers, including Otto I (912-973), Henry II (972-1024), and Emperor Frederick I (1122-1190) travelling to Italy (Schönbachler 2010).

Excavations between 1980 and 1983 suggest that two triple-apse churches (Saint Mary and Saint Martin) once stood in the area of the present-day abbey courtyard and the Church of Saint Mary (Sennhauser 2002, 40). Dated to the eighth century, the majority of the data were linked to Saint Martin. Besides the apses, structural remains included a small tunnel leading to a small crypt, thought to house the relics of St Placidus, and parts of a wall with a small window. Remains of the second church (Saint Mary) were incorporated into the existing church (Sennhauser 2002, 40). A small chapel lay between the two larger churches and thus connecting them in one large complex (Sennhauser 2002, 40).

While determining whether people were able to gain access to these sacred spaces or whether the community was closed to the public, some artefacts might suggest the monastery welcomed pilgrims – notably moulds of people praying and copies of the relic (the foot), which may have served as 'pilgrim tokens' for visitors. These moulds, however,

*Figure 39: Interior of the current abbey of Disentis (image by Peter Berger 2006).*

have not been precisely dated. Based on the historic and archaeological evidence, we can at least make note of the monastery's regular patronage up to the destruction by the Saracens in the tenth century and thereafter (Schönbachler 2010). Indeed, today the abbey stands as one of the most wealthy and successful Benedictine communities in Switzerland, evident its decoration, gold-leaf altars, and reliquaries (Fig. 39).

### The Convent of St John, Müstair

The third case study is perhaps the most isolated and most difficult monastic community to visit – an opinion admittedly influenced by my visit to the community in the winter of 2012. From Chur, the small village is roughly a three-hour journey by automobile requiring the cross of not just one but three mountain passes. This is by no means the only route to the convent – a more direct route from east can be noted if one travelled along the Venosta Valley and then turned westward into Müstair Valley. In terms of visibility, the convent can only be seen from a distance of roughly one to two kilometres – despite its tower – from both the east and west due to the hilly nature of the landscape. There are two passes associated with the monastery: the Fuorn Pass (Zernez-Val Müstair; 2149m) and the Umbrail Pass (Val Müstair-Bormio; 2501m), with only evidence that the Fuorn Pass was used during the Roman and Medieval periods (Bundi 2015). This observation thus suggests the community was only accessible by the east and west. In any case, my own perception of the monastic community as an isolated community was mirrored when I spoke with Sub-Deaconess Dominica of the convent, who believed the monastery survived the Reformation due to its location. The Sub-Deaconess, however, noted that the monastery has begun to receive more visitors since its listing as a World Heritage Site in 1988 and its part in the pilgrimage to Santiago (now a stop on the Jakobsweg/St James Way).

So while we can observe how the convent acts today as a point of pilgrimage and tourism, thus attracting people to its otherwise isolated location, what of its early medieval past? Of the three sites, the monastery was built without a martyr or an ascetic to act as a reason for its foundation. Indeed, the local history alleges Charlemagne directed the bishop of Chur to commission the monastery *c.* AD 780 as part of his 'Carolingian Renaissance' and a wave of building in the Alps which saw new monastic houses at Cazis, Mistail, Pfafers, and potentially the reason for the expansion noted at Disentis. Sennhauser (2008, 45) stresses the location of Müstair as one of strategic import: guarding not just a pass to Chur (the Fuorn Pass) but also a place to track movement to Italy from the Alps or from Italy to the Eastern parts of the Carolingian empire. Control over the Benedictine house was transferred to the bishopric of Chur in AD 881, perhaps allowing the bishopric to better control the strategic location of the monastery which connects eastern kingdoms to not just Frankish territories but also the Italian Peninsula. The importance of the monastery's location can be noted during the Swabian War (1499), when the Habsburgs attempted to gain control of the Grisons and key alpine passes by occupying the valley surrounding the convent. This event resulted in the plundering of the convent and the loss of its library (Sennhauser 1996, 43-44). While this event occurred during the late 15th century, it certainly supports the observation that the monastery occupied a strategic location.

Archaeologically, we are fortunate that much of the monastery has been excavated. The results are not only a wealth of information on the early medieval community's ancillary buildings, including farmhouses, kitchens, and a cloister but also a strong understanding of the various buildings phases of the principal church. The early medieval structure comprised a large triple apsed central church with two side chapels as well as a large courtyard with structures around it. Some debate continues whether the Chapel of the Holy Cross dates to the ninth century or the eleventh-century (Sennhauser 1996, 54). Another problem relates to access – was the entire complex walled or was there a space between the main church-cloister complex and the barns/stables to the west? We know in successive years the monastery became fortified, including a tower known as the Planta during the Swabian war (Sennhauser 1996, 45-46). While the monastery does not boast as much wealth as the abbey of Saint Maurice and Disentis abbey, the museum housed at the convent today tells a different story. Surviving Carolingian, Romanesque, and Baroque styled art and sculpture outline a story of consistent visitors and support from patrons to allow the creation of such displays. Signs of pilgrims, including pilgrim flutes and signed registers, indicate that people did visit the site throughout the medieval period. Another intriguing aspect of Müstair is how the interior and exterior of the main church has remained relatively unchanged since its first construction.

## Viewshed Analysis and Results

Building upon the observations made by personal visits as well as the archaeological evidence, this section examines the results of viewshed analyses used to explore the visibility from the monasteries. This particular methodology questions the visibility of a site within the landscape by using elevation data within ArcGIS software. Essentially, to create a viewshed, each cell between the viewpoint cell and target cell is examined for line of sight. If a cell has a higher value between the viewpoint and the target, it means that the line of sight is blocked. Thus those particular cells are not part of the viewshed (Wheatley and Gillings 2002, 180-184). While the primary aim is to explore visibility, many archaeologists have used resultant viewsheds to explore elements of site choice in terms of defensibility, control, and connectivity (Jones 2006, 523; Zamora 2011, 619). Considering the observation by archaeologists and historians alike regarding the 'strategic' location of the monasteries, I similarly question whether the resultant viewsheds reveal elements of control and connectivity, examining possible other factors to site choice.

However, as observed by many authors (Wheatley and Gillings 2002; Zamora 2011) viewshed analyses produce rather simplistic results unless certain steps are taken. The principal problem relates to the height of the viewer. If an offset is not added, the analysis uses the level of the ground as the height of the two viewing points (Offset A and B). I followed Zamora's example regarding offsets to produce a total viewshed of the sites in order to determine whether the monasteries are indeed located in a strategic or dominant position:

- Offset A= 1.5m
- Offset B= 1.5m

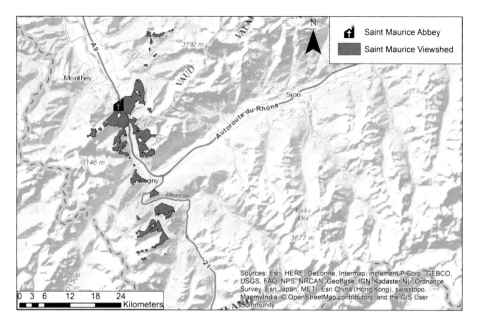

*Figure 40: Abbey of Saint-Maurice viewshed results (Image by author).*

The geographical data (geodata) utilised here were obtained from the Swiss Federal Office of Topography (SwissTopo). This includes the free 30-metre resolution digital elevation model, the Swiss rivers and lake shapefiles, and the boundaries. The analyses performed here do not utilise an algorithm to take other variables, such as vegetation, account due to access to those resources. Despite this, the results offer initial observations regarding site choice with later discussion on how the analyses can be improved in the future.

The first analyses were performed on the monastery of Saint Maurice (Fig. 40). Based on these results, the abbey would only be able to monitor movement from the south and east. This offers considerable visibility of the Roman road and river but the abbey would not be able to monitor traffic from the northwest until it passed within 1km of the abbey. Interestingly, despite its close proximity, Martigny would not have been visible from the abbey – again on account of the landscape rather than distance. The question, thus, remains whether Saint Maurice Abbey was located in the best spot to be able to view traffic as suggested by Sennhauser and Antonini.

The results on the viewshed analysis of Disentis also offered some remarkable data (Fig. 41). Despite its location on a hill, the abbey is able to view access from both the west and the south – again affirming my own observations based on site visits. The monastery is also visible from a few settlements, including Trun, Brigels, and Ruschein and logically, from higher elevation points. The results for Müstair were the most surprising – the abbey is the only site that could view access from multiple directions as well as parts of the neighbouring valley and a number of highpoints around the valley (Fig. 42).

Based on these results I argue that Müstair and St Maurice occupied the more visible locations contrasting the relatively invisible site of Disentis. In some respects, this makes sense. Both St Maurice abbey and the monastery at Müstair have ties to

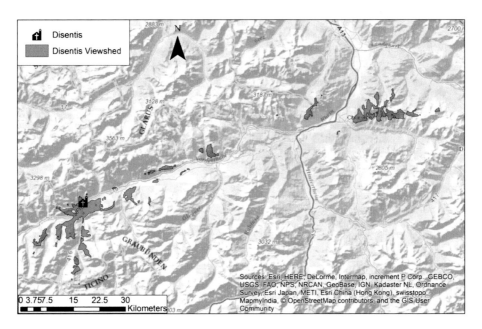

*Figure 41: Disentis Abbey viewshed results (Image by author).*

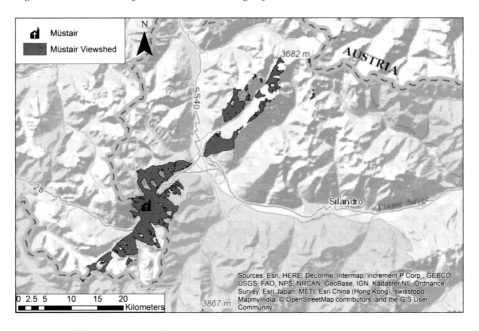

*Figure 42: Abbey of St John, Müstair viewshed results.*

royal patronage – King Sigismund in the sixth century and possibly Charlemagne with Müstair. Rosenwein and Sennhauser both comment that the location of these monasteries may have been strategically placed to keep an eye on foot traffic heading to different passes. While for St Maurice, its location near a road supports Rosenwein's idea, Müstair's relatively less known valley and access make it perhaps more difficult to

| DEBATING RELIGIOUS SPACE AND PLACE IN THE EARLY MEDIEVAL WORLD (C. AD 300-1000)

perceive the zone as a major hub of traffic, and thus I question the idea that the abbey was set up by a monarch to monitor movement.

So what is the significance behind these tests? It was already outlined that ArcGIS performs tests on models and do not truly represent reality. However, this question based approach allows us to analyse descriptions of monastic sites as 'strategically' placed communities in a manner that attempts to focus on variables such as slope and access. It also allows us to analyse the question on whether these monasteries were trying to emulate the 'desert' ideal of asceticism. In the three cases presented, the analyses demonstrated how the monasteries at Mustair and Saint-Maurice were visible in contrast to the relatively invisible Disentis while at the same time noting the nuances behind this 'visibliity'. Furthermore, this study adds to discussions of site choice and networks, a consistent theme within studies of early medieval monasticism. The medieval conference at Kalamazoo in 2016, for example, featured a session dedicated to evaluating monastic networks entitled 'Visualizing Medieval Connections: Network Analysis and Digital Mapping.

## Conclusion

This research has explored the question of visibility with respect to the monastic sites at St Maurice, Mustair, and Disentis – all based in the Alpine regions of Switzerland, a seemingly 'remote' place. While the visibility analyses performed with ArcGIS has suggested visibility would have been visible in some directions (Disentis and St Maurice) or in all directions (Mustair), visiting the sites as well as considering the sites historical context allow for more nuanced answesr to questions such as their attempt to follow a monastic ideal or their seemingly 'strategic' location as described by Rosenwein, Sennhauser and Antonini. For example, the monastery of Saint Maurice undoubtedly had more foreign visitors and pilgrims and was more visible to both local and foreign people based on its location on a road. We know this monastery had pilgrims based on its design (see Antonini in this volume on this subject) and for its relics. While the viewshed analysis denoted that it may not have been visible from the north, the through traffic of travellers heading either north or south would have led them right by the abbey. In contrast, the answers are less clear with respect to the the monastic sites found at Müstair or Disentis. While we can presume these sites known by locals, what about non-locals – *e.g.* people from neighbouring regions? Neither of these sites are located next to a key road. Whereas Disentis perhaps had the most isolated spot with the least visibility and Müstair had the most visibility, it all depends on how much traffic these places would have seen in the first place.

Finally, as with all spatial models, there are limitations. As discussed above, the quality of the results of a viewshed analysis depends greatly on the quality of the data. In the case here, including further data, including vegetation, could increase the quality of the results – perhaps even change the conclusions. For example, if the monasteries were surrounded by tall trees, the monasteries would not be visible from afar. Another variable, weather, could also impact visibility. Indeed, snow could make it difficult to view if the walls of the monasteries were white or determine access if perhaps the routes are closed based on snow accumulation. Further work on how we obtain this data would be needed to produce a more robust model.

In terms of actual access to the sites, all three had relatively open access, especially considering the wealth and the archaeological data supporting signs of pilgrims. Further analysis will be needed to establish exactly how monastic space was accessed and which zones within the complexes were considered private or closed. We can also bring weather into the question of access – winter weather and closed mountain passes today close off access to some of these sites; should we not expect similar phenomena to result in similar reactions?

While not the central focus of this paper, another observation I would like to make is the continuity of monastic space and place. In all three examples, the monastic communities are still active and still maintain the same structures or at least the same principle territory (*e.g.* the church and the surrounding courtyard). Indeed, many of Switzerland's monastic communities continue to this day or their structures continue as a church. While many of the papers in this volume have discussed aspects of continuity of space and place in terms of change from one religion to another, in terms of Christianisation and Islamisation, I believe another aspect of continuity of place relates to the idea of place-attachment theory, the ability of people to emotionally connect to a place. While the monasteries undoubtedly managed to thrive during the medieval period, denoted by their continued growth and wealth in some cases, the modern period is another case. In Switzerland, where tradition runs extremely strong in the Alpine and pre-Alpine regions, the local populations and their attachment to their places they view as culturally significant may explain why these communities are still present.

## Acknowledgements

Many thanks to Dr Douglas Mitcham and Dr Louise Rayne at the University of Leicester for suggestions and feedback on the ideas presented in this paper.

## Bibliography

*Primary Sources*

Anonymous. *The Life of the Jura Fathers: The Life and Rule of the Holy Fathers Romanus, Lupicinus, and Eugendus, Abbots of the Monasteries in the Jura Mountains* (Cistercian 274 Studies Series, 178). Translated by T. Vivian, K.Vivian, and J.B. Russell. Kalamazoo: Cistercian Publications, 1999.

Avitus of Vienne. *Avitus of Vienne: Letters and Selected Prose (Translated Texts for Historians 38)*. Translated by D. Shanzer, and I.N. Wood. Liverpool: Liverpool University Press, 2002.

Emily Dickinson. *Poems: The Originals*. Edited by M. Loomis Todd and T.W. Higginson. Raleigh: Hayes Barton Press, 2007.

Eucherius. *Passio Acaunensium Martyrum (Monumenta Germaniae Historica Scriptores Rerum Merovingicarum* 3). Edited by B. Krusch. Hannover: Impensis Bibliopolii Hahniani, 1896.

Gregory of Tours. *Glory of the Martyrs (Translated Texts for Historians 4)*. Translated by R. Van Dam. Liverpool: Liverpool University Press, 1988.

John de Bremble. *Gaufrido Suppriori Frater Johannes (Chronicles and memorials of the reign of Richard I. Volume II. Epistolæ Cantuariensis. The Letters of the Prior and Convent of Christ Church, Canterbury. A.D. 1187 to A.D. 1199)*. Edited by W. Stubbs. Cambridge: Cambridge University Press, 2012.

Sulpicius Severus. *Life of St. Martin*. Translated by A. Roberts. New York: Cosimo Inc, 1894.

## Secondary Sources

Ashmore, W. 2002. "Decisions and dispositions": Socialising spatial archaeology (Archaeology Division Distinguished Lecture, 99th AAA Annual Meeting, San Francisco, CA, November 2000). *American Anthropologist* 104/4, 1172-1183.

Bielmann, C. 2014. *A Christianisation of Switzerland? Urban and Rural Transformations in a Time of Transition – AD 300-800*. Unpublished Thesis, University of Leicester.

Bundi, M. 2015. *Ofenpass (Historisches Lexikon der Schweiz)*. *http://www.hls-dhs-dss.ch/textes/d/D8827.php* (accessed 5 May 2016).

Cassidy-Welch, M. 2001. *Monastic Spaces and their Meanings: Thirteenth-Century English Cistercian Monasteries*. Leiden: Brepols.

De Certeau, M. 1984. *The Practice of Everyday Life* (Translated by S. Rendall). Berkeley and Los Angeles: University of California Press.

Dupont Lachenal, L. 1947. L'ambon et quelques débris sculptés de St-Maurice. *Annales Valaisannes* 22, 319-340.

Eve, S.J. and Crema, E.R. 2013. A house with a view? Multi-model inference, visibility fields, and point process analysis of a Bronze Age settlement on Leskernick Hill. *Journal of Archaeological Sciences* 43, 267-277.

Jerris, R. 2002. Cult lines and hellish mountains: the development of sacred landscape in the early medieval Alps. *Journal of Medieval and Early Modern Studies* 32, 85-108.

Jones, E.E. 2006. Using viewshed analysis to explore settlement choice: a case study of the Onondaga Iroquois. *American Antiquity* 71/3, 523-538.

Kaiser, R. 1998. *Churrätien im frühen Mittelalter: Ende 5. bis Mitte 10. Jahrhundert*. Basel: Scwabe.

Lawrence, C.H. 1984. *Medieval Monasticism: Forms of Religious in Western Europe in the Middle Ages*. London: Routledge/Taylor & Francis.

Lefebvre, H. 1991. *The Production of Space* (Translated by D. Nicholson-Smith). Oxford: Blackwell.

Mazumdar, S. and Mazumdar S. 2004. Religion and place attachment: a study of sacred places. *Journal of Environmental Psychology* 24/3: 385-397.

Patrich, J. 2004. Monastic landscapes, in: Bowden, W., Lavan, L., and Machado, C. (eds). *Recent Research in the Late Antique Countryside (Late Antique Archaeology 2)*. Leiden: Brill, 413-446.

Pauli, L. 1984. *The Alps: Archaeology and Early History* (Translated by Eric Peters). London: Thames and Hudson.

Rosenwein, B.H. and Little, L.K. (eds). 1998. *Debating the Middle Ages: Issues and Readings*. Oxford: Wiley-Blackwell.

Rosenwein, B.H. 2001. One site, many meanings: Saint-Maurice d'Agaune as a place of power in the early medieval ages, in: Theuws, F., De Jong, M.B., and Van Rhijn, C. (eds). *Topographies of Power in the Early Middle Ages*. Leiden: Brill, 271-290.

Schönbachler, D. 2010. *Disentis (Historisches Lexikon der Schweiz). http://www.hls-dhs-dss.ch/textes/d/D11490.php* (accessed: 06 Feb 2016).

Sennhauser, H.R. 1996. *Müstair: Kloster St. Johann (2 Vols).* Zürich: Hochschulverlag.

Sennhauser, H.R. 2002. Cathédrales et églises abbatiales carolingiennes en Suisse. *Hortius Artium Medievalium* 8, 33-48.

Sennhauser, H.R. 2008. Monasteri del primo millennio nelle Alpi Svizzere, in: De Rubeis, F. (ed.), *Monasteri in Europa occidentale (secoli VIII – XI): topografia e strutture.* Rome: Viella, 43-65.

Stump, R.W. 2008. *The Geography of Religion: Faith, Place, and Space.* Lanham (Maryland, US): Rowman & Littlefield Publishers, Inc.

Vischer L., Schenker, L., Dellsperger, R. and Fatio, O. 1995. *Histoire du christianisme en Suisse: une perspective oecuménique.* Geneva: Labor et Fides.

Wheatley, D. and Gillings, M. 2002. *Spatial Technology and Archaeology: the archaeological applications of GIS.* London: Taylor & Francis.

Woods, D. 1994. The origin of the cult of St. Maurice. *Journal of Ecclesiastical History* 45, 385-395.

Zamora, M. 2011. Improving methods for viewshed studies in archaeology: the vertical angle, in: Jerem, E., Redő, F. and Szeverényi, V. (eds). *On the Road to Reconstructing the Past. Computer Applications and Quantitative Methods in Archaeology (CAA)* (Proceedings of the 36th International Conference. Budapest, April 2-6, 2008). Budapest: Archeaeolingua, 614-622.

# Sacred Ground

## Community and Separation in a Norse Churchyard, Greenland

*Jess Angus McCullough*

## Introduction

The Norse settled Greenland in approximately AD 985. Written sources unanimously credit Eirik the Red as the leader of the first successful colonization, who famously named the ice-covered island "Greenland" to attract more settlers (*Eirik the Red's Saga* 2, *Saga of the Greenlanders* 1, *Book of Settlements* 89). As in Iceland a century earlier, the Norse settlers arrived in a land that was empty of indigenous people, bringing a distinctly Norse way of life not in conflict with or influenced by local traditions. At the end of the tenth century, Iceland's socio-religious atmosphere was turbulent, with aggressive and sometimes violent Christian missionaries (with Norwegian backing) disrupting assemblies and bringing Iceland to the brink of sectarian conflict (Jochens 1999, 643-649; Vésteinsson 2000, 17; Byock 2001, 300). The sagas describe a settlement community of pagans, with only a few specific Christians mentioned, though the archaeological evidence demonstrates that Christianity was practiced in Greenland from the first generation of its settlement at the turn of the tenth century to the mid-fifteenth when the settlements were abandoned. While the causes of this abandonment were the primary concern of the first archaeological studies of Greenland, there exists no evidence to suggest that it was in any way catastrophic (Lynnerup 1998, 112-119; Madsen 2014, 255).

The first excavations of Norse Greenland were carried out by Lutheran missionary Hans Egede in 1721, who investigated several sites in the Eastern and Western settlements in search for the descendants of the lost Norse colonies (Fig. 43). There were some furtive antiquarian and exploratory investigations conducted over the next hundred years, but Greenland archaeology did not begin in earnest until the late-nineteenth century with Daniel Bruun's expeditions on behalf of the National Museum of Denmark (Bruun 2009, 1896). The next generation of archaeologists including Poul Nørlund and Aage Roussell were reconstructivists and rarely questioned saga-accounts

in: Bielmann, C. and Thomas, B. (eds.) 2018: *Debating Religious Space and Place in the Early Medieval World (c. AD 300-1000)*, Sidestone Press (Leiden), pp. 175-186.

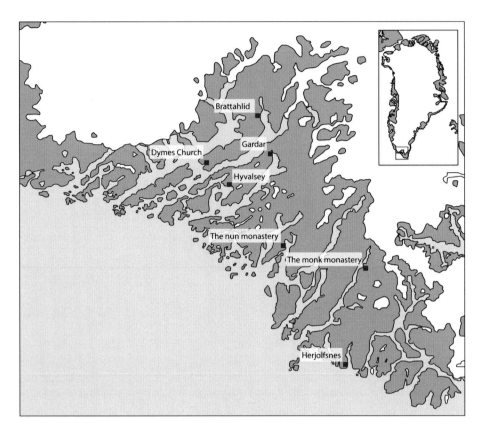

*Figure 43: The Eastern Settlement of Norse Greenland. Herjolfsnes is the southernmost church in the settlement (Map redrawn after Masae, distributed by Wikimedia Commons).*

of the settlements history. They were also responsible for conducting the largest and most comprehensive excavations to date in the decades leading up to the Second World War (Nørlund *et al.* 1930; Roussell 1936, Roussell and Degerbøl 1941; Nørlund 1971, 1924; Nørlund and Stenberger 2010). Following the war, archaeology in Green was less robust until the rise of environmental archaeology and Greenland's value in studying ecodynamics was recognized (McGovern 1981, 1985). These concerns dominated the field until a renewed interest in society and identity arrived in the 1990s and 2000s (Keller 1989; Arneborg 1998; Abrams 2009; Gräslund 2009).

Considering this brief overview of past archaeological investigations in Greenland, it is unsurprising that recent developments in the methods and theories of conversion studies have yet to be applied to Greenland comprehensively. The burials at Herjolfsnes have yet to be thoroughly examined for what they can tell us about the beliefs and practices surrounding burial in Greenland. This chapter is intended as a step in the direction of what the burials meant in a cultural context as opposed to a materialist analysis of the artefacts themselves. Was there a pattern in who was buried where? What does the use and reuse of coffins mean? What sorts of ritual practice is visible in the material record? The materials were excavated nearly 100 years ago, but such questions remain to be answered. The archaeological evidence tells a different story than the saga narrative about Greenland's acceptance of Christianity

(Abrams 2009, 55). We are told that Leif Eriksson brought Christian missionaries to Greenland at the behest of King Olaf Trygvasson, but Christian burials of individuals from the first generation of Norse settlement illustrate that there were at least some observing Christians active the settlement's earliest period (Arneborg *et al.* 2012, 13). Churches were built throughout the Eastern Settlement and likely operated in the same fashion as the proprietary system Iceland, where individual landowners built, maintained, and even officiated at the churches on their farms (Keller 1989, 132; Byock 2001, 297-301). In 1126 Greenland received its first bishop, who established his see at Garðar in the center of the Eastern Settlement. Thereafter churches were built in stone and according to recognizable European design. In total, 21 church remains have been discovered in Greenland, though it is possible that others have been lost to erosion or other taphonomical concerns.

The greater context in which Greenlandic churches must be understood is that of the medieval perception of the world and its organization. Greenland (and later L'Anse Aux Meadows on Labrador) was, culturally and politically, the westernmost outpost of European convention. The Norse settled in Greenland in the green interiors of the southern fjords. These inhabitable areas were (and are) surrounded by regions of rugged mountains and glacial ice, and clearly demarcated the physical boundaries within which the European way of life was viable. The Norse settlements of Greenland were cultural pockets of Europe nestled in a harsh and unforgiving environment. If the cultural practices of the Norse – agriculture, architecture, social and political organization, etc. – existed as a 'layer' in this naturally geographically defined area, the context of European Christendom existed as another. Christendom was made up of the places where Christians were. In the east, this traditional boundary existed in the Middle East where control of the Holy Land was contested militarily with practitioners of another Abrahamic religion – Islam – during the Crusades. In the west, there was no competing political power fighting for the symbolic centre of Judeo-Christianity, only endless wilderness populated by unfamiliar peoples. The Greenlanders existed at the edge of their geographical and spiritual spheres of influence – a 'geoconceptually' marginal space. This paper will assess the ways in which awareness of this marginality played out in the burials at E-111 Herjolfsnes.

## Church Burials

Site E-111, Herjolfsnes, is one of the final Norse churches to be used and represents a picture of the island's last stage of Norse Christianity. This fact establishes a terminus which, by comparison with other sites, demonstrates what earlier practices had been abandoned, were still in use, or were adopted by the end of the settlement. The site was established in the final decades of the tenth century. This southernmost church was built on a farm site that appears to have been selected for visual prominence and access to a natural harbor rather than for prime pasture land, located further inland. The visible church ruin on the site dates to the twelfth century, and is possibly not the first church on the site. The site was thoroughly investigated by Poul Nørlund in 1921 (Nørlund 1924) (Fig. 44).

Within the church itself are two inhumations that raise numerous questions. Nørlund's excavation of the church graves revealed only the 'faintest reminiscences

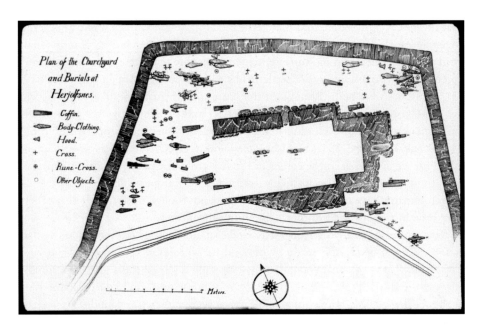

Figure 44: Plan of the Churchyard and Burials at Herjolfsnes as seen in Nørlund 1924.
Stratigraphical lines at the bottom denote erosion by the sea (Courtesy of Dartmouth College Library).

of bodies', and neither have thus far been radiocarbon dated. The first of these burials closest to the altar contains a bear tooth which has been worked in a way that suggests it was worn on the body as a pendent or perhaps amulet (Nørlund 1924, 68; Roussell 1941, 123). A similar artefact has been recovered from the tenth-century farm at E-17a Narsaq, and a possible bear amulet was excavated at W-51 Sandnes (Vebæk 1993, 32). Examples outside Greenland include bear tooth amulets from the pagan burial complex at Birka and the Brough of Birsay – the latter etched with the runic *futhark* (Gräslund 1969, 166-169; Curle 1982, 59). The significance of the bear tooth amulets may be tied to Eirik the Red as the *Floamanna saga* describes the famous Viking as part of a bear cult. The historicity of the saga is negligible (*The Saga of the People of Floi* 25, Perkins 1971). Very few Greenlandic graves contain any manner of adornment at all – those that do are almost exclusively with Christianity associated items (Lynnerup 1998, 59-60). The presence of a bear tooth need not signify a pre-Christian cult, but its associations are worth noting.

Approximately 1.5m west of the bear tooth burial, a grave was excavated which contained the wooden pommel of a knife (with owners mark) and a whale bone and pine oval box of the type used by the Inuit people of the time. The box was filled with animal tissue and blood, leading Nørlund to conclude that the box must have contained 'food for the dead person' (Nørlund 1924, 68, 225). While pre-Christian Norse burials have contained foodstuffs and the implements for preparing them, there have been no other incidences of such goods being interred in Greenland. It is possible that the box represents contact with the Inuit, perhaps even an acknowledgment of Inuit concern for the treatment of the deceased or some manner of diplomacy. The prominence of the grave's placement suggests that in life the occupant was a person of importance – and the presence of the box indicates a flexibility of practice or individual expression on the part of those who conducted the burial, whatever it may mean.

At the waist of the individual a wooden knife pommel was found, perhaps worn on a belt. No other part of the knife remains, though this is the only indication of a person being buried with a weapon in Greenland. The pommel, however, is etched with a design interpreted as an owner's mark. It is also feasible that the part of the knife symbolizing ownership was interred, and that the rest of the tool was kept by a survivor.

The term 'grave good' has been thoroughly re-evaluated in recent years, especially as regards the relation of said goods to the religious identity or identities being represented in the burial (Price 2010, 131). The presence of artefacts in any grave is deliberate and carries meaning. The meanings of the whalebone box, the knife pommel, and the bear tooth pendant may be difficult to determine, but as there is a marked absence of potentially non-Christian grave goods in Greenland, it is extraordinary that these examples reminiscent of pre-Christian practice are within the church.

Based on their placement and condition, it is possible that the graves in the church are among the oldest that survive at the site, perhaps as early as the first phase of the church in the mid-1100s. Norse paganism continued in parts of Scandinavia well into the twelfth century and that could be the case in Greenland as well. Inclusion within the church could indicate an enmeshment of social and spiritual conventions, such as a pagan member of a Christian community being shown the deference that was proper for their individual attitudes and the values of the community, as one of many possibilities.

The analysis of grave goods has until recently focused on what the goods say about the individual they accompany. It is more useful to assess them as representative of the forces at work in the world of the living, be these forces a cosmological belief structure, a sense of communal identity, or political or social performance. Rather than use the items buried with an individual to mark the ascendancy of one cosmology over another, they should be used to study the interplay between them. At the least these burials demonstrate variation in Greenlandic church burials. The presence of these items and their unique natures make it highly likely that the individuals interred within the church were seen as separate in some sense from those buried outside and without goods. Their bodies were interred with items of significance. To whom they were significant and why must for now remain a mystery.

## The Churchyard

The most famous finds from Herjolfsnes are the numerous well-preserved garments recovered from the churchyard. Some individuals were buried wearing their garments; others were buried shrouded in them. The garments themselves show signs of heavy wear and use, suggesting that the clothing selected for burial was chosen based on its physical state – heavily worn clothing was suitable for burial, presumably to make further use of the clothes in better condition (Nørlund 1924, 90).

Coffin use in Greenland has been assessed as high-status burial due to the sparsity of wood available in Greenland, a view supported by the variety of coffins used – some with no floor, some built onto one another to make double use of the valuable planks, even some made with repurposed boards (Nørlund 1924, 72; Lynnerup 1998, 60).

This functionalist interpretation may be an appropriate assessment in some cases, but evidence also suggests a desire to establish an individual space for the dead in the churchyard. The bottomless coffin, for instance, does not so much contain the body for transport as it separates the body's space in the earth, not from the bottom or the surface, but defining its location within the burial 'plane'. Attaching three walls of another coffin to a coffin already in the ground makes use of precious lumber, but it also relates the occupant of one to another, perhaps symbolizing a relation of the two in life or in death.

## Coffin 30

The most complex and involved burial at Herjolfsnes is that which occurred in Coffin 30 just outside the north wall of the church (Fig. 58). In the grave was a sturdy, lidless coffin (though Nørlund describes nail holes which indicated a lid was present initially) with interior dimensions of 1.615m in length and 43cm across at the top, narrowing to 31cm at the foot. A cross was etched on the coffin floor, 'in the bottom at the place of the breast' (Nørlund 1924, 83). Contained in the coffin were the remains of at least one individual, though remains were so thoroughly decomposed that only patches of a 'waxy substance' (likely adipocere) remained. These two patches were discovered near where the head and hips of the individual would have lain, prompting Nørlund (who believed the adipocere to be the remnants of brain material) to declare that the head of the second body lay near the hips of the first (Nørlund 1924, 61-63, 82-86). Such burials are not uncommon in Greenland, including multiple 'family burials' with apparent mothers and children interred together. Lynnerup has pointed out that such deposits can be formed from subcutaneous fat as well, and as such both patches in Coffin 30 may be from the same individual (Lynnerup 1998, 59).

Even if there was only one physical body in the coffin at the time of interment, the grave also belongs to another individual. Found in the corner of the coffin was a rune stick with the following inscription: 'This woman was laid overboard in the Greenland Sea, who was named Gudveg'. Gudveg thus is not the person whose body decomposed in Coffin 30, but her memorial was interred in the churchyard all the same.

Following the deposition of the coffins, the grave was sealed by the placement of a 1.5 tonne boulder atop the grave which was massive, unadorned, and unlikely to be a monument. Nørlund viewed this as a precaution against revenants – a belief which is widely attested to in Norse literature and archaeology as well. Nørlund's interpretation was based on the placement of the boulder itself, but a number of other factors support the theory that members of the community were concerned about the restless dead in Coffin 30 (Nørlund 1924, 63).

First, if the second adipocere deposit was brain matter, it was near the pelvic region of the body. Severing the head and placing it between the legs of a corpse has been attested to in medieval literature and archaeology as a way to silence revenants and their cultural-specific incarnation *draugr* (*The Saga of Grettir the Strong* 35; Klevnäs 2010, 169). The adipocere deposits suggest that a head decomposed still attached to its body, however, raising the question of whose head was resting at the pelvic level if indeed this is the case. As Gudveg's rune stick demonstrates, the coffin did hold – at least at a symbolic level – multiple individuals.

Second, the cross carved 'below the breast' upon the floor of the coffin is reminiscent of other robbed and disturbed medieval graves in England and Europe. Klevnäs documents a number of crosses deliberately left in older burial mounds as a means of either protecting the thieves from the vengeful dead or as a way of Christianising a previously pagan monument (Klevnäs 2010, 54).

Third, Gudveg's rune stick commemorating a woman buried at sea also calls to mind numerous examples in Norse literature and folklore connecting the *draugr* to water and drowning. Numerous drowned sailors and travellers are described in *Eyrbyggja saga* for instance (*The Saga of the People of the Eyri* 53, 54).

In Norway, folklorists like Jonas Lie collected the folk tales of the people of Halogaland during the renaissance of folklore in the 1800s wherein the *draug* – now in the form of a seaweed-covered sailor – terrorized coastal towns (Lie 1893, 1-20). *Draugr* became increasingly associated with the sea from the Middle Ages onward. Gudveg's bodily absence from the coffin and subsequent burial *in absentia* may have caused anxiety about her physical and spiritual repose among the community, prompting them to take precautions against her restlessness.

### Devotional Crosses

While only three crosses are associated with skeletal material, 58 crosses of varying quality and design have been recovered from the cemetery, suggesting that they too were buried with the dead. Burial with devotional crosses is of particular interest because it is a practice that only seems widely practiced at Herjolfsnes. The devotional crosses are, in most cases, spiked at the bottom, suggesting that they were made to be planted in the ground and prayed before or otherwise incorporated into Christian rituals. It is tempting to assign the crosses to individuals of greater or lesser prominence based on the quality and workmanship of them individually, but this cannot be said for certain and in fact may be assigning an inappropriate definition of value to these artefacts. What can be said about them is that they were deemed appropriate for inclusion in the churchyard, most likely in a funerary context, and were not deemed so valuable that they were removed as the settlement was deserted.

It is likely that the crosses were possessions of individuals or at least assigned to individuals after death. This practice is not evident in any other Greenlandic cemetery thus excavated, with the exception of a single wooden cross interred with a group burial at V-51 Sandnes and several fragments found throughout that farm (Roussell and Degerbøl 1941, 17-18). Similar crosses were also excavated from the Farm beneath the Sand in the Western Settlement (Berglund 1998, 48). The lateness of the burials at Herjolfsnes and the absence of crosses from elsewhere in Greenland may indicate that the use of devotional crosses was a part of a later phase of Greenlandic Christianity. Nørlund states that crosses such as these have clearer parallels in northern France than Scandinavia, though intriguingly very similar crosses were recovered from the ninth-tenth century establishment phase layer of the farm at Toftanes in the Faroe Islands (Nørlund 1924, 64-65; Stummann Hansen *et al.* 2013, 120-123).

## Multiple Burials and Child-graves

Burial in groups is seen at multiple sites in a number of ways. Mass graves, for instance, occur at a number of early sites such as E-29a Brattahlíð I and E-48 Igaliku. At Herjolfsnes, there are several instances of coffins being reused for subsequent interments. One grim discovery noted by Nørlund at the churchyard at Garðar was a coffin containing two skeletons, one of which had been dismembered to make room for another body while the soft tissues had still held the bones together (Nørlund *et al.* 1930, 64). A similar practice seen at Herjolfsnes is the construction of one coffin built against the side of an existing one. As stated, it has been suggested that this practice was to conserve wood, but if wood were in such short supply it is likely that those conducting the funeral would have foregone lumber altogether as is the case in many other graves in the churchyard. I propose that this manner of coffin construction was to associate the second burial with the first, perhaps as a family member or acquaintance of similar social status. The state of physical remains once interred was not of great importance in Medieval Christianity as God could reassemble the body at will (Robb and Harris 2013, 147). The mingling of and association of bodies is interesting as it combines the remains of two individuals while maintaining their separation from the rest of the churchyard.

In the widely excavated churchyards, the graves of children frequently accompany adults, such as the 'family grave' at Sandnes, though interestingly at Brattahlíð I, the earliest known churchyard, and Herjolfsnes, one of the last, we see evidence of burial clusters for subadults. In both cases these are at the western gable of the churches – a practice known in Scandinavia. The primary difference between the two clusters a slight lessening of definition at Herjolfsnes and a slightly older age-group; at Brattahlíð I foetal and neonatal remains were excavated in 1961, potentially reflective of the use of lay-baptism or an acceptance of the unbaptised into the churchyard (Lynnerup 1998, 62).

## Sacred Ground as a Concept and in Practice

Burial in Greenland represents an evolving perspective of 'holy ground' as a concept. As we see in Gudveg's coffin, the mere presence of a stick with her name on it in the ground itself speaks to the perceived importance of burial in sanctified ground, as opposed to earlier practices such as that of the Icelandic settler Aud the Deepminded (ca. AD 834-900), who according to *Landnamabok* 'was buried at the high water mark as she'd ordered, because having been baptized she didn't wish to lie in unconsecrated earth' (Palsson 2007, 56). Aud's desire to be washed away into the sea contrasts sharply with the precautionary measures seen in Gudveg's absentee grave. For Aud, a minority Christian in ninth-century Iceland, to be washed out to sea represented a sense of unity with the Christian conception of the world. It has been suggested that this belief stems from Zecharia 14:8: 'And it shall come to pass in that day, that living waters shall go out from Jerusalem: half of them to the east sea, and half of them to the last sea: they shall be in summer and in winter'. For Aud, the sea represents a connection to Jerusalem, the center of her spiritual world. For the people who carved and buried Gudveg's name, it represented the metaphorical other, and action was needed to include Gudveg among the community of deceased Christian faithful.

The earth within the churchyard became the safest place for the dead to wait for resurrection. Multiple written sources describe individuals going to great lengths to ensure this. Corpse-Lodin, for instance, is described as sailing to the remote regions in the north of Greenland to find the bodies of sailors and hunters and return them to the nearest church for Christian burial (Anon 1849, 59). Einar Sokkeson boiled down the bones of the victims of a shipwreck for the same purpose (Jones 1986, 239). Thorstein, son of Eirik the Red, died on a mission to collect his brother Thorvald's body from where it lay on the North American continent (*Saga of the Greenlanders* 5). Knud Krogh even wrote of accounts of Greenland Norse buried far from a church to be buried with a pole resting on their chest and sticking out of the ground so that the next visiting priest could pour holy water down onto the corpse and retroactively sanctify the earth (*Eirik the Red's Saga* 6; Krogh 1967, 29). In all of the sites excavated in Greenland, there have been only six cases of human remains found outside a churchyard, and these are fragmentary and not proper burials. 'Bundled' bones found at Brattahlíð I suggest that even deceased ancestors could be included in this Christian community of the dead. Such practices are well documented in other Norse contexts. Gorm the Old's reburial beneath the new Jelling church by Harald Bluetooth in the tenth century is a famous example. Odin-worshipping warrior-poet Egil Skallagrimsson was also reinterred by his children in Mosfell, Iceland (*Egil's Saga* 89; Byock 1993, 30). It is possible that the 'bundled' burials and mass grave at Brattahlíð I represent an inclusion of deceased pagans in a changing belief structure.

## Geoconceptual Marginality

Burial practices in Greenland are also reflective of a conceptual view of the physical and cultural worlds the Greenlanders inhabited, and not at odds with the prevailing views throughout Europe during the Middle Ages. To the Greenlanders and their European contemporaries, these worlds had a similar shape and their places in them were defined. This view is best exemplified by Isidore of Seville's T and O description of the earth.

Documentary evidence has shown that Church authorities had little idea where Greenland even was, and believed it to be populated with pygmies and green people, living in a part of the world so cold that people's noses would come off in the cold upon wiping (*History of the Archbishops of Hamburg-Bremen*: Appendix, Gad 1971, 62; Keller 1989, 52-59). Though geographical awareness of Greenland is not indicated on world maps until after the settlements were deserted, the limited documented contemporary knowledge consigns it to the margins of the world.

The one commonality of all burials in Greenland is a sense of enclosure within the protective boundary of churchyard, grave, or church itself. It appears that even as the Greenlanders were being described as noseless, green pygmies by their European counterparts throughout the five hundred years of settlement, they were keenly aware of their own perilous place at the edge of Christendom and the limits of the known physical world. A runestone found in the remote northern hunting grounds of Greenland demonstrates that the Greenlanders observed Rogation Day which frequently included the tradition of Beating the Bounds, where 'every country child would remember the boundary brooks and trees where he was dunked and bumped on Rogation day... which marked upon his own body the spatial limits of his world' (Camille 1992, 16).

To the Greenlanders, the churchyard was a bubble of centrality in the world's margins. This, more than anything, describes the Greenlanders sense of their place in this conceptual medieval world. Their concern for burial within a boundary of consecrated earth is evident. Within this conceptual line symbolized by the churchyard, delineation of one individual from another occurs only in a few specific ways such as burial inside the church, enclosed in a coffin or a shroud, or with a marker such as a cross or stone.

Even potentially 'problematic' burials in these cases are centrally placed. Child burials at Brattahlíð I and Herjolfsnes are buried at the gables. The boulder-capped Coffin 30 at Herjolfsnes is placed at the northeast intersection of the chancel and the nave. Burial in proximity to the church could symbolize much more than social stratification. This practice reflects a desire to bring the outside in, securing for the interred whatever spiritual benefit or protection the physical church itself could provide.

## Conclusions

The Greenlanders' sense of their place at the marginal edges of Christendom is reflected, consciously or unconsciously, in the manner and method of the Herjolfsnes burials.

Historian Robert Bartlett (1993, 174-175) writes:

> 'It is as if there were three concentric circles: one, our world, where there is no need for generalizing description because everything is taken for granted; the second, outer ring where the barbarians live, peoples whose strange customs prompt us to record them; the third, outermost ring where the principles of order dissolve and all our fears, fantasies, and projections become real.'

Greenland was clearly in Bartlett's second ring when it comes to European thought, and likely the thoughts of the European bishops sent to oversee the faith of the Greenlanders. This perception appears to have been present among the community that buried its dead at Herjolfsnes. To a Greenlander, to be buried within the churchyard was to await Christ's return as a part of their community. There was some room for variance of practice, but the primary concern was to remain within the bounds of the churchyard and by proxy within Christendom. Though to the west was a vast, mysterious land populated by what must have seemed strange races and hostile spiritual forces, the sacred boundary of the churchyard encircled a holy piece of earth, secure against the spiritual dangers of the massive empty expanses in every direction, and burial within this place was more important than the manner in which it occurred.

## Acknowledgments

The author is grateful to Dr Chantal Bielmann and Brittany Thomas for allowing me to present at the stimulating *Debating Religious Space and Place* conference at Leicester, Deirdre O'Sullivan and Dr Neil Christie for their encouragement and input, and Ms. Shannon Smith for her professional assistance in preparing this paper for publication.

## Bibliography

*Primary Sources*

Adam of Bremen. *History of the Archbishops of Hamburg-Bremen.* Translated by F. Tschan. New York: Columbia University Press, 1959.

*The Book of Settlements: Landnamabok.* Translated by H. Palsson. Winnipeg: University of Manitoba Press, 2007.

*Egil's Saga*, in: *The Complete Sagas of Icelanders: Including 49 Tales.* Translated by B. Scudder. Reykjavík: Leifur Eiríksson Publishing, 1997, 33-177.

*Eirik the Red's Saga*, in: *The Complete Sagas of Icelanders: Including 49 Tales.* Translated by K. Kunz. Reykjavík: Leifur Eiríksson Publishing, 1997, 1-18.

*The Saga of Grettir the Strong*, in: *The Complete Sagas of Icelanders: Including 49 Tales.* Translated by B. Scudder. Reykjavík: Leifur Eiríksson Publishing, 1997, 49-191.

*The Saga of the Greenlanders*, in: *The Complete Sagas of Icelanders: Including 49 Tales.* Translated by K. Kunz. Reykjavík: Leifur Eiríksson Publishing, 1997, 19-32.

*The Saga of the People of Floi*, in: *The Complete Sagas of Icelanders: Including 49 Tales.* Translated by P. Acker. Reykjavík: Leifur Eiríksson Publishing, 1997, 271-304.

*The Saga of the People of Eyri*, in: *The Complete Sagas of Icelanders: Including 49 Tales.* Translated by J. Quinn. Reykjavík: Leifur Eiríksson Publishing, 1997, 131-218.


*Secondary Sources*

Abrams, L. 2009. Early religious practice in the Greenland Settlement. *Journal of the North Atlantic* 2, 52-65.

Arneborg, J. 1998. *Man, Culture and Environment in Ancient Greenland: Report on a Research Programme.* Copenhagen: Danish National Museum & Danish Polar Center.

Arneborg, J., Lynnerup, N., Heinemeier, J., Møhl, J., Rud, N. and Sveinbjörnsdóttir, Á. 2012. Norse Greenland dietary economy ca. AD 980-ca. AD 1450: Introduction. *Journal of the North Atlantic*, Special Volume 3, 1-39.

Bartlett, R. 1994. *The Making of Europe: Conquest, Colonization, and Cultural Change, 950-1350.* Princeton, NJ: Princeton University Press.

Berglund, J. 1998. Christian symbols, in: Arneborg, J. and Gulløv, H. (eds). *Man, Culture, and Environment in Ancient Greenland. Report on a Research Programme.* Copenhagen: The Danish National Museum & Danish Polar Center, 48-54.

Bruun, D. 2009. *The Icelandic Colonization of Greenland and the Finding of Vineland.* Monographs on Greenland. Copenhagen: Museum Tusculanum Press.

Bruun, D. 1896. *Arkæologiske undersøgelser i Julianehaabs district.* Monographs on Greenland. Copenhagen: Museum Tusculanum Press.

Byock, J. 2001. *Viking Age Iceland.* New York: Penguin Books.

Byock, J. 1993. Skull and bones in Egil's Saga: a Viking, a grave, and Paget's Disease. *Viator: Medieval and Renaissance Studies* 24, 23-50.

Camille, M. 1992. *Image on the Edge: The Margins of Medieval Art.* London: Reaktion Books.

Curle, C.L. 1982. *Pictish and Norse Finds from the Brough of Birsay 1934-74.* Monograph series / Society of Antiquaries of Scotland. Edinburgh: Society of Antiquaries of Scotland.

Gad, F. 1971. *The History of Greenland.* Montreal: McGill-Queen's University Press.

Gräslund, A.-S. 2009. How did the Norsemen in Greenland see themselves? Some reflections on 'Viking identity'. *Journal of the North Atlantic* 2, 131-137.

Gräslund, A.-S. 1973. Barn i Birka. *Tor* 15, 161-179.

Charlton, E. 1849. Historical memorials of Greenland. *Dublin Review* 26, 35-73.

Jochens, J. 1999. Late and peaceful: Iceland's conversion through arbitration in 1000. *Speculum* 74/3, 621-655.

Jones, G. 1986. *The Norse Atlantic Saga: Being the Norse Voyages of Discovery and Settlement to Iceland, Greenland, and North America*, 2nd ed. Oxford: Oxford University Press.

Keller, C. 1989. *The Eastern Settlement Reconsidered. Some Analyses of Norse Medieval Greenland*. (Unpublished PhD Thesis). University of Oslo.

Klevnäs, A.M. 2010. *Whodunnit? Grave-robbery in Early Medieval Northern and Western Europe*. (Unpublished PhD Thesis). Girton College, University of Cambridge, Cambridge.

Krogh, K. 1967. *Viking Greenland*. Monographs on Greenland. Copenhagen: Museum Tusculanum Press.

Lie, J. 1893. *Weird Tales from Northern Seas, from the Danish of Jonas Lie*. Translated by R. Nisbet. Freeport: Books for Libraries Press.

Lynnerup, N. 1998. *The Greenland Norse: A Biological-anthropological Study*. Monographs on Greenland. Copenhagen: Commission for Scientific Research in Greenland.

Madsen, C.K. 2014. *Pastoral Settlement, Farming, and Hierarchy in Norse Vatnahverfi, South Greenland*. (Unpublished PhD Thesis). Copenhagen: University of Copenhagen.

McGovern, T. 1985. The Arctic frontier of Norse Greenland, in: Green, S.W. and Perlman, S.M. (eds), *The Archaeology of Frontiers and Boundaries*. Studies in Archaeology. Orlando: Academic Press, Inc, 275-323.

McGovern, T. 1981. The economics of extinction in Norse Greenland, in: Wigley, T.M.L., Ingram, M.J. and Farmer, G. (eds), *Climate and History*. Cambridge: Cambridge University Press, 404-434.

Nørlund, P. 1971. *Viking Settlers in Greenland and their Descendants during Five Hundred Years*. London: Kraus Reprint Company.

Nørlund, P. 1924. *Buried Norsemen at Herjolfsnes: An Archaeological and Historical Study*. Monographs on Greenland. Copenhagen: C.A. Reitzel.

Nørlund, P., Roussell, A. and Calvert, W.E. 1930. *Norse Ruins at Gardar: The Episcopal Seat of Mediaeval Greenland*. Copenhagen: C.A. Reitzel.

Nørlund, P. and Stenberger, M. 2010. *Brattahlid*. Monographs on Greenland. Copenhagen: Museum Tusculanum Press.

Price, N. 2010. Passing into poetry: Viking-age mortuary drama and the origins of Norse mythology. *Medieval Archaeology* 54, 123-156.

Roussell, A. 1936. *Sandnes and the Neighbouring Farms*. Monographs on Greenland. Copenhagen: C.A. Reitzel.

Roussell, A. 1941. *Farms and Churches in the Medieval Norse Settlements of Greenland*. Monographs On Greenland. Copenhagen: C.A. Reitzel

Stummann Hansen, S. 2013. Toftanes: A Viking Age farmstead in the Faroe Islands. *Acta Archaeologica* 84/1, 5-239.

Vebæk, C.L. 1993. *Narsaq – A Norse landnáma Farm*. Brenderup: Geografforlaget.

Vésteinsson, O. 2000. *The Christianization of Iceland: Priests, Power, and Social Change 1000-1300*. Oxford: Oxford University Press.

# Light and Life in the Catacombs

## Questioning the Early Christian and Early Medieval Pilgrim Experience(s)

*Neil Christie*

## Introduction

The catacombs of Rome are a much-frequented tourist hit: the fascination lies in stepping down to the deep, narrow corridors carved into the natural volcanic bedrock and trailing through the complex honeycomb of channels, brushing past and peering into emptied burial shelves, seeing the fragmented covers, and admiring the larger chambers for wealthier early Christians and their remnant, but much degraded, painted artwork. Yet modern tourists are shepherded and rushed through set route-ways, down corridors with periodic electric light and past cordons hung to prevent one from wandering off course, and are cursorily talked to by guides with set scripts leading specific language groups. Some of us academic tourists feel frustrated by this. Surely the many, foreign pilgrims of the fifth – ninth centuries AD were better treated? Surely they could 'take in' so much more? Surely much more was visible, tangible and accessible in terms of the buried past Christian citizens? How, therefore, can we build up a clear image of the pilgrim experience in their visits to Rome's catacombs? In this paper, I ask what archaeology, art and text can tell us of this experience and how it might have evolved. I ask also if better recognition will help our understanding of what pilgrims did and saw; and if it will help us in imagining better the 'feel' of early Christian and post-classical Rome and its buried (as well as its above-ground) religious places and spaces.

To do this, four aspects will be explored. First we will seek to gain a sense of how the catacombs (and perhaps other hypogea, such as those on Malta; Fig. 45) were viewed in antiquity; then an outline survey is presented of what these spaces were – their character, scale and contents – and how they evolved, from burial loci to pilgrimage foci; next critical consideration will be made of gaps in our archaeological understanding of these places, notably in terms of access, lighting and visitor experience; and finally discussion is made of important new modern explorations of these subterranean complexes. While Rome will of course be core to this paper, the ideas and issues have

in: Bielmann, C. and Thomas, B. (eds.) 2018: *Debating Religious Space and Place in the Early Medieval World (c. AD 300-1000)*, Sidestone Press (Leiden), pp. 187-208.

*Figure 45: View of part of the complex interior of an early Christian to Byzantine hypogeum at the Catacombs of St Paul, Malta. Strongly illuminated by modern electric lights, details stand out and viewers can observe the whole of the space – in contrast with the patchy flickering original light offered by oil lamps in antiquity (Image courtesy of Daniel Cilia, Malta).*

resonance for catacombs and hypogea elsewhere, and potentially also for built religious spaces. This contribution does not itself offer the fruits of original research gained from months spent deep in airless, spider-webbed subterranean vaults pestering and/or observing tourists and guides (although some periods of self-imposed isolation in the catacombs space would no doubt have generated interesting reactions), but is mainly a call to start understanding these places better and more critically in terms of how they *worked* and *were experienced*.

## Exploring the Catacombs

Before outlining the nature, scale and lifespan of the catacombs as foci for ancient burial and pilgrimage, we can start with contemporary voices to the late Roman catacomb experience, first by drawing on no less an authority than Saint Jerome, writing in the later fourth century, who here describes visits to the martyrs' tombs on Sundays with fellow students:

> 'We would visit the tombs of the apostles and martyrs and enter the crypts [galleries] excavated in the very bowels of the earth. The walls on both sides as you go in are full of dead bodies and the whole place is so murky that one seems almost to find the fulfilment of those words of the prophet 'Let them go down alone into Hell'. Here and there a little light, coming in from above ground, is sufficient to give a momentary relief from the horror of darkness; but when you go forward and find yourself once more enveloped in the utter blackness of night, the words of the poet [Virgil] come spontaneously to mind: "the very silence fills your soul with dread"' (*Commentary on Ezekial* 60 – translation cited by Milburn 1988, 22).

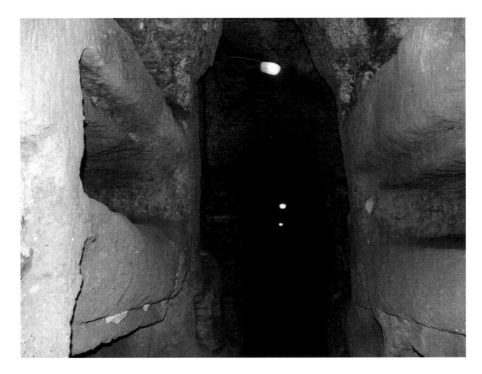

*Figure 46: Typical modern photograph of a corridor with loculi and larger tomb recesses in Rome's catacomb of San Callisto. Although lit by low wattage electric light bulbs and here 'captured' by a camera flash, this image (unlike Figure 45) gives some sense of the 'murk' described by Jerome and Prudentius in the late fourth/early fifth century (Image by User GerardM on nl.wikipedia – https://commons.wikimedia.org/w/index.php?curid=787559).*

Noticeably, this sounds less a religious experience than a regular haunt and adventure. Here excitement is roused by the limited lighting; oddly the explorers do not seem to have carried their own lamps, nor is there reference to 'regular' lamps in the galleries (perhaps, though, Jerome and his troupe eagerly strayed off the beaten main track in these catacombs).

The noted occasional skylights were multifunctional: not only ventilation spaces, early on they were wells or shafts required for removing cut rock and debris; but they also served to act as markers for larger tombs areas (*cf.* Bisconti 1999, 72-73). Such is described by the Spanish scholar and hymn-writer, Prudentius, in his account (*c.* AD 400) of a visit to the crypt of Hippolytus on Rome's *via Tiburtina*. This text gives a dramatic account of the emotions conjured up by the dark depths of a catacomb (Fig. 46):

> 'Not far from the city ramparts, in the open farmland, the mouth of the crypt gives entry to its murky pits. Into its secret recesses a steep path with curving stairs guides the way, while its winding course bars out the light. The brightness of the day comes in, however, through the opening at the top and illumines the threshold of the entrance-hall. Then as, by gradual advance, you feel that the darkness of night is closing in everywhere through the mazes of the cavern, there occur openings pierced through the roof which cast bright rays about the cave…. The shrine which

*encloses the relics of Hippolytus, that brave soul, gleams with solid silver. Wealthy hands have set in place a smooth surface of glistening panels, bright as a mirror…'* (*Peristephanon* ii – translation cited by Milburn 1988, 54).

Bisconti (1999, 73) notes how, in time, catacomb corridors were given bands of whitewash to guide pilgrims, to supplement the various skylight shafts which, he argues, became signs of 'privilege… to mark out monuments that were particularly important or decorated, so that the light could emphasise their architectural features, the iconographic programmes of frescoes and placements of marble or mosaic furnishings… In a later period of the use of the catacombs and especially when they became heavily visited in connection with the cult of martyrs, skylights became salient points of the *itinera ad sanctos*'.

## Catacombs as Tombs; Catacombs as Pilgrim Destinations

The cited descriptions from both Jerome and Prudentius seemingly belong to a time when pilgrimage on a formal, perhaps touristic, level was yet to impact fully on the catacombs – Prudentius in particular implies open access, without any organised spaces above (waiting areas, ordered stairways) and a fairly chaotic set of lower levels, badly lit except for the area of the shrine and altar before the body of Saint Hippolytus. Yet in reality the visits by these two famous fourth-century figures signify the rapid religious 'pull' or attraction of the catacombs, which was marked by increasing formal attention by the Church to the holy graves within. Below, therefore, it is worthwhile outlining the basic chronology and evolving role of the multiple catacombs of Rome, especially since this sequence is often only superficially understood by non-specialists.

Nearly 70 catacomb sites are known in the environs of Rome, with particular foci to the south-east of the city walls (the *via Appia* zone) and the north-east (the *viae Annia Nova* and *Nomentana* zone); estimates suggest a total extent of corridors and galleries of *c.* 175 km. Their locations and contents were largely forgotten in the Middle Ages, although many of their above-ground basilicae persisted, and various subterranean shrines too (Osborne 1985, 297 and 327-328 notes ongoing knowledge of names and of possible monastic input). 'Rediscovery' came slowly from the mid-15th century, with a first major 'scientific' study compiled by Antonio Bosio in his 1632 *Roma Sotterranea* – a remarkable work including plans, drawings of sarcophagi and murals, and descriptions. This study duly opened the door to multiple explorations, plus robbing and clearance of finds. Academic efforts multiplied from the mid-19th century (first via the efforts of Giovanni Battista de Rossi) and 20th century, with emphases on the artworks and, in time, epigraphy (with *c.* 40,000 inscriptions known) (A compact summary on the rediscovery and study of the catacombs is Fiocchi Nicolai 1999, 9-13; for inscriptions, see Mazzoleni 1999; early mapping, see Ghilardi 2012). But big gaps remain: in the case of the largest of the catacombs known, those of Domitilla (extending for *c.* 15 km in length on multiple levels), it is stressed how 'in the last 100 years, no new ground plan has been developed and no plan maps the current state of the galleries and their geographical extent. The inscriptions have never been studied as an entire group. The paintings are only known in part, the total number of burials has never been counted exactly and… objects fixed near the graves have not been studied… Thus, a few specialists aside, we are accustomed to not knowing the catacombs: they remain literally invisible' (Zimmermann and Eßer 2008, 59).

Despite these deficiencies, archaeologists, historians and art historians have generated a fairly secure sequence of activity related to the catacombs which we might break down into a set of seven phases, some of which overlap (see Fiocchi Nicolai 1999 for a lucid overview of the second- to seventh-century catacombs): *Phase I (second – fifth centuries AD)* comprised usage for burials and remembrance; *Phase II (fourth – fifth centuries)* included open commemoration, services, visits, and church building; *Phase III (sixth – eighth centuries)* featured no further burials, but insertion of subterranean basilicas which in part responded to ever growing levels of pilgrimage; *Phase IV (mid-eighth – later ninth centuries)* suffered thefts from catacombs of relics and bodies, followed by extensive papal relocation of such to urban shrines and diminished pilgrimage; *Phase V (10th – 15th centuries)* saw the progressive (but not total) loss of catacombs from memory; *Phase VI (16th – 18th centuries)* was marked by rediscovery and Grand Tour visits; and, finally, *Phase VII (19th – 21st centuries)* has witnessed the combined input of tourism and academic study, and a progressive awakening of heritage management needs.

Within these, besides the current Phase VII, we might recognise Phases II and III as the prime periods of targeted visits or pilgrimage and those which were marked by a notable investment in infrastructure (Fiocchi Nicolai 2000). But Phase IV also required access and movement and the strong Frankish demands for relics after Charlemagne will have entailed many formal (and also many illegal) visits to these. And even after many of the catacombs had seen the translation (=transfer) of bodies/relics into intra-mural shrines, it is evident from both textual sources and, indeed, artwork that various catacombs (or at least parts of these) were maintained: for example, Pope Benedict III (855-858) restored the Balbina cemetery near the Porta Appia, and Nicholas I (858-867) funded repairs to three sites, including St Sebastian 'in Catacumba', where he also founded a monastery (Osborne 1985, 295-296). Osborne (1985, 286-295) offers an excellent review of changes in this Phase IV (*cf.* Goodson 2007. See Geary 1990 for the relic thefts of the period).

Constantine's reign from AD 312 certainly marked a first stage of making catacombs and early Christian burials more accessible for large numbers of public: after all, various of his new churches were set over key tombs, such as those of St Peter and St Agnes, and access to see/touch these holy remains was crucial. We hear, for example, of the basilica to the martyr-saint Laurence on the *via Tiburtina* - erected:

> 'above the arenarium of the crypt; to reach the body of the martyr he [the emperor Constantine] built steps for going up and down. In that place he built an apse and decorated it with purple marble, and above the burial place he sealed it with silver, and decorated it with railings… and in front of the actual burial place in the crypt he placed a lantern of finest gold with 10 wicks weighing 20 lb, a crown of finest silver weighing 30 lb…, 2 bronze candelabra 10 ft in size, each weighing 300 lb; in front of the body of the martyr St Laurence, his passio in medallions chased with silver, with six-wick silver lanterns each weighing 15 lb.' (translation in Davis 1989, 22)

But these expansions and modifications were not just for pilgrims to see the martyrs' tombs; rather, the fourth and fifth centuries mark the main periods of burial of early Christians in Rome's catacombs – the majority housed in the galleried *loculi*, while elites were marked by chambers, paintings, and proximity to holy tombs; the growth of these family tomb-rooms is seen as reflective of the progressive conversion of Rome's middle and upper classes across the fourth century (Fiocchi Nicolai 1999, 37-46. On burials and rituals, see also Zimmermann 2012, exploring 'daily life' in the catacombs). Such investment in burials required infrastructural investment and planning by the Church and important research can still be done to try and map how systematic or *ad hoc* such works in the burial spaces were and how far components like stairways, formal entrances, above-ground basilicas were planned to assist. Either way, the indications are that these catacombs were busy places: the ordering of galleries and routeways, the increasing monumentality of *cubicula* (including possible 'banquet halls') signify regular traffic. Meanwhile, the specialised catacomb diggers – *fossores* – became a very important group of workers; alongside these we must assume Church officials to help guide visitors, both in churches above ground, and in galleries and chapels below (Mazzoleni 2000; Zimmermann 2012, 174-175).

A prominent – and very well advertised – investment in the catacombs as points of devotional pilgrimage and worship comes with the pontificate of Damasus (366-384). The focus was heavily on the aggrandisement of the tombs of the City's many martyrs and pope-saints with Damasus setting up over 60 large metrical inscriptions at these and redesigning the spaces around and over the tombs. There is strong evidence for marble panelling, tables to hold lamps and offerings, altar tables, screens, new murals, new light-shafts, enlarged entranceways, and a systematisation of approaches to and from the main venerated tombs and into the catacombs, including blocking of corridors; we see also growing competition to be buried near these holy rooms and in new funerary basilicas (Fiocchi Nicolai 1999, 49-59; Pergola 2000; Zimmermann 2012, 184-188; Thacker 2007, 30-36, viewing Damasus' promotion as 'entrepreneurial activity') (*cf.* Figures 47 and 48). The elevation of saints' feast days into major festivals will have also brought flocks of high clergy, imperial staff, and the populace to these catacombs. This investment in the 'cult of the martyrs' would provide the lifeblood for the Rome Church and clearly the flow of pilgrims helped invigorate the young Papacy (Thacker 2007, 42-49, stressing the growing role of relics in the fifth–seventh centuries; more widely, Birch 1998 and Llewellyn 1993, chapter 6).

An important reflection of the scale of the pilgrim trade and the pull of Rome's martyrs and catacombs in Phase III especially (and thus after the cessation of burials here), comes in the series of Itineraries generated from the first half of the seventh century. The *Notitia Ecclesiarum Urbis Romae* and the *De Locis Sanctis Martyrum,* both compiled *c.* AD 630/640 (but perhaps with late sixth-century precursors), centre on the suburban cemeteries, shrines and tombs/relics; they do not refer to Roman imperial monuments (Fiocchi Nicolai 2000, 223-229). While not endowed with images and useful phrases for tourists, there is good detail on direction and there are 'sight/site tick-lists' for the pilgrims – such as in this entry in the *Notitia*: 'Then proceed south along the *via Salaria* until you come to St Hermes; in the basilica there, the first at rest is Bassilla, virgin and martyr, then the martyr Maximus, and the martyr St Hermes, who is deep underground... Then further

*Figure 47: A sign of the modern pilgrim-cum-tourist experience – a multi-lingual welcome but with lots of 'do not' warnings, from taking photos to littering, using phones or smoking. As perhaps in the seventh and eighth centuries, visitors are shepherded up, talked to first and then accompanied in small groups to the actual catacombs (Image courtesy of Natalia Vásquez from Santiago, Chile).*

*Figure 48: A new tour group jostles down the steps into the San Callisto catacombs in Rome, aided by bright lights and new brick steps (Image by Viaggi Italy – http://viaggi.nanopress.it/fotogallery/cimiteri-italiani-da-visitare_7877_26.html).*

along the same road you come to the holy martyr Pamphilius, underground; you go down 24 steps here' (translation in Llewellyn 1993, 178).

The pilgrim 'traffic' grew consistently from the fourth century, and by the sixth and seventh centuries featured many high-profile figures, from bishops to kings, from close by or far afield, including from Sicily and Saxon England. These eminent figures would often visit the pope, obtain gifts, give gifts, do the tour, stay in Church-run hostels, and usually, but not always, return to their home/homeland and stimulate the next set of devout travellers (Fiocchi Nicolai 2000, 222-223). The Itineraries (though in truth only the *Notitia* gives actual directions) combine to help show an 'order' and structure to the pilgrim routes; they signify also attention to the roads servicing the shrines and catacombs; and they give a sense of the 'topografia martiriale' of Rome (Fiocchi Nicolai 2000, 224-229). What timescale was required to do the pilgrim circuit of suburban Rome is unknown, nor the time spent in each basilica and shrine, nor whether pilgrims would take rest/meals at the scattered monasteries; however, we would expect some pilgrims not doing the whole circuit, but choosing just the 'hotspots' (dependent on their own preferred saints and relics). It may also have been the case that Church officials might limit access to certain catacombs. Much of this actual experience cannot be traced, although the letters and travelogues of some pilgrims give a sense of time spent and targets made.

## Old Technologies to See, to Find and to Experience the Catacombs

After this rapid (but longer by far than what tour guides currently give!) overview of the early Christian to early medieval catacombs, their visitors and some of the textual guides, next we delve down into the actual experience of the pilgrims. We know of the goals of the many visitors – to bury, to commemorate, to visit, to worship, to work, to admire, or even to steal – and yet we still have a very limited understanding of the mechanics of the visits and especially also of what individuals could do, see and touch. Below, therefore, we consider and critically appraise some of these experiential aspects of the catacombs. First, and most crucial, is the aspect of lighting.

### Light, Lamps and Vision

Oil lamps and candles were the prime medium for lighting the catacombs and any subterranean tombs (*hypogea*) or built above-ground space in antiquity (Bisconti 1999, 82. Still a valuable overview is Leclercq 1928. For Roman Pompeii in day and night: Griffiths, *in press* a and b. See Fig. 49 here). Such lights were essential portable and fixed components in these, although we are uncertain whether these might burn constantly, or were re-lit daily, dependent on the venue. Presumably, for example, shrines, heavily venerated tombs and chambers, chapels for prayer, and stairwells, were the most regularly tended; an 11th-century attestation for the catacomb of St Valentine says '*ubi semper ardent lampades*' – 'where lamps always shine' (Osborne 1985, 313). Lamps might have been given (or sold) to individual visitors on entry, perhaps with donations anticipated for lamp, oil and blessings; this could well have been a tidy business for locals, although as the pilgrim 'industry' developed we might assume that local church priests/officials oversaw any such transactions (after all, many a catacomb entrance was overlain in time by a church). Regular services at martyr and papal tombs and the act of new burials certainly needed good lighting to assist the ceremonies. Thus, for the late fourth century, the *Apostolic Constitutions* state 'Gather together without fear [of pollution] in the cemeteries [*i.e.* catacombs] to read from the divine Scriptures and sing psalms for the martyrs who rest there, for all the saints and your brothers who rest in the Lord; and celebrate the Eucharist... in your churches and your cemeteries; and for funerals accompany the departed with psalms' (*Ap. Const.* 6.30.2; translation in Maas 2010, 277. And much earlier, in second-century North Africa, both Tertullian and Hippolytus stressed the importance of lamps and light for congregational meals – see Yasin 2009, 40).

Archaeologists, or rather ceramic specialists, have long studied lamps for their designs as a way, primarily, to date contexts and sites, to chart even religious change (*e.g.* the advent of Christian motifs or symbols on the body of the lamps), and to recognise trade contacts (From a substantial bibliography, see, for example, Anselmino 1986; Pavolini 1986; Bonifay 2005; Chrzanovski ed. 2005; plus compact summaries in Karivieri 2016. On iconographic change see the excellent paper by Talloen on materials from Sagalassos in Turkey). Lamps (or fragments of these) occur regularly in excavated contexts, whether urban, rural or military, but are not usually common finds in church excavations (*e.g.* the very compact collection of finds from the fifth- to sixth-century church and villa/*vicus* site of San Giusto in Apulia – Volpe ed. 1998, 267-268; but note how the interior reconstructions of the church here (figs. 327-335)

*Figure 49: A rather gloomy and sadly tended array of late Roman ceramic oil lamps behind a grille in the catacombs of San Callisto near the main early papal-saint tombs (Image by TripAdvisor: https://media-cdn.tripadvisor.com/media/photo-s/03/49/4f/f4/catacombs-of-st-callixtus.jpg).*

show no lighting apart from the clerestory windows). Most probably churches used metal – mainly bronze but some precious metal – lamps, both freestanding or hung, plus glass lamps, with the metal especially lost to later recycling (*cf.* Milburn 1988, 265-266). The best evidence for such comes from the rich archaeology of the early medieval monastic complex of San Vincenzo al Volturno (Molise province, southern central Italy), with metal chains from ninth-century lamp-hangers plus glass lamp fragments from the areas of the church crypt and apses (Hodges *et al.* 2011, 205-207, 261, 146-147, highlighting the fine glass lamps produced in nearby workshops). One might also note the early fifth-century description of the church of St Felix at Nola (Campania province, central Italy), whose wood ceiling 'gleamed like ivory in the light of numerous suspended lamps' (cited by Yasin 2009, 186).

Contemporary textual guidance comes from records in the *Liber Pontificalis* (Rome's 'Book of Pontiffs') of the lists of donations by popes to their own or older churches in and around Rome. We need note just two examples. Sistus/Xystus (bishop of Rome from 432-440) offered the following items to his new church of San Lorenzo/Saint Laurence: '30 silver crown lights each weighing 6 lb; 3 chandeliers each weighing 15 lb; 2 silver candelabra each weighing 30 lb; 24 bronze candlestick chandeliers in the body of the basilica; 60 bronze lights' (translation by Davis 1989, 36. Pope Hilarus (461-468) later replaced silver and gold items pilfered from churches in the Vandal sack of 455, including at San Lorenzo: a gold lantern, 2 gold lamps, a gold chandelier and 10 silver lamps – Davis 1989, 40). For the eighth and ninth centuries, we hear much of gifts of silk veils and curtains especially (to lie over altars and to hang between arches/columns – and presumably well away from open flames), but for the pontificate of Leo III (795-816) much is made in the *Liber Pontificalis* of new lighting provision in St Peter's basilica:

> '*Over the canopy of the high altar, 4 great chandeliers of fine silver, with silver-gilt candles in the centre, weighing in all 140 lb... In this same place a decorated lectern of wondrous size and beauty, of fine silver weighing 114 lb; candlesticks of fine silver to stand close to this lectern, weighing in all 49 lb; and over these candlesticks 2 cast lanterns with 2 wicks... and he [Leo] decreed they should stand on either side close to the lectern on Sundays and on saints' solemnities to shine with bright light for the reading of the holy lessons; 14 chandeliers in the presbyterium of fine silver weighing in all 332 lb 3 oz...*' (translated by Davis 1992, 207-8)

A good example of lamps from a well-excavated early Christian funerary context – unlike many of Rome's catacombs, where lamps are scattered finds, rarely tightly provenanced (Fig. 49) – is the fourth- to sixth-century 'S. Sofia' catacomb at the site of 'Ponte della Lama' near the Roman and late antique urban centre of Canosa in southeast Italy. Lamps here formed a third of all ceramic material excavated, and many were intact, often forming the sole objects left in sealed tombs (Eramo *et al.* 2013, 275-276. The authors cite concisely that the lamps 'obviously... were also used to provide light in these dark places'. However, while their study was innovative in being centred on determining the clay sources for the lamps, they nowhere discuss what the lamps actually did).

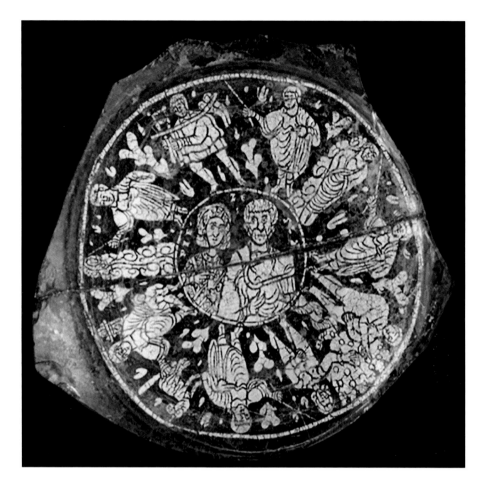

*Figure 50: A fine example of a mid-fourth-century gilded glass bowl base likely once set beside a lo-culus. The subject is a couple surrounded by scenes of salvation from the Old and New Testaments, with a toast in Greek to one of the couple – Pie! Zeses! – written in Latin script above the portraits. This base was broken from an oval dish of a shape and size convenient for serving fish. Formerly in the Wilshere and Recupero Collections of the Ashmolean Museum, it probably comes from the cata-combs of Rome (AN2007.13 Glass Fragment. Image © Ashmolean Museum, University of Oxford; description courtesy of Dr Susan Walker).*

Lamps set alongside individual *loculi* may well have been personalised items, depos-ited to symbolically light the journey of the deceased. Perhaps ritual blessings were said as these tombs were closed and the lamps set close by – recalling, for instance, words such as 'For you, Lord, are my lamp. And the Lord will lighten my darkness' and 'Your word is a lamp to my feet and a light to my paths' (*II Kings* 22, 29). Bisconti (1999, 82) stresses this mental connection with 'the eternal light illuminating paradise'.

There were other items to add to this mix of light, liturgy, religiosity and sal-vation: gilded glass bowl bases are a fairly common find in (or, rather, from) the catacombs; many hundreds of examples are known, but with the vast majority long divorced from their original context alongside *loculi* especially. These were parts of vessels, perhaps ones used in funerary offerings or rituals, deliberately broken and reduced down to their carefully decorated gilded bases which display generally fine images of saints and martyrs – such as Lawrence, Agnes or Hippolytus – or biblical scenes (Fig. 50). We cannot be certain, but cannot exclude that the scenes/images were ones once favoured by the deceased. Set in the mortar, these small objects and their gilded designs were not only distinctive objects, but we must recognise that they were also reflectors, set to glisten in nearby or passing lamplight (Bisconti 1999, 80-81; see the forthcoming work by Susan Walker).

Away from the galleries, other items will have shone and sparkled, especially within featured martyr/saint tomb rooms and shrines where services will have been performed. Here stood some of the rich 'furniture' noted already for the above-ground churches – candelabra, dishes, chalices, veils with gold thread, *etc.* The catacombs lack, however, the mosaic work which filled apses and other spaces in these churches and which, by the ninth century especially, feature gold leaf tesserae as (Heavenly) background and framing devices and which will have certainly been resplendent in the flickering candle/lamp-light. (One notable example is the San Zeno chapel of Santa Prassede, Rome, built under Pope Paschal, 817-824 – see Mackie 1995 discussing the varied iconography, including celestial flowers, jewelled borders, ornate textiles, *etc.*). Most noteworthy are the words pronounced in the mosaic inscriptions composed for early ninth-century churches like Santa Cecilia:

> *'This spacious house glitters built of varied minerals; this hall, once in time past had been ruined, the generous prelate Paschal built to a better condition, forming it on a famous foundation; these golden mysteries resound with jewelled precincts; serene in the love of God. He joined the bodies of Saint Cecilia and her companions; youth glows red in its bloom. Limbs that rested before in crypts, Rome is joyous, triumphant always, adorned forever.'* (translated in Goodson 2010, 152; cf. the dedicatory text for S. Maria in Domnica, 153)

Here Pope Paschal alludes also to the translation of bodies and relics from the catacombs to the more spacious and public arena of a city church, with ornate, powerful images duly reflecting those saints' virtues and vitality. It is striking how the inscription emphasises the mosaics and their glittering effect in response both to Heavenly light but also, of course, to light from candles and lamps.

One non-Rome example we can cite regarding lighting is from Malta: Buhagiar (2015) discusses the important early Christian and Byzantine site at Abbatija tad-Dejr comprising rock-cut church, colonnaded building and a set of four catacombs cut into the limestone and forming a quadrangular zone. Much visited from the 18th century at least and despoiled en route, excavations in the 1920s and 1930s gathered up various remaining (broken) finds around the tombs (these a mix of 'window-tombs', 'freestanding canopied tombs', burial niches, loci and chambers), which included lamp fragments. There are occasional light wells, but the excavators also recognised lamp-holes cut into the walls, and iron hooks in the ceiling of at least Catacomb I for suspending lights. What stands out is the occasional presence of paintings, decorative screens, carvings and words, all certainly meant to be seen by visitors. Scope surely exists to revisit and scrutinise such catacombs and plot the lamp settings, to experiment in showing the impact of these, observing if they correlate with displays of texts or art or are in 'set' locations (new work at Saint Augustine's Catacombs [Triq Ħal Bajada, Rabat] offers one venue for such 'tighter' modern analysis: see papers by D'Ambruoso 2013; Cardona and Farrugia 2013; Cardona and Gustafsson 2013. The work by Griffiths (in press) on Pompeian lamps shows how experimental work can be invaluable in aiding how we understand the use of light and spaces in a built and dark environment).

A further geographical aside can be made to consider lamps as potential cave and cult site offerings or marks of ritual festivities. Saradi (2011) provides a fascinating discussion for material traces of late paganism and for early Christianisation in Attica (Greece), such as at the Cave of Vari. This cult place, dedicated to Pan, the Nymphs and Apollo, lay redundant from the second century BC but was revived in the fourth century AD; here, along with many coins, a full 1000 lamps were found. While the presence of Christian symbols on some of these has been taken to support a claim of Christians rooting out this pagan revival, the symbols might simply denote current designs and not the religious adherence of the lamps' users. At the Cave of Pan on Parnes, the lamps numbered over 2000. Both caves saw also the (later?) defacing and smashing of their residual pagan statuary (Saradi 2011, 287-288. In addition, Saradi notes the excavated deposits of over 4000 lamps in the 'Fountain of the Lamps' at Corinth, some clearly connected to the worship of nymphs and water angels: 289-291).

*Other Sensory Expressions*

While the above discussion has centred on the 'technology' of sight and vision, there are other senses to consider which were – and still are – also integral to the pilgrim/visitor experience, and yet which again have seen too little academic consideration, especially by catacomb scholars. Firstly, **sound**: in an auditory sense, modern tourists (such as the University student groups I have led in Rome) often talk of the quietness of the catacombs, whether the hushed voices, the crunch or shuffle of feet in the narrow corridors, or the way that the volcanic rock seems to soak up sound. This is not far removed from the words quoted from St Jerome above, namely '… when you go forward and find yourself once more enveloped in the utter blackness of night, the words of the poet [Virgil] come spontaneously to mind: "the very silence fills your soul with dread"'. Occasionally there are 'lost' sounds – the curving corridors or lost side alleys snatching words away or releasing a few as another tour group passes by.

Secondly, **touch**: as well as the sensations felt from walking on the irregular floors with their stray pebbles, sherds and dust, visitors always run their fingers along the cut and worn tufa, around the shape of a *loculus*, and perhaps venturing a hand deeper into a recess; there is also the touch of other people, pushing you along, reassuring you, or coincidental to being gathered into the confined space of a *cubiculum* or chamber. Touching *loculi* cuttings, residual fragments of marble covers, or a sarcophagus instantly 'transport' the individual mentally (him or her usually touching without talking) and help that person to 'soak' up the antiquity of the object and place (Fig. 51). We cannot doubt that family members in the third to fifth centuries and likewise pilgrims in the sixth to ninth centuries similarly touched the fragments of inscribed and incised marble covering *loculi*, or felt the glass, ceramic, metal or wood objects and ornaments (including dolls, statuettes, coins) mortared into the *loculi* frames (Bisconti 1999, 78-81) (Fig. 50). And no doubt, on occasion, a few visitors will have (successfully) sought to extract some of these individual mementoes and symbols for themselves.

*Figure 51: Members of a tour group touching the sides of a gallery and using a pen torch in the cat-acombs beneath the early medieval church of Sant'Agnese fuori le mura, Rome (Photo by author).*

Thirdly, there is the sense of **change**: tourists are often advised that 'it can be cold in the catacombs' and to take a shawl or jacket. In part this is connected to what St Jerome says about descending into 'the very bowels of the earth', and an anticipated drop in temperature. But it is also about dropping into an alien environment, a place where you might or do not belong – or, in early Christian times, where you might not *yet* belong. Indeed, some of my students have preferred not to go down into the catacombs, either through that uncertainty of being out of place, or more often due to the anticipated sense of claustrophobia. To others of course it is exciting to descend into an otherworldly landscape, with the desire to dip into the darkened and unknown depths, thinking/hoping that you might find unopened tombs, unseen paintings, *etc.* – even though you will have been told that most catacombs currently accessible have been pretty well stripped clean. This latter sense of excitement is akin to the modern phenomenon of UrbEx – the exploration of out-of-bounds ruins (Macfarlane 2013).

Finally, a highly important ingredient is **smell**: occasionally modern tourists will state that they can smell the past or can catch a whiff of the numerous bodies that once lay encased in the catacombs. Often this might be no 'genuine' smell, but more an anticipation of such. Again, we might repeat Jerome's words about how 'The walls on both sides as you go in are full of dead bodies and the whole place is so murky…'. Nowadays the issue is far more about dampness and stale air – wholly the wrong con-ditions to preserve the surviving wall paintings of the catacombs (though the survivals are numerous – see the excellent illustrated survey by Bisconti 1999, 82-141) – but, combined, these would give that sense of a decayed murkiness of the deceased. What we currently lack of course is the smell of burning oil from the lamps and wax from candles, each burning up oxygen but providing a different olfactory experience in the early Christian and early medieval periods.

Smell also played an important part in the pilgrim and wider religious experience. Incense, fine oils and other fragrances were burnt or offered at shrines or used during services, and the chapels of the main martyrs', saints' and other venerated tombs will no doubt have been regularly serviced with pleasant fragrances. Furthermore, there is regular reference to the 'sweet smell' of martyrs' or saints' bodies which were often also claimed to be 'uncorrupted' when their tombs were opened (Geary 1990, 125, 142; Campbell 1991, 80-81 on the tomb of Saint Cuthbert. The key modern work on smelly saints is Roch 2009, who concludes that the fragrant scents were signs of their divinity and proximity to God; to breathe that smell could help one to experience that saintly divinity: 645-646. See also the excellent Harvey 2006 book on the many smells and olfactory experiences which pervaded the early Christian lived and venerated world). Brazinski and Fryxell (2013) have extended the discussion to the smells of relics – whether body parts or cloths or possessions or else secondary relics such as holy waters or oil gathered from a pilgrimage site and carried in ampullae or the like; they argue how smells helped convey 'authenticity'. Many an early Christian and early medieval pilgrim to Rome's catacombs or its other shrines will have sought to carry home some item that might be infused with the spirit of a martyr or saint. Modern photographs of a relic, sarcophagus, crypt, lamp or painting could arguably be said to be trying to 'catch' or 'hold' a piece of that past and to store it to memory.

## New Technologies to See

Some of the mystique and 'otherness' of Rome's multiple catacombs has of course been lost through concerted (if long unsystematic) academic scrutiny of their spaces and art. Through photographs in books and on the internet we can nowadays observe and ponder in comfort, catalogue and compare without the need to 'experience' first-hand the catacombs in terms of their real environment. And experts have conserved the artworks, peeling away grime, restoring faded faces and forms. The contrast is with the modern tourist experience – rushed, selective and superficial.

New technologies are further enhancing our understanding of these subterranean places. Rather than simply being told of the XX km of length, the XX numbers of galleries and their height of XX m, laser scanning is providing accurate mapping – often for the very first time – of some of these complexes. Two key recent projects have been centred on different but equally extensive catacombs at Rome, those of Santa Priscilla and of Domitilla. In the latter case, as part of an Austrian Science Fund project, Vienna's University of Technology undertook eight scan campaigns of range laser scanning across the full 15 km space (including the early Christian basilica); the 'model' generated a series of point clouds, comprising over 1.2 billion points, enabling stunning visualisation of the multiple galleries, levels and chambers of the complex (see Zimmermann and Esser 2008; Scheiblauer 2008; Scheiblauer *et al.* 2009; project web archive: *http://www.oeaw.ac.at/antike/index.php?id=37 6&L=2*. For an example outside of Rome, one can cite the 3D laser mapping of the Saint Augustine's Catacombs at Rabat on Malta: D'Ambruoso 2013) (Fig. 52). The resultant model enables interactive

*Figure 52: One sector of the laser-mapped Domitilla catacombs depicting galleries, side chambers, cubicula and intersections. The main complex is the so-called 'Galleria dei Flavi', topped by a skylight shaft (Image courtesy of Prof. N. Zimmermann and Vienna University).*

walkthroughs (see *http://www.learn.columbia.edu/treasuresofheaven/shrines/Rome/video/index.php)*, but also scope for reconsidering internal structural designs and developments. Scale and complexity in particular are illuminated, putting us even more in awe of the mechanics of creating, cutting, ordering and navigating the catacombs in the early Christian to early medieval epochs. One might highlight, however, that the impressive chamber/*cubicula* views are a first stage; a next research level would be to add in the vertical (shaft) and horizontal (lamp) lights and show how visibility/clarity would change depending on source, number, *etc.*

Equally of value in terms of this 'navigation' of the catacombs is our second example focussed on the Santa Priscilla complex. Here, the European Commission FP7 funded ROVINA project (organised between Rome, Leuven and Freiburg universities and exploring also the San Gennaro catacomb in Naples) is testing and employing robots to undertake the laser mapping of the subterranean corridors and chambers (See summary in Ziparo *et al.* 2013; project website: *http://www.rovina-project.eu/).* The project team, noticeably, describe the catacombs as 'a harsh environment... there are steep slopes, uneven grounds, challenging obstacles, drifts and debris, dangerous passages, huge unexplored areas, health hazards due to radioactive radon gas, and poor wireless connectivity. In addition, being an archaeological environment, the robots has [sic] to deal with fragile objects, artifacts, walls paintings, bones, carvings, *etc.*' (Ziparo *et al.* 2013). St Jerome and Prudentius would no doubt have sympathised with the robots on many of these issues (except in terms of wireless connectivity!), adding in their extra mix of very human emotions and senses in the navigation of the murky, damp and dusty 'crypts'.

## Discussion and Conclusion

The noted laser mapping and 3D modelling campaigns at the Domitilla catacomb – the largest known of Rome's web of such complexes – mark the start of concerted new, structured and scientific approaches to these hugely important early Christian monuments. Long a focus of antiquarian exploration – and pilfering (here building on the early medieval period of spoliation and translation) – these catacombs have suffered heavily from blinkered study, with the art of the *cubicula* too long the prime focus, leaving much of our understanding of the wider content and significance of the catacombs as superficial and fragmented. The robbing limits our explorations on some levels, but the actual structures and spaces, their interrelationships, and the associated objects (whether *in situ*, displaced or marked only by their former settings) can still be scrutinised to build a better picture of the buildings, the users, the occupants and the visitors. This paper has highlighted, questioned and in part tackled – albeit briefly – some of the angles that remain under-explored and under-appreciated: 1. the lighting, both in form (skylight shafts, lamps, candles) and setting (above, alongside, within, over), to help us understand movement, location and vision; 2. the senses, from the interplay of dark/murk and light/glitter on the eyes, to the touch of the walls and the 'furniture' of the tombs, to the smells and sounds (of silence, the dead, the past); and 3. the people themselves, since, by revisiting all these other angles, we might gain new insights into how these spaces and places evolved, functioned, were appreciated (or not) and were transformed.

Arguably, an essential approach should also be to interrogate more the modern users and stakeholders of the catacombs – from guides to religious pilgrims, to priests, to tourist-mongers, to old and young visitors alike (*cf.* papers in Scerra 2013 on heritage tourism of early Christian Malta) – since we should not at all expect a single 'experience' of the catacombs but rather a multiple array of reactions and emotions (Farrugia 2017 is an important step in this direction). Saint Jerome himself in the fourth century will have changed in his mental experience of the catacombs: in his lifetime, from visits as youth and as elder, he will have observed the catacombs developing in their role and in the scale of Church interventions; by the end of that century, one could argue that the visitor experience had been 'opened up' and moved from murky meanderings to directed devotion. Ancient lamps and modern lasers have much scope to illuminate the story further.

### Acknowledgements

My thanks first go to the editors for inviting me to add a paper to this volume, despite only having given an introductory welcome at the conference itself. For advice and assistance (of articles, images and/or ideas), I extend thanks to Prof Norbert Zimmermann (Vienna University), Dr Susan Reynolds (Ashmolean Museum, Oxford) and David Griffiths (PhD candidate, University of Leicester – but Dr Griffiths by the time of submission of this volume to the printers); to Glen Farrugia (recent PhD, University of Leicester, but based on Malta) for putting me in contact with photographer Daniel

Cilia who kindly supplied the splendid Figure 45; and to Natalia Vásquez in distant Chile for sharing her Rome tour photos and providing my Figure 47.

## Bibliography

### Primary Sources

*Liber Pontificalis (The Book of Pontiffs)*. Translated by R. Davis. Translated Texts for Historians. Latin Series V. Liverpool: Liverpool University Press, 1989.

*Lives of the Eighth-Century Popes*. Translated by R. Davis. Translated Texts for Historians 13. Liverpool: Liverpool University Press, 1992.

### Secondary Sources

Anselmino, L. 1986. Le lucerne tardoantiche: produzione e cronologia, in: Giardina, A. (ed.), *Società romana e impero tardoantico. III. Le merci, gli insediamenti*. Rome & Bari: Einaudi, 227-240.

Birch, D. 1998. *Pilgrimage to Rome in the Middle Ages. Continuity and Change*. Woodbridge: Boydell.

Bisconti, F. 1999. The decoration of Roman catacombs, in: Fiocchi Nicolai, V., Bisconti, F. and Mazzoleni, D. (eds), *The Christian Catacombs of Rome. History, Decoration, Inscriptions*. Regensburg: Schnell & Steiner, 70-145.

Bonifay, M. 2005. Observations sur la typologie des lampes africaines (III-VII siècles), in: Chrzanovski, L. (ed.), *Actes du 1er Congrès international d'études sur le luminaire antique (Nyon-Genève, 29 Sept – 4 Oct. 2003)*. Lychnological Acts 1: Instrumentum 31. Chauvigny, 31-38.

Brazinski, P.A. and Fryxell, A.R.P. 2013. The smell of relics: authenticating saintly bones and the role of scent in the sensory experience of medieval Christian veneration. *Papers from the Institute of Archaeology* 23/1, 1-15.

Buhagiar, M. 2014. The early Christian site at Abbatija tad-Dejr: archaeological and art historical insights, in: Buhagiar, M. (ed.), *Essays on the Archaeology and Ancient History of the Maltese Islands. Bronze Age to Byzantine*. Maltese Social Studies Series No 22. Sta Venera: Midsea Books, 197-211.

Campbell, P. (ed.) 1991. *The Anglo-Saxons*. London: Penguin.

Cardona, D. and Farrugia, G. 2013. The St Augustine's Catacombs complex: history and general description, in: Scerra, S. (ed.), *Archaeotur. Gestione integrata e promozione dei siti archeologici a Ragusa e Malta. Integrated Management and Promotion of Archaeological Sites in Ragusa and Malta. I siti archeologici del periodo tardoantico. The Archaeological Sites of Late Antiquity*. Palermo: Assessorato dei Beni Culturali e dell'Identità Siciliana, 55-66.

Cardona, D. and Gustafsson, A. 2013. Excavations at St Augustine's Catacombs: a preliminary report, in: Scerra, S. (ed.), *Archaeotur. Gestione integrata e promozione dei siti archeologici a Ragusa e Malta. Integrated Management and Promotion of Archaeological Sites in Ragusa and Malta. I siti archeologici del periodo tardoantico. The Archaeological Sites of Late Antiquity*. Palermo: Assessorato dei Beni Culturali e dell'Identità Siciliana, 67-74.

Chrzanovski, L. (ed.) 2005. *Actes du 1er Congrès international d'études sur le luminaire antique (Nyon-Genève, 29 Sept – 4 Oct. 2003)*. Lychnological Acts 1: Instrumentum 31. Chauvigny.

D'Ambruoso, G. 2013. 3D documentation at St Augustine's Catacombs, Triq Hal Bajada, Rabat – Malta, in: Scerra (ed.), *Archaeotur. Gestione integrata e promozione dei siti archeologici a Ragusa e Malta. Integrated Management and Promotion of Archaeological Sites in Ragusa and Malta. I siti archeologici del periodo tardoantico. The Archaeological Sites of Late Antiquity*. Palermo: Assessorato dei Beni Culturali e dell'Identità Siciliana, 48-54.

Eramo, G., Giannossa, L.C., Rocco, A., Mangone, A., Graziano, S.F. and Laviano, R. 2013. Oil lamps from the catacombs of Canosa (Apulia, fourth to sixth centuries AD): technological features and typological imitation. *Archaeometry* 56/ 3, 375-391.

Farrugia, G. 2017. *The Presentation and Interpretation of Early-Christian Heritage in Malta: Past, Present and Future*. Unpublished PhD, University of Leicester, UK.

Fiocchi Nicolai, V. 1999. The origin and development of Roman catacombs, in: Fiocchi Nicolai, V., Bisconti, F. and Mazzoleni, D. (eds), *The Christian Catacombs of Rome. History, Decoration, Inscriptions*. Regensburg: Schnell & Steiner, 8-69.

Fiocchi Nicolai, V. 2000. *Sacra martyrium loca circuire*: percorsi di visita dei pellegrini nei santuari martiriali del suburbio romano, in: Pani Ermini, L. (ed.), Christiana Loca. *Lo spazio cristiano nella Roma del primo millennio*. Rome: Fratelli Palombi Editori, 221-230.

Fiocchi Nicolai, V., Bisconti, F. and Mazzoleni, D. 1999. *The Christian Catacombs of Rome. History, Decoration, Inscriptions*. Regensburg: Schnell & Steiner.

Geary, P. 1990. *Furta Sacra. Thefts of Relics in the Central Middle Ages*. Princeton: University Press.

Ghilardi, M. 2012. "ut exitum reperirent, signis notabant loca". La nascita della cartografia di Roma sottoterranea Cristiana, in: Bevilacqua, M. and Fagiolo, M. (eds), *Piante di Roma dal Rinascimento ai castati*. Rome: Artemide Edizioni, 168-181.

Goodson, C.J. 2007. Building for bodies: the architecture of saint veneration in early medieval Rome, in: Carragáin, É. Ó and Neuman de Vegvar, C. (eds), *Roma Felix – Formation and Reflections of Medieval Rome. Church, Faith and Culture in the Medieval West*. Farnham: Ashgate, 51-79.

Goodson, C.J. 2010. *The Rome of Pope Paschal II. Papal Power, Urban Renovation, Church Rebuilding and Relic Translation, 817-824*. Cambridge & New York: Cambridge University Press.

Griffiths, D.G. in press (a). Household consumption of artificial light at Pompeii, in: Papadopoulos, C. and Moyes, H. (eds), *Oxford Handbook of Light in Archaeology*. Oxford: Oxbow.

Griffiths, D.G. in press (b). Commercialization of the night at Pompeii, in: Veal, R. and Leitch, V. (eds), *Fuel and Fire in the Roman World*. Cambridge: McDonald Institute for Archaeological Research Series.

Harvey, S.A. 2006. *Scenting Salvation: Ancient Christianity and the Olfactory Imagination*. Berkeley: University of California Press.

Hodges, R., Leppard, S. and Mitchell, J. 2011. *San Vincenzo Maggiore and its Workshops*. Archaeological Monographs of the British School at Rome 17. London: The British School at Rome.

Karivieri, A. 2016. Lamp: metal; Lamp: pottery, in: Corby Finney, P. (ed.), *The Eerdmans Encyclopedia of Early Christian Art and Archaeology*. Grand Rapids: William B. Eeerdmans Publishing, 36-37, 37-39.

Lavan, L. and Mulryan, M. (eds) 2011. *The Archaeology of Late Antique Paganism*. Late Antique Archaeology 7. Leiden: Brill.

Leclercq, H. 1928. Lampes, in: Cabrol. F. and Leclercq, H., *Dictionnaire d'archéologie chrétienne et de liturgie*. Vol 8.1, Paris: Letouzey et Ané, 1086-1221.

Llewellyn, P. 1993. *Rome in the Dark Ages*. London: Constable.

Maas, M. 2010. *Readings in Late Antiquity. A Sourcebook. 2nd Edition*. London & New York: Routledge.

Macfarlane, R. 2013. The strange world of urban exploration. *The Guardian* on-line 20 September 2013 (*http://www.theguardian.com/books/2013/sep/20/urban-exploration-robert-macfarlane-bradley-garrett*).

Mackie, G. 1995. Abstract and vegetal design in the San Zeno chapel, Rome: the ornamental setting of an early medieval funerary programme. *Papers of the British School at Rome* LXIII, 159-182.

Mancinelli, F. 1981. *Catacombs of Rome*. Florence: Scala.

Mazzoleni, D. 1999. Inscriptions in Roman catacombs, in: Fiocchi Nicolai, V., Bisconti, F. and Mazzoleni, D. (eds), *The Christian Catacombs of Rome. History, Decoration, Inscriptions*. Regensburg: Schnell & Steiner, 146-185.

Mazzoleni, D. 2000. Fossori e artigiani nella società Cristiana, in: Pani Ermini, L. (ed.), Christiana Loca. *Lo spazio cristiano nella Roma del primo millennio*. Rome: Fratelli Palombi Editori, 251-255.

Milburn, R. 1988. *Early Christian Art and Architecture*. Aldershot: Scolar Press/Berkeley & Los Angeles: University of California Press.

Osborne, J. 1985. The Roman catacombs in the Middle Ages. *Papers of the British School at Rome* LIII, 278-328.

Pani Ermini, L. (ed.) 2000. Christiana Loca. *Lo spazio cristiano nella Roma del primo millennio*. Rome: Fratelli Palombi Editori.

Pavolini, C. 1986. La circolazione delle lucerne in terra sigillata Africana, in: Giardina, A. (ed.), *Società romana e impero tardoantico. III. Le merci, gli insediamenti*. Rome & Bari: Einaudi, 241-250.

Pergola, P. 2000. Dai cimiteri ai santuari martiriali (IV – VIII secolo), in: Pani Ermini, L. (ed.), Christiana Loca. *Lo spazio cristiano nella Roma del primo millennio*. Rome: Fratelli Palombi Editori, 99-105.

Roch, M. 2009. *L'intelligence d'un sens: odeurs miraculeuses et odorat dans l'Occident du Haut Moyen Âge (Ve-VIIIe siècles)*. Turnhout: Brepols.

Saradi, H. 2011. Late paganism and Christianization in Greece, in: Lavan, L. and Mulryan, M. (eds), *The Archaeology of Late Antique Paganism*. Late Antique Archaeology 7. Leiden: Brill, 263-309.

Scerra, S. (ed.) 2013. *Archaeotur. Gestione integrata e promozione dei siti archeologici a Ragusa e Malta. Integrated Management and Promotion of Archaeological Sites in Ragusa and Malta. I siti archeologici del periodo tardoantico. The Archaeological Sites of Late Antiquity*. Palermo: Assessorato dei Beni Culturali e dell'Identità Siciliana.

Scheiblauer, C. 2008. Domitilla Catacomb Walkthrough – dealing with more than 1 billion points, in: *Proceedings of the 13th International Congress on Cultural Heritage and New Technologies*. Vienna.

Scheiblauer, C., Zimmermann, N. and Wimmer 2009. Interactive Domitilla Catacomb exploration, in: Debattista, K., Perlingieri, C., Pitzalis, D. and Spina, S. (eds), *VAST 2009 – The 10th International Symposium on Virtual Reality, Archaeology and Cultural Heritage*. Eurographics Symposium Proceedings. Aire-la Ville: Eurographics Association, 65-72.

Talloen, P. 2011. From pagan to Christian: religious iconography in material culture from Sagalassos, in: Lavan, L. and Mulryan, M. (eds), *The Archaeology of Late Antique Paganism*. Late Antique Archaeology 7. Leiden: Brill, 575-607.

Thacker, A. 2007. Rome of the martyrs: saints, cults and relics, fourth to seventh centuries, in: Carragáin, É. Ó and Neuman de Vegvar, C. (eds), *Roma Felix – Formation and Reflections of Medieval Rome*. Church, Faith and Culture in the Medieval West. Farnham: Ashgate, 13-49.

Volpe, G. (ed.) 1998. *San Giusto. La villa, le ecclesiae. Primi risultati dagli scavi nel sito rurale di San Giusto (Lucera): 1995-1997*. Scavi e ricerche 8. Bari: Edipuglia.

Walker, S. *in press. Saints and Salvation: Gold-glass, Sarcophagi and Inscribed Memorials from the Catacombs of Rome*. Cambridge & New York: British School at Rome/ Cambridge University Press.

Yasin, A.M. 2009. *Saints and Church Spaces in the Late Antique Mediterranean. Architecture, Cult, and Community*. Cambridge & New York: Cambridge University Press.

Zimmermann, N. 2013. Die Alltagswelt der römischen Katakomben, in: Eich, P. and Faber, E. (eds), *Religiöser Alltag in der Spätantike*. Potsdamer Altertumswissenschaftliche Beiträge 44. Stuttgart, 169-200.

Zimmermann, N. and Eßer, G. 2008. Showing the invisible – documentation and research on the Roman Domitilla catacomb based on Image-Laser-Scanning and 3D-Modelling, in: Posluschny, A. Lambers, K. and Herzog, I. (eds), *Layers of Perception. Proceedings of the 35th International Conference on Computer Applications and Quantitative Methods in Archaeology (CAA), Berlin, Germany, April 2-6, 2007*. Bonn, 58-64.

Ziparo, V.A., Zaratti, M., Grisetti, G., Bonanni, T., Serafin, J., Di Cicco, M., Proesmans, M., van Gool, L., Vysotska, O., Bogoslavskyi, I. and Stachniss, C. 2013. Exploration and mapping of catacombs with mobile robots, in: *Proceedings for the 2013 IEEE International Symposium on Safety Security and Rescue Robotics*. Institute of Electrical and Electronics Engineers.

# Conclusion

## Looking for Beliefs and Visions in Archaeology

*Deirdre O'Sullivan*

*The Disappearing Island*
*Once we presumed to found ourselves for good*
*Between its blue hills and those sandless shores*
*Where we spent our desperate night in prayer and vigil,*

*Once we had gathered driftwood, made a hearth*
*And hung our cauldron like a firmament,*
*The island broke beneath us like a wave.*

*The land sustaining us seemed to hold firm*
*Only when we embraced it in extremis.*
*All I believe that happened there was vision.*
(Seamus Heaney, The Haw Lantern, 1987)

In his elegant tribute to the seventh-century Irish monk Brendan's pilgrim voyage into the Atlantic, and his encounter with the divine on a whale's back, which he mistakes for an island, Seamus Heaney beautifully captures both the immanence and transience of sacred space, and the importance of spiritual experience. Such insights are intangible but crucial to understanding how spaces become spiritual places, different from the everyday, although not necessarily apart from it.

In this case, the 'island', wholly a part of the natural biological rather than geological world, is destroyed by innocent human need; but the whale, doubtless with a few blisters on her back, survives; and trusting in their God and in the power of their own faith, Brendan and his little band manage to do the same. What remains for us is a traveller's tale, remediated by a great poet, an expert in understanding human experience.

This chapter serves as an endnote to this collection of studies on medieval sacred space, a field of study in which I have laboured for many years. My personal offering,

in: Bielmann, C. and Thomas, B. (eds.) 2018: *Debating Religious Space and Place in the Early Medieval World (c. AD 300-1000)*, Sidestone Press (Leiden), pp. 209-218.

however, is a perspective informed by a research project centred on much more recent creations of religious places. The insights offered by this research serve to broaden the horizons of the materiality of medieval faith, beyond the formally designated buildings and particular practices on which medievalists so often focus.

Traditional archaeological pathways into sacred places most commonly investigate cemeteries, architecture and religious iconography. As the papers in this volume demonstrate, these are still significant areas of academic endeavour, in many cases essential stages in the creation of intelligible frameworks for less immediately accessible understandings. But as they also demonstrate, contemporary scholarship is no longer content to stay within this comfort zone. The questions are no longer about 'what' or 'when', but also' how' and 'why'. We may never get very satisfactory answers to these more probing issues, but we can usefully engage with them. We cannot experience early medieval sacred places in the same way that the faith communities of the Middle Ages encountered them, but we can strive to understand that experience in intelligent and creative ways, using identifiable and even in some cases measurable tools and evidence.

My own insights into sacred spaces and places have been recently widened by my involvement with a project that aims to document and understand the ways in which the newly created places of worship of the faiths of South Asia have been incorporated into the urban landscape of Leicester (UK), and the meanings which these new places possess for both their own faith communities and the neighbourhoods in which they are situated (O'Sullivan and Young 2013; 2016). I come, as most archaeologists do, from a tradition in which the study of physical form lies at the heart of a rather hierarchical approach to sacred places. This approach underpins architectural and art historical readings of places of worship, which are identified and classified on the basis of a formal typology, surveyed, described, illustrated and rated on a sliding scale of architectural merit, primacy or state of preservation, and 'authenticity'. The project, which is ongoing, sets out to see if such approaches have continuing value, and whether there is something further to be learnt from the modern world about sacred spaces and places.

As the most religiously diverse city in Britain outside London, Leicester has a good selection of mosques, Hindu temples or mandirs, and Sikh gurdwaras. Although a few of these are purpose-built, what makes most them interesting to the archaeologist is the fact that the great majority are housed in buildings originally designed for a very different purpose; they are new plants in old soil. Sometimes these are places of worship of a different faith. The Leicester Jain Centre, for example, is housed in a former congregational church; it has been provided with a new façade and interior fittings, including some Jain stained glass, but it is still clearly recognisable as a former chapel in the interior. The most recent major introduction, the BAPS Shree Swaminarayan temple on Gipsy Lane, built in 2011, presents an exotic exterior, which totally masks its earlier use as a textile factory.

Such physical alterations may often be structurally quite minor, though the transformation in the use of space is quite profound. The largest Sikh temple in the city, the Guru Tegh Bahadur gurdwara, serves as a good example of the ways in which new purposes transform the space. Located in an industrial suburb planned at the end of 19th century, it was formerly a shoe warehouse. From the outside its present purpose is evident in the addition of a domed porch and some further external embellishments, including the flagpost with the orange flag of Sikhism, the *nishan sahib*. The open plan frame of the warehouse has proved very suitable for the accommodation of large prayer halls on the first floor, and a big kitchen and *langar* hall on the ground floor to prepare free community food, the provision of which is an essential part of Sikh devotional practice. The building also houses a museum, a gym, a crèche and a day care centre for the elderly, as well as a Punjabi school and a translation service.

The history and development of the building can be traced in a conventional sense using documentary sources, including early maps, trade directories and Building Register plans but the specifics of this history are of no serious cultural relevance to its present use. The stanchions of the original building serve as pillars in the prayer halls, but have been masked by mirrors and other decorative strategies. When the main frontage was renewed in 2000, double-glazed windows with stained-glass panels which incorporate Sikh symbols and short texts were inserted; facilities for hand-washing, an important prelude to worship, have been added at a number of points on most floors. The management committee is currently investigating the addition of solar panels to assist with energy bills.

We have spent some time interviewing and conversing with visitors to the gurdwara, aiming to establish what the building 'meant' to the Sikh faith community, and which activities and places were especially valued. Entrance to the building is formally observed: on arrival at the gurdwara, visitors sometimes touch the post of the *nishan sahib,* or the threshold, and may leave offerings. Some interviewees commented briefly on the nature of their spiritual experiences. Sikh worship involves both individual prayer and communal worship or *kirtan,* both of which take place in the prayer hall, where there is a constant stream of devotees, coming singly or in family groups. The focus of prayer in the hall is the Sikh holy book, the *Guru Grant Sahib*, and reading aloud from the text is a key devotional practice. Participation in festivals is also valued, an occasion where people 'could come together'.

A prayer visit could be combined with a visit to the *langar* hall to share the food being served there, but this was not automatic. Individuals helped with the Punjabi school for children during the week, and doing charitable work was also common; this included collecting clothes and food for redistribution, and looking after homeless people, something which many saw as a function of the *langar* hall. The gurdwara also raises significant funds for regular UK charities.

The previous history of the building as a shoe warehouse was potentially an issue; footwear is considered unclean by Sikhs, and must always be removed in the reception area. When asked about this directly however, the response was usually that its former use was of no relevance. In this context, one interviewee noted that another gurdwara in the city, the Dashmesh Gurdwara on Gypsy Lane, had been a public house. Alcohol is prohibited in gurdwaras, so the point being made here is, again, simply that the earlier use of the place did not matter. The areas set aside for prayer are permeable; respondents invariably expressed perfect ease with the idea that non-Sikhs could visit them and share food, and it was clear during our visits that a number of local Muslims regularly used the gurdwara for social purposes, including *langar*.

There are paradoxes. For example, notwithstanding the commonly-voiced view that the building 'didn't matter', a number of interviewees expressed a strong attachment and the reasons for this seem mostly related to personal biography. One woman, who had been a member of the community that helped raise the money for the acquisition of the building, said that her attachment was based on the fact that she lived locally and had raised her children here; it was where she met her friends and relatives on a regular basis, and she felt valued for helping out and doing charitable work. A young man recognised the building as an important local landmark. By extension, for many it was the centre of the Sikh community in the area, and for a family of recent migrants from the EU, it was their first port of call in seeking to integrate with the city and find employment. Notifications of funerals were posted in the gurdwara, often in both English and Punjabi, but the dead were otherwise visibly absent.

Interviewees usually stated that they visited other gurdwaras in the city – 'it doesn't matter to which temple you go – people are very welcoming' and at least one respondent also visited places of other faiths. Visiting was seen as a good way to get to know people in a new place. One visitor from Birmingham illustrated this by a visit to his brother in Switzerland. Another respondent was aware of tensions between gurdwara communities; however this was set down to the management, not the faith.

Architecture was not completely irrelevant however. The visual and spiritual qualities of temples elsewhere are not ignored; pictures of impressive gurdwaras in India and Pakistan are displayed on the walls of the *langar* hall, and, notwithstanding the fact that pilgrimage has no formal role in Sikh worship, the Golden Temple in Amritsar was clearly a very important destination; respondents, if they had not yet visited, often aspired to do so.

It is apparent from this example – and it can be paralleled at many other places of worship in the city – that the concept of the sacred cannot be simply mapped onto physical space on a decreasing radius of privileged access. More important, however is that it is also clear that the interface between place and faith is performative – people encounter the sacred primarily through what they do, rather than where they are, or who they are. And what they do – preparing and sharing food, caring for the young and the elderly, and generally helping with the daily negotiation of the everyday – covers a much wider range of activities than those normally admitted into archaeological understandings of the sacred. A dichotomy between the sacred and the profane, so often deployed in scholarly theorising, is invisible.

I offer this case study as a useful insight rather than a direct analogy for the papers presented here, which engage with a range of situations and places in the pagan, Christian and Islamic worlds of the first millennium. At the heart of these studies is the concept of place, a social and cognitive ordering and naming of dimensional space. Place is a key element in the human sense of belonging, and the difference between space and place is central to our current understanding of how we order the world. Archaeological understandings of place are sometimes unnecessarily constrained by the formal classification of monuments and sites into different sorts of 'place', but our experience of place is much more deeply layered than the simple recognition of change in the use of space, or stratigraphy. Time is a key dimension of the differential use of space to create place, for example; a space that is used for one purpose may be experienced as something very different, and by a different group of people, on a seasonal or even daily basis.

Debate about the nature of place is very wide-ranging within the social sciences and humanities, to the extent that the concept is now so over-theorised that, like 'society', 'community' and 'identity', it may have has lost much of its semantic utility. For this reason, I will confine my discussion to exploring a number of specific concepts of place that are of particular relevance to consideration of the sacred.

One of the most widely deployed concepts is that of a 'place of memory', a term developed by the French scholar Pierre Nora in the 1980s, and widely deployed ever since, especially in heritage studies (Nora 1989; 1992-98). His concept of a *'lieu de memoire'*, translates literally as place of memory, but it has also been interpreted as a 'realm of memory'. Nora never intended that the concept should be simply applied to physical places, although it does encompass them; some of the original case studies included the French national anthem (Vovelle 1998), and particular historical events or ceremonies, such as the celebration of Bastille Day (Amalvi 1998). A place of memory is where a collective memory is created, developed and revisited, accruing significance over time; but this significance can change, wax and wane. In the present context, pilgrimage destinations serve as excellent exemplars, the city of Jerusalem, for example acting as an enduring and complex place of memory for a range of religious faiths. The fact that it was located conceptually at the centre of Christendom is only one consideration among many that have sustained the myriad experiences and readings of the place. Jose Carvahal Lopez here argues that the construction of the Dome of the Rock on the Temple Mount represents an incorporation of memory into a 'new' place, to serve as a Muslim devotional focus as well as legitimating a place of memory. In this case, the aims of the caliph Abd-al-Mālik are fulfilled to this day; but other initiatives by the powerful to deploy the power of religious belief had more uncertain outcomes. Brittany Thomas' careful deconstruction of the use of space and decoration within San Vitale in Ravenna evaluates the extent to which Bishop Maximian aimed to engage with a public audience in his showcasing of Imperial authority. The showcase may seem obvious today, but it is by no means certain that it was accessed by anyone other than the members of a privileged elite in the sixth century.

As discussed above, place may be also be viewed as performative, *i.e.* where certain things happen. A number of the papers included here address the issue of experience quite explicitly. In his exploration of accessing the Roman catacombs, Neil Christie reviews how catacombs were experienced by their visitors, the darkness and flickering light a key part of the medieval encounter, the spiritual nature of the pilgrim visit marked out on the lamps that they carried, which were taken away as testimony to both their physical and spiritual journey. The fact that we cannot calculate the scale of such pilgrim traffic in any detail is frustrating, but we still have the realisation that the visitors, aware that they were moving among the bones of martyrs and saints as well as more ordinary mortals, had a privileged encounter with a place of memory. A visit to the catacombs thus served as a personal testimony to the creation myths of the Christian faith, as well as a devotional practice.

When such practices cease to be relevant, as for example with the urban civic ceremonials of the cities of Late Antiquity, it could be argued that the place itself ceases to be, although of course there may be very visible signs of its former role. Pilar Diarte Blasco proposes that in Iberia this can be seen as a shift from the public to the private use of a place, and that the subsequent 'Christianisation' of towns and cities fills a gap left by the abandonment of the Imperial cult. However, she argues that this is best understood in terms of individual place biographies, rather than some kind of uniform process operational across the region.

'Occupying the same space' does not necessarily mean 'living in the same place'. Segregation can be an important dynamic in societies, whether or not it is formally or culturally prescribed, by exclusion or community identity, people either seeking out or forced into defining and delimiting their home space on the basis of connections and creed. The extent of segregation within the multi-faith communities of the Mediterranean in the first millennium is a theme barely explored by historians; but although it is not possible to investigate this on a wide scale, the practice of catacomb burial offers some insights from archaeologists. The tradition of catacomb burial predates the adoption of Christianity in Rome, and was practiced in other parts of Italy; on the basis of inscriptions, Glen Farrugia demonstrates that on Malta, pagan, Christians and Jews were using the same burial places although some degree of segregation is still apparent.

In this context it is appropriate to address the issue of continuity, a recurrent theme in many assessments of sacred places. The concept of 'continuity' in which a place or focus of worship transfers from one set of beliefs to another is considered in a number of papers, and here archaeological skills provide a useful critical framework. The simplest way of interpreting 'continuity' may involve no more than the basic fact that a place remains 'a place' rather than a space; as my contemporary example makes clear, it is not a blank on which the forms of a new system of belief may simply be imposed. A place has already been named and serves as an existing node in both a physical and conceptual landscape, offering practical resources for the implementation of new visions, including such basic things as stonework for spolia as well as an optimal location and the natural resources of the land.

Sacred places can have a post life, and a new life. This does not rely on the existence of some kind of holy aura, emanating from the ground, but on the fact that they are also places of memory and community activity. In her deconstruction of the use of Roman forums in Classical and late antique cites, Diarte Blasco has carefully reframed the apparent dereliction of public space as a transition from public to private, evidence for the decline of municipal authority, and/or the active opportunism of citizens in putting the formal public spaces to new uses. One kind of place therefore becomes another – with a different functionality takes over the physical centre of a late antique city. This is relevant because the concept of public space was intimately tied to both imperial authority and correct religious practice within Roman urban culture. The later use of these spaces as *necropolei* – heretofore confined to extramural zones – reflects an important shift – not just in what citizens could do with their own towns, but in changing attitudes to purity and pollution, and the right place for dead bodies in an urban environment.

The Christian concept of a community of the living and the dead is evident in the changes taking place in the late antique cities of Iberia, where, as Diarte Blasco demonstrates, the idea that Christians should be buried next to, and in some cases within their places of worship, takes hold in the course of the fifth and sixth centuries. Cutting across Classical ideas of purity and pollution, the introduction of burial grounds within the walls of towns and cities is a manifest shift away from the public urban order of Imperial times.

This ultimately resulted in a very stable realisation of faith for Christians in the West but there were many stations on the way, especially in the countryside, and considerable variation from region to region. As Francesca Garanzini reveals, Christian churches equipped with baptisteries offering pastoral care under the direction of bishops were clearly operational in rural northern Italy by the sixth century, but this was far from the case elsewhere. In his study of cemeteries in North-East England, Stephen Sherlock demonstrates that the new burial grounds created to serve Christian communities did not necessarily result in 'permanent' places, even when it seems that they contained the graves of the powerful, as at Street House Farm, where it seems that the cemetery may only have been in use for a generation, and was swiftly lost to memory.

The monastic communities that dominate so much discussion of religion in the early medieval west are often viewed as living in a place apart, their primary concern an exclusionary devotion, but it can be argued that this is an over-polarisation of both their places and their practices. Stephen Ling here presents the case that at least by Carolingian times, monastic cloisters are best viewed as 'porous walls', their inhabitants directly engaging with the secular clergy and secular communities who were welcomed into the formally segregated claustral space in the interests of education and orthodoxy.

The concept of the unity of the living and the dead reaches its fulfilment in the creation of the medieval parish structures of the 10th-12th centuries, where a place-based community, with territorial boundaries, worshiped collectively in a parish church and expected to be buried in the surrounding churchyard. This can best be seen as elements of a continuum, not an opposition; the church and churchyard stood for the relationship between the faithful and the faithful departed, where the prayers of the faithful could relieve the sufferings of their dead ancestors and relatives in the hereafter. This 'norm' was only developing in North-Western Europe when the first European settlers arrived in Greenland, but it seems to have provided a powerful spiritual and conceptual overcoat there, the identity of individuals and communities strongly tied to the conjuncture of place of burial and place of worship.

Finally, place also involves appreciation of 'where you are in the world'. This was not simply experienced in a purely spatial or material sense; it involved engagement with a cognitive landscape, informed by belief and holy writ. Such landscapes can be identified through the texts that encode them, even if the point is not made explicit. Reading Jerusalem as a model for the Church itself – the 'heavenly Jerusalem' is a well-developed exegesis within western Christian tradition, but it is increasingly appreciated that more localised understandings of place follow similar approaches to geography. For example, Tom O'Loughlin has argued that St Patrick's awareness of the importance of his own labours derives from his belief that by taking Christianity to the ends of the known world, his mission presaged the second coming of Christ (O'Loughlin 1999, 42-47). Adamnan's treatment of the topography of Iona has been read by Jennifer O'Reilly as a homology of Biblical terrain, in which Columba's activities take place within a landscape that directly references the Old and New Testaments (O'Reilly 1997). I have argued that the phenomenon of the tides, perceived as daily visible evidence of divine intervention, leant special significance to the island of Lindisfarne (O'Sullivan 2001). The need for a 'desert' in which Christian ascetics could test their spiritual fitness is widely acknowledged in discussions of monastic place selection (e.g. O'Loughlin 1997). Much of this discussion is rhetorical, but it can be explored on the ground. Using viewshed analysis convincingly in the Alpine landscape,

Chantal Bielmann here identifies the physical salience of the early monastic sites, even where they seem physically remote.

Eschatological readings are necessarily grounded in the obvious authority of major writers and actors in the promotion of a Christian worldview, but they must surely also have formed part of a wider, popular understanding of place. In the case of the first Greenlanders, McCullough argues that this involved an understanding of their geo-conceptual marginality, far into the Ocean, at the absolute limit of Christendom, where St Patrick had located himself five centuries earlier. The need to 'belong' within the Christian world involved the recognition of the dangers of the Ocean, a special if dangerous place in Christian geographical understanding, on which the Greenlanders were ultimately dependant for their material welfare. The consecrated earth of the parish churchyard offered an opportunity to affirm their right to be included among the faithful, despite their remoteness from the mainstream of the Christian church.

The tradition of polarising the 'sacred' and the 'profane' in archaeological writings owes much to nineteenth- and early twentieth-century anthropological discourse. Such scholars were usually committed to an evolutionary perspective, in which creeds and beliefs could be allocated to formal taxonomies. Not simply obsessed with the classification of faith practices and beliefs into different strata of sophistication, they were also usually deeply hostile to them, in an intellectual environment informed by a profound materialism, often accompanied by an active anti-clericalism. The study of medieval religion became, and for many still is, an attempt to impose a 'rational' understanding on what were often classed as 'irrational' beliefs – in the existence of divine beings, or the intercessory powers of the dead; anxieties – fear of possible damnation and a future of perpetual suffering in Hell; and aspirations – salvation, whether in the form of a journey to the Asphodel Meadows, Heaven or Valhalla.

Such beliefs were very real for people in the past – they are still relevant for billions in the present. Materialism has thereby often set severe limitations on our understanding of what early medieval sacred places are actually about. They are often simply cast as crude expressions of power, authority and access to resources of human labour and raw materials, where the masses could be appropriately deluded, through lurid didactic iconography or impressive architecture, and exploited, through requisitioning of their meagre resources for supposed spiritual benefits. A privileged few, passing themselves off as religious experts, controlled the material realities, whether through direct management of property and economic surplus, or self-identification as a spiritual elite, who practised personal and collective austerity as a demonstration of their superior access to divine authority. This approach is a bit of a caricature, but I would argue that has some traction in archaeologists' explanations of the own evidence.

One does not have to share a religious faith to appreciate how sincerely it may be held, or the fact that it may inform a very wide range of human actions. As a result of my own encounters with new places of worship I would now argue that prayer is more important than architecture; cultural reference, and social engagement more significant than aesthetic value or expert verdict; and heresy of heresies – burial not very important at all. But perhaps these are just the values I have acquired in the 21st century.

It remains a source of ongoing frustration that both archaeological and historical approaches to sacred space are too often reductionist, perceiving change and significance in purely material terms. For this has also had very wide implications for how 'sacred

DEBATING RELIGIOUS SPACE AND PLACE IN THE EARLY MEDIEVAL WORLD (C. AD 300-1000)

places' have been globally recognised, conserved and monumentalised, or re-conceived as 'historic assets', including World Heritage sites. These are our formal tactics in the 21st century; not necessarily wrong (although that could be disputed) but certainly insufficient to frame experiences of sacred places in medieval times. Whatever the universal value of Brendan's experience, his whale happily entirely eludes UNESCO policies and strategies, as well as GIS analysis, spatial syntax, or the connoisseurship or formal study of architecture or landscape. In seeking a vision of the sacred, we must be aware of the paradox that it will ultimately always elude us; but the inability to know all of something, is no justification for the argument that we cannot know any of it.

## Bibliography

Amalvi, C. 1998. Bastille Day: from *Dies Irae* to Holiday, in: Nora, P. (ed.), *Realms of Memory: the Construction of the French Past, 3 vols*. New York: Columbia University Press, 117-159.

Nora, P. 1989. Between Memory and History: Les Lieux de Mémoire. *Representations* 26 (Special Issue: Memory and Counter-Memory), 7-24.

Nora P. (ed.) 1992-98. *Realms of Memory: the Construction of the French Past, 3 vols*. New York: Columbia University Press.

O'Loughlin, T. 1997. Living in the Ocean, in: Bourke, C. (ed.), *Studies in the Cult of St Columba*. Dublin: Four Courts Press, 11-23.

O'Loughlin, T. 1999. *Saint Patrick: the Man and his Works*. London: SPCK.

O'Reilly, J. 1997. Reading the Scriptures in the Life of Columba, in: Bourke, C. (ed.), *Studies in the Cult of St Columba*. Dublin: Four Courts Press, 80-106.

O'Sullivan, D.M. 2001. Space silence and shortage on Lindisfarne: the archaeology of asceticism, in: Hamerow, H. and McGregor, A. (eds), *Image and Power in the Archaeology of Early Medieval Britain. Essays in Honour of Rosemary Cramp*. Oxford: Oxbow, 33-52.

O'Sullivan, D. and Young, R. 2012. A world apart? Translating the archaeology of the sacred in the modern world. *World Archaeology* 44/3, 342-358.

Vovelle, M. 1998. La Marseillaise: War or Peace, in: Nora, P. (ed.), *Realms of Memory: the Construction of the French Past, 3 vols*. New York: Columbia University Press, 29-74.

Young, R. and O'Sullivan, D. 2016. South Asian Buddhist viharas translated to the UK, in: *Proceedings of the Society for Buddhist Art and Archaeology*, 1st Conference 2015.